Crossing the Plate

Crossing the Plate

*The Upswing in Runs Scored
by Major League Teams,
1993 to 1997*

by
RUSSELL O. WRIGHT

McFarland & Company, Inc., Publishers
Jefferson, North Carolina and London

British Library Cataloguing-in-Publication data are available

Library of Congress Cataloguing-in-Publication Data

Wright, Russell O.
    Crossing the plate : the upswing in runs scored by major league
teams, 1993 to 1997 / by Russell O. Wright.
      p.   cm.
    Includes index.
    ISBN 0-7864-0536-8 (sewn softcover : 50# alkaline paper) ∞
    1. Baseball—Offense—United States—Statistics. 2. Baseball
teams—Rating of—United States. 3. Major League Baseball
(Organization) I. Title.
GV867.7.W75   1998
796.357'2—dc21   98-20511
                                     CIP

Manufactured in the United States of America

McFarland & Company, Inc., Publishers
  Box 611, Jefferson, North Carolina 28640

*Dedicated
to
Halina*

Acknowledgments

The primary sources for this book were the tenth edition of *The Baseball Encyclopedia* published by Macmillan and the fifth edition of *Total Baseball* published by Viking. Data for 1997 came from *The Sporting News* published by The Sporting News Publishing Company and *USA Today Baseball Weekly* published by Gannett Co., Inc.

I want to acknowledge the work done by the *Los Angeles Times* in upgrading the baseball information available in its sports section. This makes it possible to get most of the data needed to know how the game is changing without consulting other less timely reference sources, and the additional coverage provided during the baseball season gives much better background for the game on and off the field. I hope they will continue to increase the level of detail in the information they provide.

I also want to thank Paul Pedroni for the effort he has made over the years to make it possible for us to attend opening day at Dodger Stadium. It counts as true devotion to the game considering he is a dedicated fan of the Giants and he places the Dodgers high on his enemy list.

Contents

List of Figures

Part I: League Comparisons

Part IV: The Future

List of Tables

Part III: Team Summaries

Part IV: The Future

Preface

In 1992 McFarland & Company, Inc., published *The Evolution of Baseball*, my first statistical history of baseball. The book had a starting point of 1903, when the National League (basically formed in 1876) and the American League (formed in 1901) agreed on common rules for the game on the field, agreed to stop raiding each other's players, and agreed on the cities in which the teams in each league would play (a combination of cities and teams that remained unchanged for the next 50 years). This was the true beginning of the two leagues as we know them today.

The emphasis of *The Evolution of Baseball* was on long-term changes in the game during the century as shown by changes in league and team statistics (rather than individual statistics). Data were presented on a per-game basis to account for the different number of games played in different years, and averages over five and ten year periods were used to show how the game evolved as it cycled between periods when first defense and then offense had the upper hand.

As shown in the book, offense peaked in the two decades following the rule changes favoring offense that took place in 1920 to end the so-called "dead ball" era from 1903 through 1919 (as the book also shows, it would be more accurate to call this period the "dirty ball" era). Pitchers slowly began to gain the upper hand again after World War II, and although home runs continued to grow through the 1950s, runs were still in a long-term period of decline when a change in the strike zone in favor of pitchers, which was intended to reduce the number of home runs, was initiated in 1963. This change killed offense from 1963 through 1968, and it led directly to a fundamental change in the game in the American League with the introduction of the designated hitter in 1973.

By the late 1980s runs had returned to the levels of the 1950s in the American League, even though they were well below the peaks of the 1930s. But in the National League, without the designated hitter, runs continued to decline. There was an upturn in 1987, but in the long-term view taken by *The Evolution of Baseball*, the decline in runs in the National League since the late 1950s was clear. The end of the nine decades I intended to cover in the book came in 1989, and I wrote in the conclusion that offense would continue to decline in the National League, in spite of the 1987 surge, unless there was a fundamental change that would have an effect similar to that produced by the designated hitter in the American League. By 1992 National League offense had hit bottom.

1

In a note published in the *SABR Bulletin*, the monthly publication of the Society for American Baseball Research, I pointed out that the 3.88 runs per game averaged by the National League in 1992 was the lowest since the "Year of the Pitcher" in 1968, the last year the 1963-68 rule changes favoring pitchers were in effect. Further, except for three years in the 1963-68 period, the National League's 3.88 level was its lowest since the dead ball days of 1919.

Additional proof of the decline in offense in the National League was that the league batting average from 1988 through 1992 was .251, the lowest five year average since 1915 through 1919 outside the 1963-68 period. The low year (1989) of .246 in the 1988-92 period was the third lowest year in the 80 seasons since 1909. Only 1963 and 1968 in the 1963-68 doldrums were lower.

A final point was that the double play rate, which is strongly dependent on the number of runners reaching base (which is why the poorest teams in the league often are near the top in double plays), also had declined dramatically in the National League. In 1991 the National League averaged only 0.79 double plays per game. In spite of the much better fielding levels today, that was the lowest level in the National League since 1919. The nature of the game in the National League had truly returned to the dead ball period.

But although my prediction of a continued decline in National League offense came true, what appears to be a long-term reversal started in 1993. This was due partly to the maturation of a fundamental change in hitting strategy and training that traces its roots to the adoption of the designated hitter in the American League in 1973. This change is discussed in detail below. The reversal was also due to the consequences of expansion in 1993. Expansion brought major league baseball to the mile high city of Denver, where the air is thin and the ball travels nine percent further than a ball hit with the same force and at the same angle at sea level. This means that a fly ball traveling 330 feet for an out at sea level becomes a 360 foot home run in Denver. Similarly, a curve ball with a lot of bite at sea level does not break as sharply in Denver. The result is more hits and more runs. Offense in the National League has benefited greatly from the big hitters favored by the Colorado Rockies and the addition of Coors Field to the stadiums in the league. Certainly "arcade" baseball in Denver was a big factor in the National League's offensive outburst in 1993-97.

But the fundamental change in hitting strategy and training also played a major role. It has enhanced the effect of the designated hitter in the American League to the extent that the league set its all-time home run record in 1996. Four of the five highest years in league history in hitting home runs came between 1994 and 1997, and in 1996 the American League also came close to its all-time records for runs that were set in the 1930s. But the change in hitting strategy also led to all-time records in strikeouts in both leagues. This is the price hitters at all levels are now willing to pay for increased offense.

The results of this new strategy became clear while I was writing my second statistical history of baseball. It was called *The Best of Teams, the Worst of Teams*, and was published by McFarland in 1995. My basic reason for writing the book was that *The Evolution of Baseball* had focused on the leading teams for limited key measures such as runs, home runs, winning percentage, and ERA. This was consistent with the desire to show changes in the game over time at the league and team levels. But after writing the book I wanted to know what teams were best for other measures like doubles and triples and stolen bases. I wanted to know what teams had the best and worst strikeout and walk records from the standpoint of both pitchers and hitters. I wanted to know what teams had the best and worst performances for all the common measures of the game over five year periods as well as just one very good or very bad year. And most of all I wanted to know the bests and worsts for all the teams, not just the leaders.

I answered all of these questions (and much more) in *The Best of Teams, the Worst of Teams*. The book covered the period from 1903 through 1994, the last year before it was published, and in extending the data through this period I tracked the offensive surge that began in the expansion year of 1993 and was continuing full force in 1994 up to the time of the strike. The surge continued in 1995, and it soared to new heights in 1996 before declining somewhat in 1997 (possibly due to interleague play). League run scoring records set more than 60 years ago were being approached, and the expansion teams were setting franchise records for offensive output. But there were great differences in the way runs were being scored in the 1990s compared to the way they were scored in the peaks in offense that took place in the 1920s and 1930s.

The difference between these periods of high offense is another focus of this book. Home runs account for a much higher percentage of runs scored today than in the previous record years of the 1920s and 1930s. But batting averages are much lower today, and strikeout records are being set at a rate that exceeds even the 1963-68 period, when the pitcher was the undisputed king of baseball. This is dramatically different than the case in the huge offensive surge of the 1920s when records for all-time *lows* in strikeouts were recorded.

The offensive records of today have their origin in the designated hitter rule that was established in the American League in 1973. Today nearly all forms of organized baseball, especially including colleges and high schools, use the designated hitter rule. Essentially, the only organization in baseball in the United States today that does not use the designated hitter rule is the National League. The designated hitter rule is intended to increase offense, and so it has. Below the professional baseball level, the rule has been aided by the universal use of aluminum bats. They were introduced as a cost saving measure because they rarely break and thus greatly reduce the cost of replacement bats. But they have had a strong impact on offensive output.

Aluminum bats increase offense not only because the impact given to the ball at contact is enhanced with an aluminum bat compared to a wooden bat. Another factor is that aluminum bats are so hard to break that pitchers pitching inside gain no advantage from their effort. A major league pitcher pitching hard inside can break the handle of a wooden bat swung by a hitter who cannot handle the pitch. With an aluminum bat the result is a "ping" and a handle hit over the infield. All players coming up through high school ranks and onward toward the major leagues learn to play with aluminum bats and the designated hitter rule.

The resulting strategy is offense and "hitting it out." There is no disgrace in striking out, and batting average is irrelevant if the hitter drives in lots of runs. This means hitters go for a big swing (even with two strikes) with a light bat that permits high bat speed. Strikeouts increase dramatically, but so do home runs and runs. Further, a player intent on making it to the major leagues now includes serious weight lifting as part of his training. For hitters it is as big a part of training as any other aspect. Stronger players with lighter bats who take big swings with impunity as far as strikeouts are concerned have been slowly accumulating in the major leagues for several years. In 1993 they reached critical mass and the small explosion started in that year is still growing.

One result of this fundamental change in strategy is that every team is taking part in the home run derby. Even the teams at the bottom of the list in hitting home runs are hitting them on average at a higher rate than in the past. In the prior offensive outburst of the 1920s and 1930s, home run hitters were scattered throughout the leagues. As late as 1927, Babe Ruth hit more home runs in a season by himself than any other *team* in the American League. Today everyone hits them out, some teams more than others, but all at a high level. The American League, with the designated hitter, continues to set home run records while it hits 17 percent more home runs than does the National League.

There has been a lot of discussion about a "lively" ball, but that discussion is just as wrong today as it was 75 years ago. No one ever complains about the introduction of a "dead" ball in years such as 1992 when the National League hit its present day bottom in offense. Poor pitching has also been blamed, and expansion certainly reduces the average quality of pitchers, but the same is true for all players. As measured by strikeouts and strikeout-to-walk ratios, pitchers are as effective today as at any time in the past except perhaps for the 1963-68 period when the rules were bent in their favor. The key to the new offensive surge in the major leagues is the new hitters who have grown up in the new game of weight lifting, lighter bats, swinging for the fences regardless of strike count, and stroking the ball in a way that maximizes home runs and extra-base hits.

The main purpose of this book is to show how recent data through 1997 support such a conclusion. The Introduction explains how the data is presented in the book in a manner that permits you to draw your own conclusions.

Introduction

Data are shown in this book on both a per game and total year basis. Data on a per game basis permit both leagues and teams to be compared in different time frames regardless of the number of games played. With the adoption of the 154 game schedule in 1904, the number of games played in both leagues was reasonably consistent in each season except for the reductions in 1918 and 1919 resulting from World War I. But this changed with the advent of expansion in 1961 and the introduction of the 162 game schedule in 1962. The unfortunately high frequency of strikes in subsequent years also produced differences in the total number of games played in a given season. Thus, comparisons between league results in different time frames are meaningful only on a per game basis. Further, knowing there were 2,742 home runs hit in the American League in 1996 is not nearly as useful as knowing that the average number of home runs per team per game in the American League in 1996 was 1.21.

The number of games played by different teams in different time frames also varies for the same reasons as those noted for the leagues. But there is an additional factor that applies to teams. Before the advent of lights, domes, and synthetic surfaces, many teams played more games than the total of games won and lost due to extra games played to make up for tie games halted by darkness or rain. The differences may balance out between the leagues, but for an individual team there can be wide differences by season. Thus, comparing teams in different time frames also requires the use of per game data.

But yearly totals for a team have meaning for fans regardless of the number of games played in a season. For example, the New York Yankees held the record for total home runs in a season with their mark of 240 in 1961 until it was broken by the 1996 Baltimore Orioles who hit 257 (as shown in Part II, the 1996 and 1997 Mariners and the 1996 A's also broke the record of the 1961 Yankees). The Yankees' record of 1.47 home runs per game in 1961 was actually broken by the Cleveland Indians in 1994 when they hit 1.48 home runs per game. But no notice was made of this because the Indians hit only 167 home runs in 1994 due to the strike (the Indians set their team record for total home runs in 1997 even though their per game level in 1997 was well below their 1994 mark).

Thus, in this book, totals as well as per game data are shown for all the teams. The per game data permit direct comparisons between teams, but including the totals permits the book to be used as a reference source for record performances measured in the same way they are in the standard record book. Thus, both total year and per game records for all the teams for the measures used in the book can be determined from the tables in this book.

In calculating averages over a period of years, all years are considered equal regardless of the number of games played. For example, per game records for a five year period are determined by adding the per game values for each year and dividing by five. This gives a different result than adding the totals for the specific measure being considered for the five year period and dividing by the total number of games played over that period. Making all years equal avoids giving extra weight to years having more games played.

The book is divided into four parts. Part I compares the leagues and shows league records for the measures in the book while Part II does the same for the teams. Part III shows individual summaries for each team. Part IV shows the trends for the last decade for both leagues for the measures in the book, and it provides a summary and forecast for the new game that has evolved in the 1990s.

Part I begins with two tables (one for each league) that show the highest year for each of the measures in the book for the offensive peaks in the 1920s and 1930s and the present peak in the 1990s. The peak five year period that surrounds the peak year is also shown. This gives a dramatic comparison of the differences between the offensive peaks of the 1920s and the 1930s and the peak of the 1990s. Each table is accompanied by explanatory text that makes clear the differences and explains why they exist. A third table then summarizes the record years in both leagues for each of the key measures.

The next set of eight tables in Part I shows the highest years for each league for each of the key measures. This puts the offensive peaks in perspective over the century. For example, of the 10 highest years for home runs in the American League, 4 of the top 5 came in the 1990s (1996, 1994, 1997, and 1995 in rank order) and 3 of the top 7 came in the 1980s (1987, 1986, and 1985 in rank order). The last 3 years on the list came in the 1960s. However, it is highly likely that the next 3 years in the league will displace the years from the 1960s. This means that within 3 years there will be no years from the 1960s on the list, and in 5 years 1987 probably will be only year before 1994 on the list. This is as clear a measure as can be made of the fact that the peak decade for hitting home runs in the American League is taking place right now.

As a National League example, the list for the top ten years for strikeouts has 5 years from the 1990s. The 4 years at the top are 1997, 1996, 1995, and 1994 in rank order. The only years from the 1963-68 period when pitchers were king are 1965 in 8th place and 1963 in 10th. Both years almost surely will be gone from the list in 3 years. As far as strikeouts are concerned, the most dominant decade for pitchers in the National League is the 1990s. Those who claim today's pitchers are unusually poor should take another look at the data.

The last seven figures in Part I compare the decade averages for the key measures for both leagues in graphs that cover the century from 1903 through 1997. Both leagues are shown on one graph for each measure to make clear the differences in the leagues over the century. The "decade" averages cover only 1903-09 at beginning of the graph and 1990-97 and the end of the graph, since 1903 and 1997 mark the first and last years for the data in the book. But the prime purpose of the graphs is to show trends over time, and the truncated decades do not detract from this purpose. The league averages for the five years from 1993 through 1997 are also shown in the graphs to provide added perspective to the variations over time. The 1993-97 data shows clearly how close the new offensive peaks of the 1990s are to the prior offensive peaks of the 1920s and 1930s.

Before going on to Part II, Team Comparisons, it is necessary to make a distinction between the terms "peak years" and "ranked years." Peak years is used to identify listings that show the peak value for a measure as recorded by each of the 14 teams in each leagues. The teams are listed in order of the highest peak the franchise has reached during its existence in the league. Such a listing does not constitute a listing of the 14 highest years in the league's history for the particular measure. Generally teams near the top of the list will have had several years below their peak year that are still higher than the peak year of teams further down the list. The intention of peak year lists is simply to show the peak year for each of the 14 teams. This is the place to look to find a peak for your favorite team.

Ranked years is used to define lists that show the highest 10 (or 15) years ever recorded for a particular measure in each league regardless of how many times one team may appear on the list. This is the place to find all-time bests in a league even though your favorite team may not appear on the list at all. For example, the Yankees occupy 10 of the top 15 spots for the most runs scored per game in a year in the American League (Table 2-16). Your favorite team may not appear on this list because of the dominance of the Yankees. But your favorite team is sure to appear on the list of peak years for runs in the American League (Table 2-1) since that list specifically includes the best single year for each of the 14 American League teams.

The same distinction between peak years and ranked years is used in Part I, but because Part I applies only to the two leagues, and each league is shown on the "peak" and "ranked" tables, the distinction is not of great importance. But it is very important in understanding the data listed in Part II.

Part II, Team Comparisons, begins by showing the peak year for each team for the eight key measures used in the book. For runs, home runs, doubles, strikeouts, and walks, separate tables by league show both per game and total year peaks. For batting average, ERA, and strikeout-to-walk ratio, per game and total year data are identical because each of these measures is a ratio. Thus, a single table containing data for both leagues is used for each measure. The first section of Part II concludes with tables that show which teams set the all-time peaks for the eight key measures in league.

Thus, the first 15 tables in Part II make it possible to find the peak performance for a team of interest regardless of whether or not the peak for the team was the best ever for the league for that measure. Also, the clustering of record years for a specific measure is a good indication of the changing nature of the game over time. For example, Table 2-3, which lists the peak years for home runs for American League teams, shows that 10 of the 14 teams had their single year peak performance between 1987 and 1997. This confirms that the American League continues to set home run records. Otherwise, the peak years would spread out over a long time frame because an exceptional outburst by one great team in franchise history can stay as a team record for many years in spite of trends in the league. For example, one of the four American League teams setting records before 1987 is the 1961 Yankees. Their peak year was the all-time major league record at the time, and the record stood for 35 years.

The last 13 tables in Part II show ranked years rather than peak years for teams in each league for the eight key measures. As previously discussed, ranked years show the 10 or 15 highest years in league history regardless of how many times teams from one franchise appear on the list. These tables make it possible to determine if records are clustering in a specific time frame, and they also make it possible to determine if one team dominates a measure. For example, Table 2-25 with the 10 highest ranked years for strikeouts in the National League shows that 9 of the 10 teams set their records in the 1990s. The only exception is the 1969 Astros who previously held the major league record until the Braves broke it on a per game basis in 1994 and a total year basis in 1996. The Astros will probably fall out of the top ten list in the next 5 years. The Braves hold 3 of the top 4 positions on the per game list (and 4 of 10 overall), and the 1996 Braves have the top spot on the total year list. The Braves of the middle 1990s are the all-time strikeout kings of the National League. But the Dodgers are not far behind, and most other teams are also setting franchise records in the 1990s. The National League is in the middle of a strikeout frenzy, a frenzy that likely will be the standard performance in years to come.

Part III of the book, Team Summaries, shows the peak years for all 28 teams for the eight key measures. The peaks are show on both a per game and total year basis. This makes it possible to determine the peak year for a given team on whichever basis is of most interest. In addition, the per game peaks in franchise history are compared to the per game average for the five years during the offensive outburst from 1993 through 1997. This indicates the direction the team is presently heading.

At the end of Part III, the per game averages for the 3 top teams from 1993 through 1997 are put in rank order for each league. This shows at a glance the top teams in each league for the 1993-97 period as defined by the eight key measures. The degree to which the leading teams dominated their league is discussed in the accompanying text. The Rockies have one of the largest differences between a team average and the league average. For example, the Rockies averaged 1.23 home runs per game from 1993 through 1997, even though they struggled as an expansion team in their first year of 1993. This means the Rockies hit home runs at a rate 31 percent higher than the league average over the five year period.

The Rockies are even farther ahead of the league on a yearly basis. In 1997 they were 55 percent above the National League average in hitting home runs as they set the all-time National League record both for home runs per game and total home runs in one year. In essence, Coors Field produces the same effect on the Rockies as the designated hitter produces on American League teams. This makes the Rockies look like an American League team when it comes to hitting home runs and scoring runs. But like the Fenway Park Red Sox before them, tailoring their team to their park leads to a shortage of pitching, and this keeps the Rockies from beating out the hated Dodgers (just as the Red Sox could not beat out the hated Yankees for the same reason).

Part IV shows results from 1987 through 1997 for the key measures in both the American and National leagues. For both leagues, 1987 marks the last offensive spike before 1993. The decline from 1987 and the sharp rise that began in both leagues in 1993 is clearly evident. Both leagues are shown on the same graph for each measure, so it is possible to see at a glance the difference between the leagues for these measures over this recent time frame.

To give added perspective to the graphs, Part IV begins with a table showing the ratios between the leagues for the key measures before and after the start of the designated hitter in 1973. This table, together with the graphs, helps to make clear how offense has dominated baseball since 1993 and why it seems likely to continue to do so. But Part IV concludes with a summary of the best and worst teams for winning percentage for the 1993-97 period, and the accompanying analysis shows that even in the era of the big swing the defining factor for the winners is pitching. It is now a game of high offense (which I and many other fans prefer), but the winners are still the teams with the best pitching.

Some final comments need to be made about the eight key measures used in the book (runs, home runs, doubles, batting average, ERA, strikeouts, walks, and strikeout-to-walk ratios). These measures were chosen because they define not only whether offense or defense has the upper hand in specific time frames, they also define changes in the way the game is played on the field. The most important measure in baseball is runs, and measuring the variation in runs over time is enough to determine if we are in a period when offense or defense has the upper hand. But the other measures permit us to determine how the nature of the game is changing as well. For example, as the tables and graphs in the four parts of the book show, when runs in the 1990s rose to approach the levels of the 1920s and 1930s, home runs soared and batting averages fell compared to the previous period. In the 1990s, strikeouts hit record highs as runs increased while in the 1920s strikeouts hit record lows as runs increased. Reviewing data of this type tells us much about the differences in the game between the 1920s and the 1990s.

But there is another aspect to the eight key measures chosen. These are the most fundamental measures in the game. It is not necessary to be a statistician to understand these basic measures. Even the most casual fan recognizes each of the measures, and current data is available in most daily newspaper. Thus, for anyone who wishes to follow future results for their favorite team(s), the only source needed is their daily newspaper. That should add to the utility of the information provided in this book.

Record highs rather than lows are shown for walks and ERA values. This is partly because record highs for these measures accompany periods of high offense, and partly because the records lows for these measures for the original teams all occurred in the early years of the century. This is especially true of ERA because the manner in which ERA is defined leads to artificially low values in periods when errors are high as they were in the early 1900s.

The "high" ERAs of the 1990s must be put in perspective when they are used by some to support a claim that the present offensive outburst is due to a lack of pitching skill. For example, the percentage of "unearned" runs in the 1920s in the American League was 16.1 percent. In the 1990s so far it is 9.1 percent. The American League ERA of 4.11 in the 1920s (runs averaged 4.90) would be 4.50 in the 1990s if unearned runs were proportional to errors. This is consistent with the actual ERA of 4.42 for the American League so far in the 1990s (runs have averaged 4.80). Since errors continue to fall in both leagues (the all-time lows set in 1995 in the American League and 1992 in the National League were both closely approached in 1997), ERA levels will appear to be at record highs even if runs allowed are lower than prior peaks. Again, one must study the data before jumping to "obvious" conclusions that are not necessarily so obvious.

Ratios are used often in the book to compare league values or to compare the 1993-97 period to earlier periods. Usually the ratio is of the higher value to the lower value no matter which league or period has the higher value. This makes it easy to translate the ratio to a percentage. All ratios shown are based on actual computer values. They will not necessarily agree with what a reader obtains by dividing the values shown. This is because the values in the book are shown only to two decimal places while the computer ratio considers all decimal places.

Part I
League Comparisons

American League Peak Years

Table 1-1 compares offensive peaks for the American League in the 1930s and 1990s. As discussed in the Introduction, the key measure for defining an offensive peak is runs scored. All other measures simply help indicate the way the game was being played at the time a run scoring peak was reached. Thus, the years selected in Table 1-1 are the years in which a peak was reached for runs in a single year and in a five year period. The other measures show the values reached in the specific year or five year period chosen for runs, but these values do not necessarily reflect peaks for the other measures. The peak values for all of the other measures are shown in Table 1-3, which shows the highest value ever reached for each measure regardless of the year in which it was reached.

All values shown in Table 1-1 (and in all of Part I) are on a per game basis only ("per game" throughout the book means per game per team). This is because totals on a league basis have little meaning. Knowing the American League averaged 5.67 runs per game in 1936, the highest average ever for runs, tells us exactly what level of scoring was taking place in the league. Knowing that the total number of runs scored in the American League in 1936 was 7,009 tells us essentially nothing at all. For example, there were 10,527 runs scored in the American League in 1979, 50.2 percent more than in 1936. Further, on a per game basis, 1979 was the highest run scoring year for the league since 1950. But the American League only scored 4.67 runs per game in 1979, exactly 1.0 runs per game (or 17.6 percent) fewer than it had in the record year of 1936. On a league basis totals provide no basis at all for comparison.

With 1936 as the highest single year for scoring runs, the 1935-39 period was the highest five year period for scoring runs in the American League. As shown in Table 1-1, the league averaged 5.67 runs per game in 1936 and 5.31 runs per game from 1935 through 1939. The average of 5.39 runs per game scored in 1996 is the third highest year for the American League, with 1930 at 5.41 runs per game just edging out 1996 for second place. Similarly, the 5.06 runs per game scored in the American League from 1993 through 1997 is third behind the 5.18 runs per game scored from 1930 through 1934. Further, 1994 through 1996 marks the first time the American League averaged more than 5.00 runs per game 3 years in a row since the end of the 1930s. These comparisons confirm that the two major offensive peaks in run scoring in the American League came in the decade of the 1930s and 60 years later in the 1990s.

The ratios of the 1993-97 data to the 1935-39 data in Table 1-1 show the differences in the way the game was played in the two decades. Home runs set an all-time high in 1996 at 1.21 per game, twice the rate of 0.61 in 1936. From 1993 through 1997, home runs were 1.08 per game compared to 0.63 from 1935 through 1939, a ratio of 1.71. When runs reached their all-time peak in 1936, the explosion of home runs that began with the era of Babe Ruth in 1920 was still far below the level of 1996. Serial offense in which a series of hits drives runners around the bases was a much bigger factor in 1936 than in 1996. In 1996 the key to a big inning was a three-run home run. But the big swing for home runs reduced batting averages and increased strikeouts as shown in Figure 1-1.

Table 1-1. American League Peak Runs Periods

	Single Year		Five Years		
	1936	1996	1935-39	1993-97	Ratio
Runs	5.67	5.39	5.31	5.06	1.05
Home Runs	0.61	1.21	0.63	1.08	1.71
Doubles	1.94	1.86	1.81	1.80	1.01
BatAvg.	.289	.277	.282	.271	1.04
ERA	5.04	4.99	4.70	4.68	1.01
Strikeouts	3.26	6.20	3.41	6.06	1.78
Walks	3.93	3.79	3.86	3.65	1.06
SO/W Ratio	0.83	1.64	0.88	1.66	1.88

Batting averages were 12 points lower in 1996 compared to 1936, and 11 points lower in the 1993-97 period compared to the 1935-39 period. This is a significant difference in batting average even though the ratio is only 1.04. ERA differences are smaller than those in runs because error rates in the 1990s are much lower than those in 1930s. As explained in the Introduction, constant error rates would make the differences in ERA consistent with the difference in runs.

The biggest change is in strikeouts and strikeout-to-walk ratios. Strikeouts grew by a ratio of 1.78 from the 1930s to the 1990s, more than the increase in home runs. Walks were lower in the 1990s, and thus the SO/W ratio was higher by a ratio of 1.88. This is the largest difference among the measures shown. Strikeout-to-walk ratios have long been a key measure of pitcher efficiency. Thus, based on this measure, pitching in the 1990s was better than in the 1930s. This supports the concept that the home run outburst in the 1990s is due to hitters who are trained to focus on hitting home runs at the expense of serial offense.

Table 1-2 compares offensive peaks for the National League near 1930 and in the 1990s. As discussed in the Introduction and in the text accompanying Table 1-1, an offensive peak is defined by runs scored. All other measures indicate the way the game was being played at the time a runs peak was reached. The years shown in Table 1-2 are years in which a peak was reached for runs in a single year and in a five year period. The other measures show the values reached in the one year or five year period chosen for runs, but these values do not necessarily reflect peaks for the other measures. The peak values for each of the individual measures are shown in Table 1-3 which lists the highest value ever reached for each measure regardless of the year in which it was reached.

The values shown in Table 1-2 are on a per game basis. This is because totals on a league basis have little meaning. Knowing the National League averaged 5.68 runs per game in 1930, the highest average ever in the majors for runs in a single year, tells us exactly what level of scoring was taking place in the league. Knowing that the total number of runs scored in the National League in 1930 was 7,025 tells us essentially nothing at all. For example, there were 10,190 runs scored in the National League in 1993, 45 percent more than in 1930. But the National League only scored 4.49 runs per game in 1993, 1.19 runs per game (or 21 percent) fewer than it had in the record year of 1930. On a league basis, only per game comparisons are meaningful.

With 1930 as the highest single year for scoring runs, the period from 1926 through 1930 was the highest five year period for scoring runs in the National League. As shown in Table 1-2, the league averaged 5.68 runs per game in 1930 and 4.97 runs per game from 1926 through 1930. But the performance of the National League in 1930 has to be put in perspective. There was a huge surge in scoring runs in the National League in 1929 and 1930. As shown in *The Evolution of Baseball*, this was the culmination of an offensive upturn that started in 1921. The upturn was due to rule changes hampering pitchers (which led to a much cleaner ball being put into play on a regular basis), favorable changes in park dimensions, and the trend to a game featuring hitting that Babe Ruth triggered in 1920. But while American League offense grew steadily from 1920 through the 1930s with a peak in 1936, the National League spurted upwards in the 1920s with a sharp peak in 1930, and then declined sharply afterwards.

For example, the American League scored more than 5 runs per game 14 times before the 1990s, with 13 of those years coming in the 1920s and 1930s (the exception was 1950). The National League went over 5 runs per game only 4 times, just barely getting over in 1922 and 1925, and then soaring to 5.36 in 1929 and 5.68 in 1930 (Table 1-4). In 1931 the league fell back to 4.48 runs per game and dipped to 3.97 in 1933 before recovering somewhat a few years later. Thus, comparisons with only 1930 are somewhat misleading in the National League. Comparisons over five year periods are more meaningful.

Accordingly, the ratios of 1993-97 data to 1926-30 data in Table 1-2 provide a better picture of the differences in the two periods of high offense. Runs were 8 percent higher (ratio of 1.08) in the 1926-30 period, but the National League scored more runs in the 1993-97 period than in any other such period since 1930. Home runs were 82 percent higher in 1993 through 1997, meaning serial offense was a much bigger factor in 1926 through 1930 than in 1993 through 1997. But the big swing for home runs in the 1990s dramatically reduced batting averages while increasing strikeouts. Because of the lack of the designated hitter, these changes are larger in the National League than in the American League. This is shown by the larger ratios in Table 1-2 compared to those in Table 1-1.

Table 1-2. National League Peak Runs Periods

	Single Year		Five Years		
	1930	1996	1926-30	1993-97	Ratio
Runs	5.68	4.68	4.97	4.61	1.08
Home Runs	0.72	0.98	0.52	0.94	1.82
Doubles	1.93	1.67	1.70	1.68	1.02
BatAvg.	.303	.262	.288	.264	1.09
ERA	4.97	4.21	4.28	4.17	1.03
Strikeouts	3.12	6.73	2.85	6.47	2.27
Walks	2.98	3.31	2.97	3.28	1.10
SO/W Ratio	1.04	2.03	0.96	1.97	2.05

The league batting average was 41 points lower in 1996 compared to the huge offensive surge of 1930, and it was 24 points lower in the respective five year periods. Swinging for the fences (and better pitchers) produce lower batting averages today. The combination also produces more strikeouts and higher strikeout-to-walk ratios. Strikeouts increased by a ratio of 2.27 (127 percent) from the 1920s to the 1990s. Walks were 10 percent higher in the 1990s, and thus the SO/W ratio was higher by a ratio of "only" 2.05.

Strikeout-to-walk ratios have long been a key measure of pitcher efficiency. Thus this measure confirms that pitching in the 1990s is better than in the 1920s. This supports the concept that the home run outburst in the 1990s is due to hitters who are trained to focus on hitting home runs at the expense of serial offense. But without the designated hitter, the higher level of home runs in the National League is not enough to regain the higher run levels of the 1920s, even if run scoring in the 1990s is at its highest sustained level in 60 years.

Table 1-3 shows the highest values ever reached in the American and National Leagues for each of the key measures used in this book. The values are shown on a per game basis together with the year in which the peak was reached. Years from the 1990s are shown in boldface. The ratio of the American League and National League peaks are also shown. At the end of Part I, Figures 1-1 through 1-8 show the measures over the decades using data from *The Evolution of Baseball*. Thus, the peak values for each league as discussed below can be put in perspective by comparing the peaks to the trends over the century.

Runs--In spite of the fact that the American League has scored more runs on average than the National League during the century, the record for the highest run scoring year is held by the National League. The record was set in 1930 when the National League had its sharp peak in offense as discussed in the text accompanying Table 1-2. The American League just missed the record by 0.01 runs in 1936, its peak year. The two values are so close that the ratio of the peaks rounds off to 1.00.

Home Runs--Although home runs are often associated with the American League due to the famous "Bronx Bombers" of the Yankees, the National League averaged 0.54 home runs per game compared to 0.51 for the American League from 1903 through 1972 (see *The Evolution of Baseball*). The American League took the lead after the designated hitter was born in 1973. The all-time home run record in the league was set in 1996 at 1.21 home runs per game. The National League reached its peak in 1955 as Hank Aaron and Eddie Mathews were leading the Braves to all-time records for home runs on the road. Even though the Colorado Rockies set an all-time league record for home runs in one year in 1997, the National League has not managed to top its 1955 peak. The American League record is 18 percent above the National League peak (ratio of 1.18).

Doubles--The peaks are nearly the same for each league, and each was reached in the same year as the peak year for runs. The leagues were usually close in doubles except for an American League edge from 1920 through 1940, but the American League has taken a larger lead in the 1990s.

Batting Average--The National League set the all-time record at .303 during its huge offensive spike in 1930. It's the only time an entire league batted over .300, but there have been seven years over .290 (Table 1-7). The American League set its record at .292 in 1921, just after the rule changes favoring hitters were made in 1920. The importance of these rule changes in producing an increase in batting averages is emphasized by the fact that the 10 highest batting averages in both leagues took place between 1921 and 1930 except for one last spike in the American League in 1936.

ERA--As expected, the ERA peaks matched the runs peaks in both leagues. The ERA difference is a little more than that for runs because the National League had a higher error rate in 1930 than the American League had in 1936.

Strikeouts--Both leagues had similar strikeout rates until the designated hitter arrived in 1973. They both set all-time records in 1997, with the National League leading the American League (with the DH) by 7 percent (ratio of 1.07).

Walks--The American League held a big edge over the National League in walks from 1910 through 1970. Both leagues had sharp unexplained increases near 1950, and thus both leagues set their all-time highs near 1950 with the American League 24 percent ahead of the National League (ratio of 1.24).

Strikeout-to-Walk Ratio--Higher strikeouts and lower walks give the National League an automatic edge in this measure. Both leagues hit their peaks at the end of the 1963-68 period when rule changes favored pitchers.

Table 1-3. All-Time Peaks for Key Measures

	American League		National League		
	Per Game	Year	Per Game	Year	Ratio
Runs	5.67	1936	5.68	1930	1.00
Home Runs	1.21	**1996**	1.03	1955	1.18
Doubles	1.94	1936	1.93	1930	1.01
BatAvg.	.292	1921	.303	1930	1.04
ERA	5.04	1936	4.97	1930	1.01
Strikeouts	6.38	**1997**	6.83	**1997**	1.07
Walks	4.55	1949	3.67	1950	1.24
SO/W Ratio	1.99	1967	2.22	1968	1.12

In summary, strikeout records are being set on an ongoing basis in both leagues (the record year prior to 1997 was 1996). The big swing producing the strikeouts is also producing ongoing home run records in the American League while the National League continues high but below its 1955 peak. Similarly, doubles are high in each league but below the 1930s peaks. Recent increases in walks will probably keep SO/W records in both leagues intact. The peak records for walks and batting average in both leagues are not likely to be exceeded, while runs and ERA records are being approached only in the American League.

To gain perspective from the standpoint of how the game was played in different time periods, it is necessary to know when highs were reached in several years rather than just one all-time peak year. Thus, Tables 1-4 through 1-11 show the top ten years in both leagues for each measure (top 15 for runs). This makes it possible to identify periods when peaks were reached in a cluster of years rather than at different times spread over the century.

Table 1-4 shows the 15 highest years for runs per game in the American and National leagues. Years from the 1990s are shown in boldface. The rankings for runs are extended to the top 15 rather than the top 10 because of the importance of runs in determining offensive peaks, and because no years from the 1990s in the National League make the top 10 list.

American League--In the American League, the 5.39 runs per game recorded in 1996 ranks third on the list. For most of the season 1996 ranked second on the list, but a decline late in the year pulled 1996 down to third place, 0.02 runs per game behind 1930. Similarly, 1994 ranks seventh on the list, but 1932, 1937, and 1994 are essentially in a three-way tie for fifth place. The difference between 1932 in fifth place and 1994 in seventh place is only 0.007 runs per game.

Although 1994 was a strike year, the average runs per game may actually have been helped by the strike because run scoring often declines late in every season. This is because the teams in contention really bear down to hold the opposition in check, while the teams out of contention bring up their younger players who are not capable of producing runs at a major league level.

The strike worked in reverse in 1995 because the strike affected the beginning of the year. Thus, run scoring got off to a slow start and then suffered the normal decline at the end of the year. The result was that 1995 only ranks 14th on the list, but ranking 14th out of 98 years still means it was a year with scoring well above average.

Of the top 15 years, 9 took place in the 1930s, 2 in the 1920s, 3 in the 1990s, and one in the 1950s (1950 was the last year the American League averaged over 5.00 runs per game before 1994, but both 1929 and 1933 also reached the 5.00 mark although they did not make the top 15 list). This confirms that the 1990s represent the best offensive outburst since the 1930s, and the peak reached in 1996 was the highest scoring year in the American League since 1936, a gap of exactly 60 years.

National League--Most of the National League years rank well behind those of the American League. Only in 1930 did the National League have a higher runs per game average in any ranking position than the American League. The first place mark of 5.68 runs per game is 0.01 runs per game ahead of the first place mark of 5.67 in the American League. Every subsequent number is lower in the National League. The National League had only 4 years at 5.00 runs per game or better compared to 17 such years in the American League. The offensive peak in the 1990s placed 1996, 1995, and 1994 on the top 15 list in the National League, but 1996 was only in 11th place on the list compared to the third place ranking for 1996 in the American League. The difference between the leagues in the 1990s is the designated hitter. The difference between the leagues in the 1930 was the amazing record of the Yankees in that decade (Table 2-16).

The National League has 5 years from the 1920s on the list, 4 from the 1930s, 3 from the 1990s, 2 from the 1950s, and, perhaps most surprisingly of all, one from the dead ball period (1903). The Reds set their all-time runs per game record in 1903. They have not been able to top it in the succeeding 95 seasons, and the Reds did not even lead the National League in scoring in 1903. The National League itself has not been able to exceed the 1903 level in any year since 1930. But 1996 was the highest scoring year in the National League since 1953, a gap of 43 years compared to the 60 year gap in the American League (1936 to 1996). The National League clearly would have to adopt the designated hitter rule to approach its prior record highs.

Table 1-4. AL/NL Highest Ranked Years for Runs

	American League			National League	
Rank	Per Game	Year	Rank	Per Game	Year
1	5.67	1936	1	5.68	1930
2	5.41	1930	2	5.36	1929
3	5.39	**1996**	3	5.06	1925
4	5.37	1938	4	5.00	1922
5	5.23	1932	5	4.85	1923
6	5.23	1937	6	4.78	1903
7	5.23	**1994**	7	4.75	1953
8	5.21	1939	8	4.71	1936
9	5.20	1925	9	4.71	1935
10	5.14	1931	10	4.70	1928
11	5.13	1934	11	4.68	**1996**
12	5.12	1921	12	4.68	1934
13	5.09	1935	13	4.66	1950
14	5.07	**1995**	14	4.63	**1995**
15	5.04	1950	15	4.62	**1994**

The relative positions of 1994, 1995, and 1996 on the ranking list in the American and National Leagues is a good indication of the difference that the designated hitter brings to the game in the 1990s. The American League not only approached its prior peaks in 1996, it scored more runs per game in that year than any year in the history of the National League except for the huge spike of 1930. The results are similar in the rankings for home runs and doubles that follow in Table 1-5 and Table 1-6 respectively.

Table 1-5 shows the ten highest years for home runs per game in the American and National leagues. Years from the 1990s are shown in boldface.

American League--The American League set its all-time record for home runs in 1996. The prior record was set in 1987, the last offensive peak in the majors before the middle 1990s. With 1994 in third place on the top ten list, 1997 in fourth, and 1995 in fifth, the American League is clearly in the midst of its highest long-term surge in home runs in the century. If the list were extended past the top ten, 1993 would show up in 13th place.

Table 1-5 shows that this tendency for hitting home runs at a high level for several years in a row has been the hallmark of the American League. The three years from 1985 through 1987 are second, sixth, and seventh on the list (in reverse order), and 1962, 1964, and 1961 occupy positions eight through ten respectively. Home runs averaged 0.95 per game during the 3 years from the 1960s, 1.04 per game from 1985 through 1987, and 1.12 per game from 1993 through 1997. This steady increase from the 1960s to the 1990s puts the 4 years from 1993 through 1997 nearly 18 percent above the 3 years from the 1960s.

Only the decades of the 1960s, 1980s, and 1990s appear on the top ten list (1963 is in 11th place, 1982 in 12th, and 1993 in 13th). This is because the American League began to hit home runs at record levels after teams learned how to use the designated hitter in the decade after its introduction in 1973. The recent trend to hitters whose strategy is to hit it out and who use weight training to be sure they can simply increases the rate at which home run records are set.

There is no reason to expect the record home run pace to stop. Hitters see that hitting home runs brings the best artistic and financial payoffs; fans like high offense, especially when it is built around home runs; new stadiums are usually friendly to home runs; and baseball has a long way to go to match the weight lifting techniques that have become commonplace in other sports. In the next several years the upward trend can be expected to continue.

National League--The National League trailed the American League by 23 percent in home runs per game in 1996 (0.98 compared to 1.21), but 1996 ranks third on the National League top ten list. Further, 1994 ranks seventh, 1997 ranks eighth, and 1995 ranks ninth. The National League hit its peak in home runs in the 1950s. Both runs and home runs declined regularly thereafter, and the National League fell well behind the American League after the designated hitter arrived in 1973. The advent of hitters who can hit it out in the 1990s has brought the National League back to the level of the 1950s, but the league has not yet been able to top its peaks of 1955 and 1956. From 1955 through 1958 the National League averaged 0.98 home runs per game compared to 0.96 home runs per game from 1994 through 1997. As was the case in runs per game, without the designated hitter the National League cannot quite reach its prior peaks in home runs per game.

The average of 0.98 home runs per game reached in 1996 is the highest in the National League since 1956, a gap of exactly 40 years. That is consistent with the fact that 5 of the top 10 years on the list are from the 1950s (1959 and 1954 are 12th and 13th respectively with 1987 11th). With 4 years from the 1990s, 1961 represents the only other decade than the 1950s and 1990s to make the list. The National League was ahead of its 1955 pace early in 1996, but, as mentioned before, offense often falls off at the end of the year, and that decline kept the National League from setting a home run record in 1996. The National League is close enough to its all-time high to possibly match it in a future year, but it will be harder to match the prior average peak over five years.

Table 1-5. AL/NL Highest Ranked Years for Home Runs

	American League			National League	
Rank	Per Game	Year	Rank	Per Game	Year
1	1.21	**1996**	1	1.03	1955
2	1.16	1987	2	0.98	1956
3	1.11	**1994**	3	0.98	**1996**
4	1.09	**1997**	4	0.97	1961
5	1.07	**1995**	5	0.96	1953
6	1.01	1986	6	0.96	1958
7	0.96	1985	7	0.95	**1994**
8	0.96	1962	8	0.95	**1997**
9	0.95	1964	9	0.95	**1995**
10	0.95	1961	10	0.95	1957

Comparing home runs before and after 1973, the year that the designated hitter was introduced, shows substantial differences in the two leagues. For the 6 years on its list that came before 1973, the National League averaged 0.98 home runs per game. For the 3 years before 1973 on its list, the American League averaged 0.95 home runs per game. But for the 7 years on its list after 1973, the American League averaged 1.09 home runs per game. This is far ahead of the 0.96 home runs per game averaged by the National League for the four years on its list that came after 1973. In summary, the average for the American League was 1.09 per game for the years after 1973 and 0.95 home runs per game for the years before 1973. The National League actually declined after 1973, averaging 0.98 before and 0.96 after. These results are a good measure of the difference that the designated hitter makes in the two leagues.

Table 1-6 shows the ten highest years for doubles per game in the American and National leagues. Years from the 1990s are shown in boldface.

American League--The American League set its all-time record for doubles in 1936 (the same year the league set its all-time record for runs). Eight of the top 10 years on the list came between 1927 and 1937, the highest period for American League offense before the 1990s. Two years from the 1990s are on the list (1996 is in 5th place and 1994 in 7th), but both years would be one place higher if each team in the league had hit just one more double in 1996 and 1994 (1997 misses the list by a total of only two doubles for the league as a whole).

Even as it stands, 1996 is the highest year for doubles per game in the American League since the record year of 1936. The rate of doubles per game in 1996 is more impressive when the much higher level of home runs in 1996 as compared to 1936 is considered. In 1936, the American League hit what was then a record level of 0.61 home runs per game (Table 1-1). The combined total of home runs and doubles per game in 1936 was 2.55, with more than 3 doubles being hit for every home run. In 1996 the American League hit 1.21 home runs per game, and the combined total of home runs and doubles was 3.07 per game, with about 1.5 doubles being hit for every home run.

This comparison highlights the fact that in the 1990s a much higher proportion of long fly balls into the gap are going over the fence rather than hitting it on the bounce or on the fly. Further, of the balls staying in the park, a higher percentage were being run down and caught by the greatly improved fielding in 1996 compared to 1936 (the error rate in 1936 was 65 percent higher than that for 1996). The fact that doubles were as high as they were in 1996 is due to the greater average speed of hitters and the disdain for hitting defensively with two strikes. There were, however, many more singles per game in 1936 compared to 1996. This produced a higher batting average overall in 1936. There were also more triples per game in 1936. In 1996, fewer well hit balls stayed in the park, and those that did were more likely to be caught or cut off.

National League--In the peak years for doubles in the major leagues in the 1920s and 1930s, the National League trailed the American League by about 10 percent in doubles per game. In spite of the designated hitter, the difference has decreased to about 7 percent in the 1990s. The National League record of 1.93 doubles per game, set in the league's huge offensive surge in 1930, is just behind the American League record of 1.94. But the difference increases as we move down the top 10 list. The pattern of teams from the 1920s, 1930s, and 1990s is similar in both leagues, but the average of doubles per game is constantly lower on the National League list.

Seven of the top 10 years for doubles in the National League came between 1925 and 1936, even though runs in the league peaked between 1926 and 1930. As in the American League, the 3 years from the 1990s (1994, 1995, and 1997) on the National League list rank in the lower half of the list. But while the most recent peak in the National League (1994) marks a 65 year high in doubles per game, the combined total of home runs and doubles in 1994 was only 2.68. Unlike the American League, the recent combined total in the National League was only a little higher than the total of 2.65 doubles and home runs per game in the prior record year for doubles in 1930. Part of the reason the 1990s total was nearly the same as the 1930s total in the National League while the 1990s total was much higher in the American League is that 1930 in the National League was a year of dramatically high offense. But the difference does reflect well the present difference between the leagues.

Table 1-6. AL/NL Highest Ranked Years for Doubles

American League			National League		
Rank	Per Game	Year	Rank	Per Game	Year
1	1.94	1936	1	1.93	1930
2	1.93	1930	2	1.85	1932
3	1.88	1931	3	1.83	1929
4	1.86	1932	4	1.77	1931
5	1.86	**1996**	5	1.73	1934
6	1.84	1937	6	1.73	**1994**
7	1.84	**1994**	7	1.73	1925
8	1.83	1927	8	1.72	**1997**
9	1.82	1929	9	1.67	**1995**
10	1.81	1935	10	1.67	1936

The recent American League peak for doubles in 1996 was only 4 percent below the league record. The recent National League peak for doubles in 1994 was 10 percent below the league record. The American League set an all-time home run record in 1996. The National League was 5 percent below its 1955 record with its recent peak in home runs in 1996, and it was nearly 8 percent below the home run record when it peaked in doubles in 1994. This means that in spite of its offensive surge in the 1990s, the National League is far from its doubles peaks in the 1930s, and it is also well below its home run peaks in the 1950s. The prime difference between the leagues today is that the American League is very close to its prior offensive records and is setting all-time home run records. The National League is well behind its prior offensive records and is still missing its home run record. The difference is the designated hitter.

Table 1-7 shows the ten highest years for batting average in the American and National leagues. Years from the 1990s are normally shown in boldface, but there are no such years in Table 1-7. The most recent year shown in the table for the American League is 1936, and the most recent year shown for the National League is 1930.

American League--The American League set its all-time record for batting average in 1921, the year after the new rules of 1920 outlawing various "doctored" pitches (including spitballs) were in effect. With new balls being put into play much more often (in 1916 the Cubs and Reds played a full game with just one ball), and better yarn available after World War I, the average ball in play was much cleaner and much easier to hit than its counterpart before 1920. The so-called "dead ball" era was over, but a more proper name would have been the "dirty ball" era. The true introduction of a more lively ball came when the cork-centered ball was patented in 1909. Its use in the following seasons produced a peak in offense in 1911 and 1912. Pitchers responded by doctoring the ball in any way possible, and by 1914 offense was headed back down towards its previous levels. Suddenly changing the rules in 1920 produced another peak in offense, but this one was to last almost two decades.

The fact that the surge in offense was primarily a result of pitchers losing their edge due to changes in the rules is supported by the fact that strikeouts reached all-time lows in the 1920s in both leagues. A "more lively" ball might go farther when hit, but it would not necessarily be easier to hit. However, a cleaner ball that came in relatively straight over the plate was definitely easier to hit and batting averages soared. But pitchers slowly began to respond with new pitches (such as the curve ball and the slider), and in the American League averages never got as high again as they were in 1921. In 1936, led by the Yankees, the American League had its fourth best batting average ever as it set the league record for runs per game (Table 2-1). Otherwise, the best years for the American League for batting average came between 1921 and 1930.

National League--The National League also had a dramatic increase in batting average in 1921. A new record was reached in 1922 and it stood until 1929. Then an all-time peak was reached in 1930, the only year batting averages in either league exceeded .300. The .303 mark for the National League in 1930 was 15 points ahead of the American League in that year and 11 points ahead of the American League's record year in 1921 (the National League mark in 1929 also exceeded the American League record). For the National League, 1921 only ranks fifth on the top 10 list. Both leagues used a ball with higher seams in 1931 (permitting a better grip for curve balls) in an effort to cut down on the number of home runs, but the National League used a different cover. Batting averages in the National League fell by 26 points and home runs fell by almost 50 percent. This marked the end of record batting averages for the National League.

The American League only lost 10 points with their new ball in 1931. They led the National League in batting average the rest of the decade except in 1934, the year both leagues agreed finally to use the same (American League) ball. The National League trailed badly from 1936 through 1938 as the Yankees dominated the major leagues in a way that has never been repeated, and this cemented the perception that the National League was a "pitcher's league" while the American League was a "hitter's league." This difference dissolved during World War II, and the National League was a more potent offensive force than the American League in the 1950s. But neither league was able to come close to the batting averages of the 1930s, let alone the soaring levels of the 1920s.

Table 1-7. AL/NL Highest Ranked Years for Batting Average

American League			National League		
Rank	Per Game	Year	Rank	Per Game	Year
1	.292	1921	1	.303	1930
2	.292	1925	2	.294	1929
3	.290	1924	3	.292	1922
4	.289	1936	4	.292	1925
5	.288	1930	5	.289	1921
6	.285	1927	6	.286	1923
7	.285	1922	7	.284	1924
8	.284	1929	8	.282	1927
9	.284	1920	9	.281	1928
10	.282	1923	10	.280	1926

The 1930s marked the end of high batting averages in both leagues. The American League had a batting average of .279 in 1939. In 1996 the American League hit .277, the highest average in the league since 1939, a span of 57 years. But the 1996 mark was still well below those on the American League's top 10 list as well as below the 1939 mark. Similarly, the National League had a batting average of .272 in 1939. In 1994, the National League had a batting average of .267, the highest average in the league since 1939, a span of 55 years. But the 1994 mark was far below those on the National League's top 10 list, and was well below the 1939 mark. The American League has led the National League in batting average in every year since the designated hitter arrived in 1973, and the 15 point difference recorded in 1996 matched 1989 for the largest difference between the leagues since 1973.

Table 1-8 shows the ten highest years for ERA (earned run average) in the American and National leagues. Years from the 1990s are shown in boldface.

American League--On a league basis the runs scored on offense should directly track runs given up on defense, and thus it could be expected that the list for highest earned runs would be essentially identical to the list for highest runs scored (Table 1-4). But because of the great decrease in errors during the century, earned run averages today are much higher than would be expected based on the ratio of runs scored today to runs scored in the past.

For example, as explained in the Introduction, the percentage of "unearned" runs scored in the 1920s in the American League was 16.1 percent. To date in the 1990s the percentage is 9.1 percent. This is due primarily to the fact that errors per game in the 1920s were nearly 90 percent higher than in the 1990s. But because by definition all runs scored following an error that would have ended an inning are listed as "unearned runs," the exact effect of errors on ERA depends on when the errors were committed. The question of timing becomes more and more important as the number of errors declines. The net result is that ERA levels appear high today compared to prior high-run periods, when in fact the ERA levels of the 1920s and 1930s were in essence "subsidized" by the higher error rates in those decades.

Thus, 1996, 1994, 1995, and 1997 are 2nd, 3rd, 5th, and 10th respectively in Table 1-8, while on the highest runs list (Table 1-4) these 4 years rank only 3rd, 7th, 14th, and 19th respectively. With the American league near its prior runs peaks, and with errors continuing to decline (the league set an all-time low in 1995), in future years the American League could set an all-time record for ERA even if it does not set a runs record. This will not indicate that today's pitchers are much worse than their counterparts from the 1920s and 1930s. In fact, without the designated hitter in the lineup before 1973, one can argue that today's pitchers in the American League are superior to their counterparts in the 1920s and 1930s in spite of many claims to the contrary.

National League--The National League also has had a dramatic decline in errors since the 1920s, and the same analysis that applies to American League ERA levels also applies to National League ERA levels. This is confirmed by the fact that, in the National League, 1996, 1994, 1997, and 1995 rank 5th, 6th, 7th and 8th respectively in Table 1-8, while on the high runs list (Table 1-4) 1996, 1994, 1997, and 1995 rank 11th, 15th, 17th, and 14th respectively. The prime difference in the National League as compared to the American League is that 1930 and 1929 were such high offensive peaks in the National League that the ERA levels for these years are far above the rest of the years on the list. For example, the highest ERA in Table 1-8 for the National League (1930) is 21.2 percent above the ERA level in 10th place (1922) and 15.9 percent above the ERA mark in third place (1953).

In the American League the top ERA value is only 10.5 percent above the ERA level in 10th place and 5.0 percent above that in third place. This demonstrates once again how 1929 and 1930 in the National League form a huge offensive statistical peak in the history of the league in the Twentieth Century. Even with the much lower error levels of today, the National League will almost surely never exceed the ERA levels of 1929 and 1930 unless the National League adopts the designated hitter rule (or all games in the league are played in Coors Field in Denver). If the National League continues to score runs at the 1996 level and errors continue to decline, it may be possible to record an ERA mark above 1953 in third place, but a higher level is very unlikely.

Table 1-8. AL/NL Highest Ranked Years for ERA

American League			National League		
Rank	Per Game	Year	Rank	Per Game	Year
1	5.04	1936	1	4.97	1930
2	4.99	**1996**	2	4.71	1929
3	4.80	**1994**	3	4.29	1953
4	4.79	1938	4	4.27	1925
5	4.71	**1995**	5	4.21	**1996**
6	4.65	1930	6	4.21	**1994**
7	4.62	1937	7	4.20	**1997**
8	4.62	1939	8	4.18	**1995**
9	4.58	1950	9	4.14	1950
10	4.56	**1997**	10	4.10	1922

In spite of the huge difference between 1929 and 1930 as compared to other years in the National League, the peak ERA levels for the American League are still well above the peak National League levels. This is consistent with the fact that the top 15 years for run scoring in the American League are well ahead of the top 15 in the National League (Table 1-4) except for first place where the National League's 5.68 mark in 1930 just barely edges the 5.67 mark for the American League in 1936. But since errors declined between 1930 and 1936, the peak ERA mark for the American League in 1936 is higher than the National League peak ERA mark in 1930. These differences also reflect the fact that the American League outscored the National League by wide margins in the 1930s due to the high-scoring Yankees, and the American League is presently outscoring the National League by a wide margin due to the designated hitter.

Table 1-9 shows the ten highest years for strikeouts per game in the American and National leagues. Years from the 1990s are shown in boldface.

American League--Present strikeout rates support the contention that hitters are concentrating on driving the ball and taking big swings regardless of the strike count. The attitude in the game today is that there is no disgrace in striking out at a high rate as long as the hitter also produces high levels of home runs and runs driven in. This was true of unique hitters like Babe Ruth in the 1920s, but today it is true of nearly every hitter in the league. This is why strikeout records in the majors cluster in three relatively recent periods.

The highest strikeout levels accompany the offensive peak of the 1990s. The next period for high strikeouts is 1986 and 1987 which was the last offensive peak immediately preceding the one in the 1990s. The last period for high strikeouts was from 1963 through 1968 when the rules were changed to favor pitchers and offense collapsed. This last period can be taken as a calibration of the level to which strikeouts can be driven when pitchers are completely in control. The fact that strikeout levels from the 1963-68 period are being eclipsed by the offensive peak of the 1990s proves that hitters have ignored strikeouts in favor of the big swing and hitting it out.

With the designated hitter being born in 1973 (essentially in response to the domination of pitchers in the 1963-68 period), it would be expected that strikeouts in the American League would never again reach the levels of the 1963-68 period. This means that the 1963-68 period should occupy the top positions in the strikeout list. But the peak level for strikeouts in the American League came in 1997, and 1997, 1996, 1994, and 1995 hold 4 of the top 6 positions. The 1963-68 period holds 5 of the top 10 positions, and the other year in the top 10 came in 1987, the last offensive peak prior to the 1990s.

This result infers that if there were no designated hitter in the American League, the high strikeout peaks of the 1963-68 period would be almost completely surpassed by the strikeout rates taking place today. This is exactly what is happening in the National League.

National League--Without the designated hitter, the National League still sends its pitchers to the plate to be blown away by the opposing pitcher. The result of this absurdity, coupled with the big swing discussed above, is that the National League is presently in a strikeout frenzy. It breaks its strikeout records every successive year as the desire to hit it out overwhelms all other forms of hitting. The top 4 positions on the National League list are occupied by 1997, 1996, 1995, and 1994 in that order. The next 2 highest years are 1986 and 1987, the last offensive peak before the 1990s. The 1963-68 period occupies only three places on the list (the 1990s occupy 5 places), and there is every reason to believe that in four more years the peaks of the 1963-68 period will have disappeared from the list for good.

The absence of the designated hitter in the National League makes it the ideal "laboratory" for determining the effect on the strikeout rate of the way the game is played today because it can be compared directly with the 1963-68 period. Rule changes have a great effect on the game as demonstrated by the changes in favor of hitters in 1920, and the changes in favor of pitchers in 1963 (which were eliminated in 1969). But changes in the style of play also have a great effect. Babe Ruth demonstrated this in the 1920s with respect to hitting home runs, and the move to the big swing at any place in the count in the 1990s demonstrates this with respect to strikeouts. Without the designated hitter, the National League should continue to break its strikeout records indefinitely.

Table 1-9. AL/NL Highest Ranked Years for Strikeouts

American League			National League		
Rank	Per Game	Year	Rank	Per Game	Year
1	6.38	**1997**	1	6.83	**1997**
2	6.20	**1996**	2	6.73	**1996**
3	6.14	1967	3	6.61	**1995**
4	6.12	1964	4	6.32	**1994**
5	6.03	**1994**	5	6.01	1986
6	6.00	**1995**	6	6.00	1987
7	5.95	1965	7	5.98	1969
8	5.94	1968	8	5.93	1965
9	5.93	1987	9	5.90	**1991**
10	5.89	1966	10	5.88	1963

The fact that the National League continues to increase its rate of strikeouts is not just an issue of minor statistical importance. The reason strikeouts used to be viewed with disdain for all but the very strongest hitters is the fact that the strikeout is not "just another out" as it has often been called. With runners on base the strikeout is the worst kind of out (excluding, of course, a double play ground ball, and even certain kinds of double plays can result in a run being scored). When the batter strikes out, no runner advances. A situation that has a given probability of producing a run immediately moves to a lower probability. Other kinds of outs that move the runners up a base can maintain the probability of producing a run. The higher level of strikeouts in spite of the surge in hitting home runs is one reason why the National League is not close to its previous records for scoring runs.

Table 1-10 shows the ten highest years for walks per game in the American and National leagues. Years from the 1990s are normally shown in boldface, but there are no such years in Table 1-10. The most recent year shown in the table for the American League is 1956, and the most recent year shown for the National League is 1975.

American League--Peak periods for walks have a mystical flavor in both leagues. Figure 1-7 shows that the American League was always at a higher level than the National League except before 1910, when it was much lower, and in the 1970s and 1980s, when the leagues were nearly the same. But both leagues had a huge spike in walks centered around 1949. The American League was much higher than the National League in this period, but both leagues increased dramatically over their previous and subsequent levels. This effect is discussed at length in my book *The Evolution of Baseball*, but no reason for it has ever been found. The strike zone was changed in 1950 in a way that favored hitters, but walks generally declined from their peaks after 1950, the opposite of what would have been expected. Further, the almost identical pattern of strikeouts in the two leagues over the decades (Figure 1-6) makes it hard to make a case for a de facto difference in strike zones, especially at the time the huge surge in walks was taking place. This odd effect is simply a statistical fact.

The result of these patterns is that years from the period from 1948 through 1956 occupy 6 of the top 10 places on the American League list including the top 4 places. Years from 1936 through 1941 occupy the remaining places on the list. Further, although 1956 in 4th place is only 6.6 percent higher than 1941 in 10th place, 1949 at the top of the list is 19.4 percent above 1941. This demonstrates how sharp the spike was in 1949.

My previous books show that walks are a pitcher's option in that they are issued preferentially to teams with big hitters. But although the period around 1950 was one of good offense in the league, it was far below the 1930s and the 1990s. Still, the years from the 1950 era dominate the list with only 3 years from the 1930s and none from the 1990s making the top 10 (1996 and 1995 do rank 12th and 15th while 1939 and 1934 rank 13th and 14th respectively).

National League--The National League shows the same pattern as the American League in the era around 1950. Years during the period from 1946 through 1954 occupy 7 of the top 10 years on the list including the top 3 positions. But because the National League generally had much lower walks than the American League before 1970, the pattern in the National League is much different after the peak near 1950. The period from 1970 through 1975 occupies the remaining 3 years on the top 10 list in the National League. This is due primarily to expansion as the Expos, Padres, and Astros set all-time team records for walks in 1970, 1974, and 1975 respectively. The records set by the Expos and Padres were the 2nd and 3rd worse years ever in the league.

But except for 1997 in 11th place, there are no years from the 1993-97 period even in the top 20 on the National League list. This is a consistent pattern in the National League. By far the league's biggest offensive outburst in scoring runs came in the 1920s and there are no years from that decade even close to making the top 10 list for walks. The league's top years for home runs came from 1955 through 1959, but the only year from that period close to making the top 10 list is 1955 in 12th place. Considering the huge spike in the 1946-54 period, it is not clear if 1955 is part of that spike or a reaction to the record for home runs that was set in that year in the National League. Whatever the cause, the peak in walks around the 1950 era dominates the rest of the century.

Table 1-10. AL/NL Highest Ranked Years for Walks

	American League			National League	
Rank	Per Game	Year	Rank	Per Game	Year
1	4.55	1949	1	3.67	1950
2	4.37	1950	2	3.60	1947
3	4.23	1948	3	3.58	1954
4	4.06	1956	4	3.56	1970
5	4.02	1938	5	3.55	1948
6	3.96	1951	6	3.54	1949
7	3.93	1936	7	3.54	1946
8	3.89	1955	8	3.52	1951
9	3.84	1937	9	3.51	1974
10	3.81	1941	10	3.47	1975

In the 1990s the American League is once again moving well ahead of the National League in walks. In the 1970s the National League led the American League for the first time in 70 years. This was because the National League rose to a level near its all-time highs in the 1970s while the American League fell to its lowest levels in over 50 years. As is usual in walks, there is no clear reason why either of these things happened. The American League moved slightly ahead again in the 1980s, but so far in the 1990s the American League is 9.7 percent ahead of the National League. This is the highest difference since the 1960s for average walks in a decade. Further, the level of walks in the American League in 1996 was its highest since 1956. It appears the level of walks in the American League is rising in response to increasing offense, but the National League remains consistently inconsistent.

Table 1-11 shows the ten highest years for strikeout-to-walk (SO/W) ratios in the American and National leagues. Years from 1990s are shown in boldface.

American League--As might be expected, the highest strikeout-to-walk ratios in the American League came during the 1963-68 period when the rules were changed to favor pitchers. Every year from the 1963-68 period appears on the top 10 list, accounting for 6 of the 10 places including the top 3 positions. Strikeouts were high and walks were low in the 1963-68 period, and thus, with only two exceptions, every year from 1963 through 1968 was a record year compared to the years before 1963.

The two exceptions are 1903 and 1904. The American League set major league lows for walks in these years, and thus the SO/W ratios were very high. This was because batters had a hard time adjusting to what was then a new rule in the American League. Before 1903, foul balls were not counted as strikes. When the American League and the National League agreed on common rules in 1903 (one of the reasons this book and my other books start in 1903), the American League adopted the rule already in effect in the National League that foul balls would count as strikes until the batter had two strikes. Batters found themselves relatively quickly behind in the count compared to prior years and walks fell sharply until hitters adjusted to the new rule.

The other years on the American League top 10 list are 1972 and 1997. For the American League, 1972 was a continuation of the 1963-68 period. Although the rules favoring pitchers were modified in 1969, the American League recovered very little from the drought of runs in the 1963-68 period. In 1972 the league scored fewer runs than in all but one year of the 1963-68 period. Pitchers were as dominant as ever, and the result was the designated hitter rule in 1973. This caused a decline in SO/W ratios, and the only year on the top 10 list after 1972 is the record strikeout year of 1997 when there was a drop in walks compared to the earlier years in the 1993-97 big swing period. Thus, although walks are much higher in 1993 through 1997 in the American League than they were in 1963 through 1968, the record level of strikeouts in 1997 made that year a top ten year for SO/W ratio.

National League--The 1963-68 period was also a record time for SO/W ratios in the National League. As in the American League, every year in the 1963-68 period is on the top 10 list. But in the National League the 6 years in the 1963-68 period occupy 6 of the top 7 places on the list, and every one of these years is higher than the record year of 1967 in the American League. Further, without the designated hitter in the National League, years from the 1990s hold the 4 positions on the list not held by the 1963-68 period. After 1965 in 5th place, the 7 years from 1991 through 1997 fill 7 of the next 9 positions. Only 1988 in 11th place (not shown on the list) manages to break the hold the 1963-68 and 1991-97 periods have on the top 14 places for SO/W ratios.

The fact that years from the 1963-68 and 1994-97 periods fill the top 10 list reflects the changes in the game after 1992. Pitchers dominated in the 1963-68 period thanks to the rule changes in their favor. Pitchers cannot be said to be dominant in the 1994-97 period in light of the offensive outburst in this period, but the league is still at a very high level in SO/W ratios because pitchers are setting records in strikeouts. When such a traditional measure of pitching effectiveness as SO/W ratio is near record highs in the league while home runs are also near record highs, and runs are at their highest levels in nearly 70 years, it is a clear sign that the game has changed. Pitchers are blowing away hitters at record levels while hitters are torching pitchers at near record levels.

Table 1-11. AL/NL Highest Ranked Years for SO/W Ratios

American League			National League		
Rank	Per Game	Year	Rank	Per Game	Year
1	1.99	1967	1	2.22	1968
2	1.98	1968	2	2.11	1966
3	1.93	1966	3	2.11	1964
4	1.92	1904	4	2.09	1963
5	1.90	1964	5	2.04	1965
6	1.85	1903	6	2.03	**1996**
7	1.84	**1997**	7	2.03	1967
8	1.83	1963	8	2.00	**1995**
9	1.82	1965	9	1.99	**1997**
10	1.77	1972	10	1.95	**1994**

The reason that both hitters and pitchers in the National League are equally effective based on these measures is the change to the big swing regardless of the strike count. Hitters make contact less often (hence the increase in strikeouts), but when they do make contact the ball jumps out of the park (helped by higher bat speeds due to stronger hitters and the effect of the altitude at Coors Field). Similar changes are taking place in the American League, but with the designated hitter the American League hits home runs and scores runs at a much higher level than the National League. The pitchers in the American League are faced with a bigger challenge due to the designated hitter, and the lower level of strikeouts (and higher walks) in the league reduces the SO/W ratio. For example, while the American League scored 15 percent more runs than the National League in 1996, the National League led in SO/W ratio by 24 percent.

Figure 1-1 shows runs per game by decade from the 1900s through the 1990s for the American and National leagues. The figure also shows runs per game for the five year offensive outburst from 1993 through 1997. Since both the 1900s and 1990s are not full ten year "decades," the specific years in each period are shown in the first column below the graph. The remaining columns show the exact runs scored in each period, and the ratios of the two league values with the higher value compared to the lower value.

American League--The run scoring peaks for the AL in the 1920s and 1930s that were discussed in the preceding tables are clearly shown in Figure 1-1. Runs per game fell sharply after the 1930s, and by the 1960s they approached the low levels reached early in the century. But after the introduction of the designated hitter in 1973, runs by decade steadily increased in the AL (Figure 4-1 shows yearly variations since 1987). Further, runs per game in the offensive outburst during the 1993-97 period came within 3 percent of the record set in 1935-39 (Table 1-1). Thus, in the 1990s, with the help of the designated hitter, the AL was close to its highest run scoring levels ever. Seven of the 14 teams in the league set all-time records in the 1990s for runs per game (Table 2-1).

The greatest difference between the AL and the NL came in the 1930s when the AL outscored the NL by a ratio of 1.136 or 13.6 percent. The AL is ahead by 9.1 percent so far in the 1990s, just behind the 1980s as the second highest ratio ever. For the five years from 1993 through 1997, the AL outscored the NL by 9.9 percent. The AL jumped well ahead of the NL in scoring runs in the 1980s thanks to the designated hitter, and the AL continued to hold its margin as the overall level of offense increased in the 1990s.

National League--Run scoring by decade in the NL peaked in the 1920s (the peak individual year for the league was 1930 as shown in Table 1-2), and the NL declined by nearly 14 percent in runs per game from the 1920s through the 1980s. The 1990s began even lower than the 1980s, but the offensive surge that started with expansion (and the Colorado Rockies) in 1993 lifted NL runs per game by 1997 to their highest levels since the 1930s. But because of the poor start in the 1990s, the National League for the full decade of the 1990s will be hard pressed to beat its mark of the 1950s, let alone the 1930s or 1920s.

As shown in Part II, the Colorado Rockies are scoring runs at a much higher level than the rest of the National League teams. This means that although the NL overall is scoring much better in the 1990s than in prior decades, it will not return to its record levels anytime soon. Further, without the designated hitter, the NL continues to stay well behind the AL in scoring runs in spite of the general offensive upsurge of the 1990s. This difference may disappear if any proposed realignment of the leagues results in the DH being adopted in the NL.

Figure 1-2 shows that the differences between the leagues in home runs is even greater than the differences between the leagues in runs.

Figure 1-1. AL/NL Runs Per Game by Decade

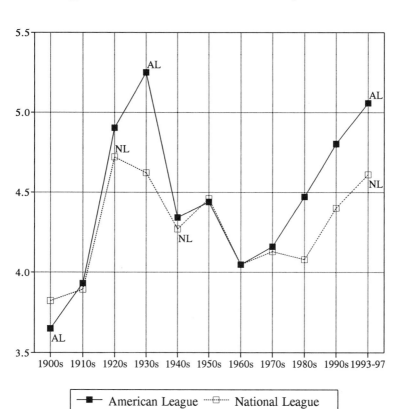

Period	AL Runs Per Game	NL Runs Per Game	AL/NL Ratios
1903-09	3.65	3.82	1.048
1910-19	3.93	3.89	1.010
1920-29	4.90	4.72	1.038
1930-39	5.25	4.62	1.136
1940-49	4.34	4.27	1.018
1950-59	4.44	4.46	1.005
1960-69	4.05	4.05	1.000
1970-79	4.16	4.13	1.006
1980-89	4.47	4.08	1.095
1990-97	4.80	4.40	1.091
1993-97	5.06	4.61	1.099

Figure 1-2 shows home runs per game by decade from the 1900s through the 1990s for the American and National leagues. The figure also shows home runs per game for the five year offensive outburst from 1993 through 1997. Since both the 1900s and 1990s are not full ten year "decades," the specific years in each period are shown in the first column below the graph. The remaining columns show the exact home runs per game hit in each period, and the ratios of the two league values with the higher value compared to the lower value.

American League--The AL will set its all-time record for home runs per game for a decade in the 1990s as the level for 1990 through 1997 is already 10 percent ahead of the previous record decade of the 1980s. The AL set its all-time record for a single year in 1996 (Table 1-5). The AL trailed the NL in home runs per game by 0.53 to 0.51 for the 1903-72 period, but since the DH was born in 1973, the AL has never failed to hit more home runs per game in a season than the NL (Figure 4-2 shows yearly variations since 1987). Eight of the 14 teams in the AL set all-time records in the 1990s for home runs per game (Table 2-3), with 4 of those teams setting their records in 1996 alone. Further, 7 of the top 10 individual years in the AL came in the 1990s (Table 2-18). The greatest era for hitting home runs in the AL is right now.

The largest difference between the AL and the NL came in the 1980s when the AL led by a ratio of 1.258 or 25.8 percent (the NL led the AL by 19.2 percent in the 1950s). The AL is ahead by 14.1 percent so far in the 1990s, and for the five years from 1993 through 1997, the AL led by 15.0 percent. The NL closed the gap somewhat in the 1990s thanks to the Colorado Rockies and the increased emphasis on the home run, but the designated hitter will keep the AL well ahead of the NL.

National League--Home runs per game in the NL peaked in the 1950s (its best year was 1955 as shown in Table 1-3), and the NL declined by nearly 23 percent in home runs per game from the 1950s through the 1980s. The 1990s began only a little ahead of the 1980s, but the offensive surge that started with expansion (and the Colorado Rockies) in 1993 lifted NL home runs per game in 1996 to their highest level since 1956. However, because of the slow start, it is unlikely the NL for the full decade of the 1990s will match its record of the 1950s. The five year average of 0.94 for the 1993-97 period also trails the league's five year record of 0.97 for the 1955-59 period.

As shown in Part II, the Colorado Rockies hit home runs at a much higher rate than the rest of the league. They set the all-time league record in 1997, and are the only team from the 1990s to appear on the league's top ten list for home runs per game in a season (Table 2-19). The Rockies must maintain their pace to keep the NL close to its 1950s peaks. But the NL has reversed a 40 year decline in home runs since the 1950s. Although it remains well behind the AL, the NL today is enjoying its second best era ever in hitting home runs.

Figure 1-2. AL/NL Home Runs Per Game by Decade

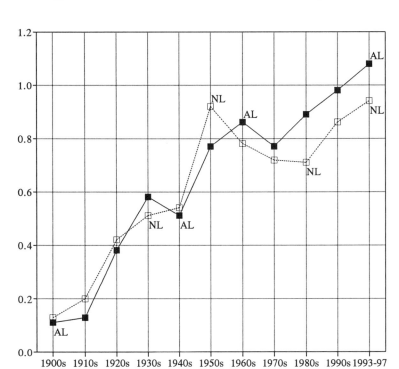

Period	AL HR Per Game	NL HR Per Game	AL/NL Ratios
1903-09	0.11	0.13	1.118
1910-19	0.13	0.20	1.505
1920-29	0.38	0.42	1.113
1930-39	0.58	0.51	1.134
1940-49	0.51	0.54	1.047
1950-59	0.77	0.92	1.192
1960-69	0.86	0.78	1.099
1970-79	0.77	0.72	1.064
1980-89	0.89	0.71	1.258
1990-97	0.98	0.86	1.141
1993-97	1.08	0.94	1.150

Figure 1-3 shows doubles per game by decade from the 1900s through the 1990s for the American and National leagues. The figure also shows doubles per game for the five year offensive outburst from 1993 through 1997. Since both the 1900s and 1990s are not full ten year "decades," the specific years in each period are shown in the first column below the graph. The remaining columns show the exact doubles hit in each period, and the ratios of the two league values with the higher value compared to the lower value.

American League--The AL set its all-time record for doubles per game for a decade in the 1930s, the same decade in which it set its runs records. Doubles declined with runs in the following decades, but the offensive surge that began in 1993 brought doubles per game back to near record levels in the 1993-97 period. 1996 and 1994 rank 5th and 7th on the AL top ten list for doubles, and 1997 nearly ties for 10th (Table 1-6). If this rate continues, the 1990s could match the 1920s as the 2nd highest decade ever for doubles per game in the AL. Three of the original 8 teams (Red Sox, Twins, and Yankees) set franchise records for doubles in the 1990s. This means that 9 of the 14 teams in the AL set franchise records for doubles per game in the 1990s (Table 2-5). This is partly due to the high offensive level in the 1993-97 period, and partly due to the fact that the average player today is faster than his counterpart in the 1930s.

The largest difference between the AL and the NL came in the 1920s when the AL led by a ratio of 1.108 or 10.8 percent. In the 1990s the AL led by 6.9 percent. This is not quite as high as the 1930s when the level of doubles was nearly identical to that of the 1993-97 period. The NL led the AL in doubles for three straight decades from the 1940s through the 1970s until the DH put the AL back on top again in the 1980s and 1990s.

National League--The peak decade for doubles per game for the NL was the 1930s, even though NL runs peaked in the 1920s. Doubles in the NL declined as offense declined after the 1930s, but even after the DH was born in 1973 the NL stayed closer to the AL in doubles than in home runs. The offensive peak in the 1993-97 period produced a higher surge in doubles than in runs or home runs in the NL. 1994, 1995, and 1996 all made the top 10 list in the NL (Table 1-6), and then 1997 took over 8th on the list and pushed 1996 into 11th. 1994 was the best year for doubles per game in the NL since 1932. As a result, the 1990s are the 2nd best decade in doubles per game for the NL, and the 1993-97 period nearly matches the record level of 1.69 set in the full decade of the 1930s.

NL runs, home runs, and batting average in the 1990s, although at high levels historically, are all well below previous peaks in the league. But doubles are nearly the same as the previous peak. It appears this is due to the greater average speed of the players today as compared to the 1930s. It might also be due in part to artificial surfaces where the ball gets by the fielder faster than before, even though the fielders are much more skilled than ever before.

Figure 1-3. AL/NL Doubles Per Game by Decade

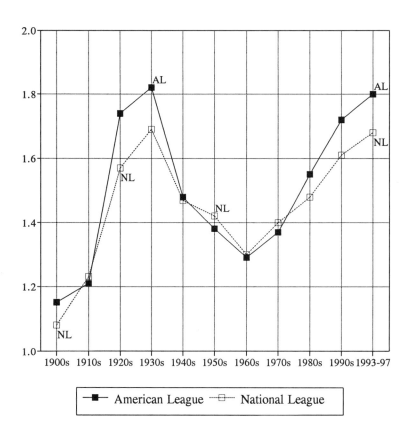

Period	AL 2B Per Game	NL 2B Per Game	AL/NL Ratios
1903-09	1.15	1.08	1.066
1910-19	1.21	1.23	1.015
1920-29	1.74	1.57	1.108
1930-39	1.82	1.69	1.079
1940-49	1.48	1.47	1.006
1950-59	1.38	1.42	1.026
1960-69	1.29	1.30	1.013
1970-79	1.37	1.40	1.023
1980-89	1.55	1.48	1.045
1990-97	1.72	1.61	1.069
1993-97	1.80	1.68	1.073

Figure 1-4 shows batting average by decade from the 1900s through the 1990s for the American and National leagues. The figure also shows batting average for the five year offensive outburst from 1993 through 1997. Since both the 1900s and 1990s are not full ten year "decades," the specific years in each period are shown in the first column below the graph. The remaining columns show the exact batting average in each period, and the ratios of the two league values with the higher value compared to the lower value.

American League--The AL set its all-time record for batting average in the 1920s, the same decade in which the NL set its record. This was due to the dramatic rule changes of 1920 and other changes which are described in the text accompanying Table 1-7. There was an immediate surge in batting average and the AL set its all-time record in 1921, a record that has stood for 76 years. Similarly, the record average for the decade of the 1920s has stood for seven decades. Batting averages in the AL were in "free fall" from the end of the 1930s onward. This effect was ignored by the powers that be in baseball, and when the rules were changed in the 1963-68 period to favor pitchers (and decrease home runs), AL batting averages fell to their lowest levels ever, including the so-called "dead ball" period (as previously noted, the "dirty ball" period would be a much more accurate name for the first two decades of the century).

The result of the death of offense in the 1960s was the birth of the designated hitter in the AL. The NL did not fall off as much at that time and thus did not adopt the new rule. The AL, after leading the NL in batting average by as much as one point in only 1 of the first 8 decades of the century (the 1930s), took a big lead in the 1980s and 1990s. The result was much more offense in the AL.

National League--The NL peaked in batting average in the 1920s for the same reasons that caused the AL peak. The NL set its all-time record in the big explosion of 1930, but the other 9 places on the top 10 list are taken by the years between 1921 and 1929 (Table 1-7). The NL declined steadily after 1930 and hit bottom in the 1960s as a result of the rule changes in the 1963-68 period. But the NL did not fall as far as the AL, and thus the NL did not see a need for the DH. It seemed to be a proper choice when the NL matched the AL in batting average in the 1970s, but the NL fell behind in the 1980s and has not been close to the AL in batting average (or runs and home runs) since. The batting average for the NL from the 1960s through the 1980s was the same or lower than it was from 1910 though 1919, a decade that was part of the so-called "dead ball" period.

The NL broke out of its dead ball batting averages in the offensive outburst that began in 1993. Averages for the 1990s are back to the levels of the 1950s, and the league batting average in the 1993-97 period is higher than in any similar period since the 1930s. But it is still well below the levels of the 1920s and 1930s. NL runs are similarly far below those periods in spite of the 1993-97 offensive surge and the huge increase in home runs since the 1920s.

Figure 1-4. AL/NL Batting Average by Decade

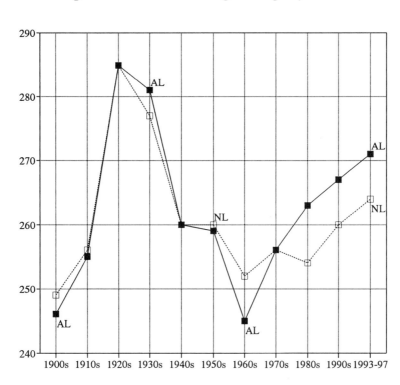

Period	AL Batting Avg.	NL Batting Avg.	AL/NL Ratios
1903-09	246	249	1.013
1910-19	255	256	1.002
1920-29	285	285	1.002
1930-39	281	277	1.014
1940-49	260	260	1.000
1950-59	259	260	1.007
1960-69	245	252	1.029
1970-79	256	256	1.003
1980-89	263	254	1.033
1990-97	267	260	1.028
1993-97	271	264	1.029

Figure 1-5 shows ERA by decade from the 1900s through the 1990s for the American and National leagues. The figure also shows ERA for the five year offensive outburst from 1993 through 1997. Since both the 1900s and 1990s are not full ten year "decades," the specific years in each period are shown in the first column below the graph. The remaining columns show the exact ERA in each period, and the ratios of the two league values with the higher value compared to the lower value.

American League--ERA values would be expected to track runs on a league basis, but a glance at Figure 1-1 shows that the ERA plot in Figure 1-5 is much more "compressed" than the plot for runs in Figure 1-1. This is a direct result of the manner in which ERA is determined and the fact that errors have been decreasing in both leagues throughout the century. If an error extends an inning, all runs scored after that error are defined as "unearned" no matter how hard the pitcher is hit. This means that in periods with high error levels ERA values will appear artificially low compared to periods when errors are much lower.

The original 16 teams all set their records for low ERA in the "dead ball" era in the first two decades of the century. This is only partly because run scoring was in fact at low levels in that era. Errors were also very high compared to today (errors per game have declined by 60 percent since the first decade of the century). The result is that earned runs were only 72 percent of runs scored from 1903 through 1909 while in the 1990s earned runs are 91 percent of runs scored. An ERA of 2.75 in the 1903-09 period would be 3.50 in the 1990s. More specifically, in the AL, the league ERA in the 1910-19 period was 2.93 with an earned run percentage of 74.6 percent. In the 1960s the earned run percentage was 88.6 percent. This would make the 2.93 ERA equivalent to an ERA of 3.48 in the 1960s. The actual ERA in the 1960s was 3.59. "Dead ball" era pitchers were not much different than their 1960s counterparts after all.

The result of this effect is that ERA values in the AL are at all-time highs in the 1990s even though runs are not. The difference is not in the quality of the pitching. The difference is in the quality of the fielding. With errors still declining in both leagues, ERA as presently defined is an almost meaningless measure today. Deducting runs due to baserunners reaching base on an error or scoring as a result of an error may be reasonable, but otherwise runs allowed is a suitable measure of pitching quality today. After all, a pitcher's ERA is not increased as the result of great defensive plays that save runs.

National League--The analysis for the NL is the same as for the AL. The only difference is that the NL for some reason commits more errors than the AL and has done so since the 1940s. The gap has grown since the 1940s even as errors in both leagues keep declining. It is not due to the DH not playing in the field because the gap was largest in the 1960s before the DH was born. There is no clear reason for it, but it is persistent and statistically significant.

Figure 1-5. AL/NL ERA by Decade

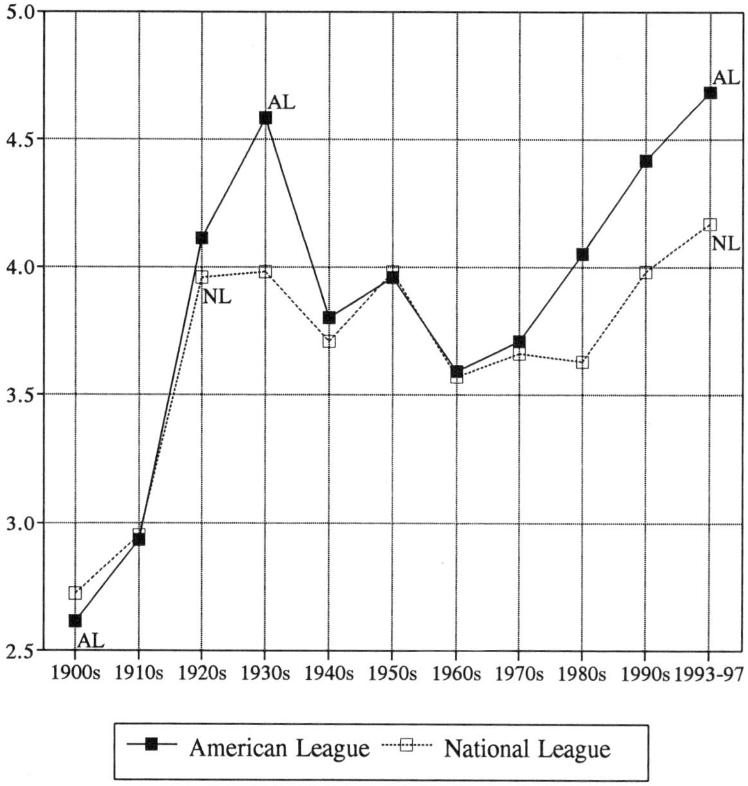

Period	AL ERA	NL ERA	AL/NL Ratios
1903-09	2.61	2.72	1.040
1910-19	2.93	2.95	1.009
1920-29	4.11	3.96	1.039
1930-39	4.58	3.98	1.152
1940-49	3.80	3.71	1.025
1950-59	3.96	3.98	1.004
1960-69	3.59	3.57	1.005
1970-79	3.71	3.66	1.012
1980-89	4.05	3.63	1.116
1990-97	4.42	3.98	1.111
1993-97	4.68	4.17	1.122

Figure 1-6 shows strikeouts per game by decade from the 1900s through the 1990s for the American and National leagues. The figure also shows strikeouts per game for the five year offensive outburst from 1993 through 1997. Since both the 1900s and 1990s are not full ten year "decades," the specific years in each period are shown in the first column below the graph. The remaining columns show the exact strikeouts in each period, and the ratios of the two leagues with the higher value compared to the lower value.

American League--Strikeouts decreased sharply in the 1920s. This was a result of the changes outlined in the text accompanying Table 1-7. Pitchers lost their tools and were dominated by hitters. If the dramatic increase in offense in the 1920s was caused by a "more lively" ball, there would be no reason for strikeouts to decrease. A more lively ball is not easier to hit. But if the increase in offense was due to the many rule changes that did in fact make the ball easier to hit, strikeouts would decline. That is exactly what happened in both leagues.

Pitchers quickly began to accommodate to the changes, and strikeouts increased steadily through the 1950s, and then hit new peaks in the 1960s when the rules were changed in favor of pitchers in 1963. The reversal of the rule changes in 1969 caused strikeouts to decline in the 1970s, and the addition of the DH in 1973 caused the AL to fall well below the NL in strikeouts for the first time in the century. The AL has remained well below ever since.

The AL set its all-time highs for strikeouts in the 1993-97 period because the strategy of the big swing is to ignore strikeouts in favor of trying to drive the ball at all points in the count. Years from this period occupy 4 of the top 6 places on the top 10 list with 1997 in first place (Table 1-9).

National League--The NL tracked the AL in strikeouts for most of the century, with the major difference occurring after the AL adopted the DH in 1973. Since this difference is fully explained by the DH, there is nothing in strikeout data that supports claims of the NL being a "pitcher's league" or the league umpires having a different strike zone than their counterparts in the AL. What the strikeout data do support is the fact that the offensive outburst of the 1920s was due to pitchers being overwhelmed by the rule changes in 1920, and the fact that the offensive outburst of the 1990s is primarily due to the strikeout being ignored by the strategy of the big swing (and the skill and training of today's hitters that makes the big swing productive).

Five of the top 10 ten years for strikeouts in the NL came in the 1990s (Table 1-9), including the top 4 years of 1997 through 1994 (1993 is in 11th place). Strikeouts in the decade of the 1990s are more than twice as high as in the decade of the 1920s (in 1997 strikeouts accounted for 25 percent of all outs in a game). If the NL eventually adopts the DH as part of league realignment, 1997 may stand as a historical peak in strikeouts for both leagues. Otherwise, strikeouts in the NL can be expected to increase indefinitely.

Figure 1-6. AL/NL Strikeouts Per Game by Decade

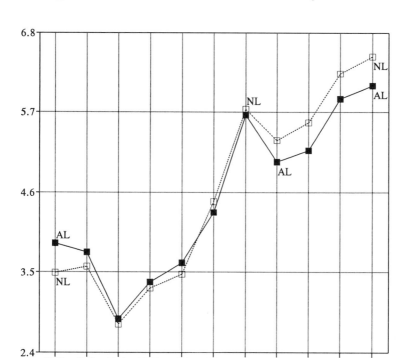

Period	AL SO Per Game	NL SO Per Game	AL/NL Ratios
1903-09	3.89	3.49	1.114
1910-19	3.77	3.58	1.052
1920-29	2.85	2.78	1.025
1930-39	3.36	3.28	1.024
1940-49	3.62	3.47	1.044
1950-59	4.32	4.47	1.035
1960-69	5.66	5.74	1.014
1970-79	5.01	5.31	1.061
1980-89	5.17	5.55	1.073
1990-97	5.88	6.23	1.060
1993-97	6.06	6.47	1.067

Figure 1-7 shows walks per game by decade from the 1900s through the 1990s for the American and National leagues. The figure also shows walks per game for the five year offensive outburst from 1993 through 1997. Since both the 1900s and 1990s are not full ten year "decades," the specific years in each period are shown in the first column below the graph. The remaining columns show the exact walks in each period, and the ratios of the two leagues with the higher value compared to the lower value.

American League--As discussed in the text accompanying Table 1-10, walks are one measure in baseball that seem to have little relationship to the way the game was being played at different points in the century. AL walks per game were so low in 1903 and 1904 that these years still remain on the top 10 list for SO/W ratio in spite of the dramatic increase in strikeouts later in the century (Table 1-11). But walks in the 1905-09 period were 15 percent higher than in the 1903-04 period (a big increase over such a small increment of time), and walks in the 1910-19 period were 35 percent higher than in the 1903-09 period. This put the AL ahead of the NL in the second decade and the AL stayed far ahead of the NL until the 1970s.

By the 1930s walks were 60 percent higher than in the 1903-09 period, and they climbed slowly from that level to an all-time peak in the 1950s. The 10 highest years for walks in the AL came between 1936 and 1956 (Table 1-10), with an especially sharp peak around 1950. No individual year in the 1990s is close to the peaks around 1950, even though the average of the 1993-97 period is not dramatically far from the average of the 1950s.

Walks fell sharply after the 1950s as would be expected due to the rule changes favorable to pitchers in the 1960s. But AL walks stayed low even after the 1960s before climbing again in the 1990s. Walks are primarily a pitcher's decision, but it is not easy to determine exactly what they are deciding.

National League--Ignoring the AL pattern, walks in the NL were nearly constant for the first 4 decades in spite of the increase in offense that started in the 1920s. NL walks soared in the 1940s and peaked around 1950 at the same time the AL peaked. However, after dipping in the 1960s in response to the rule changes favoring pitchers, NL walks rebounded to high levels in the 1970s. This gave the NL higher walks than the AL for the first time since the first decade of the century, and 3 years from the 1970s make the NL top 10 list for walks (Table 1-10). NL and AL walks stayed nearly equal in the 1970s and 1980s, but when AL walks increased in response to the offensive surge in the 1990s NL walks changed very little just as they had in the offensive surge of the 1920s.

It is not clear what will happen to NL walks in the future even if they adopt the DH. The pattern of strikeouts in Figure 1-7 argues against any de facto difference in the strike zone in the two leagues, but there is no satisfactory explanation for the different pattern of walks over the century.

Figure 1-7. AL/NL Walks Per Game by Decade

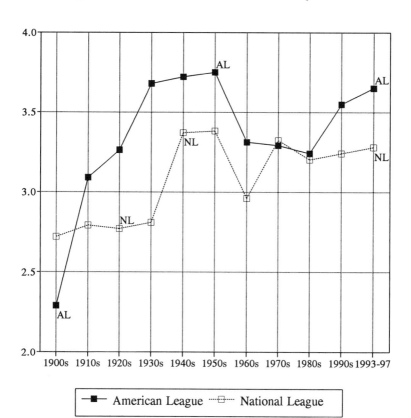

Period	AL Walks Per Game	NL Walks Per Game	AL/NL Ratios
1903-09	2.29	2.72	1.190
1910-19	3.09	2.79	1.108
1920-29	3.26	2.77	1.176
1930-39	3.68	2.81	1.309
1940-49	3.72	3.37	1.105
1950-59	3.75	3.38	1.111
1960-69	3.31	2.96	1.118
1970-79	3.29	3.32	1.009
1980-89	3.24	3.20	1.011
1990-97	3.55	3.24	1.097
1993-97	3.65	3.28	1.112

Figure 1-8 shows strikeout-to-walk ratios by decade from the 1900s through the 1990s for the American and National leagues. The figure also shows SO/W ratios for the five year offensive outburst from 1993 through 1997. Since both the 1900s and 1990s are not full ten year "decades," the specific years in each period are shown in the first column below the graph. The remaining columns show the exact SO/W ratios in each period, and the ratios of the two league values with the higher value compared to the lower value.

American League--As shown in Figure 1-7, walks were so low in AL in the first decade that the league recorded a SO/W ratio for the decade that was not topped by either league until the 1960s when the rules were changed to favor pitchers. The AL just barely topped the record (1.71 to 1.70), and the years of 1904 and 1903 are 4th and 6th respectively on the top 10 list (Table 1-11). They will remain on the list indefinitely as long as the AL continues to use the DH.

SO/W ratios fell to record lows in the 1920s when strikeouts fell to record lows as pitchers lost their "doctored" pitches in the rule changes of 1920. It is hard to imagine today that in the full decade of the 1920s, AL pitchers only recorded 81 strikeouts for every 100 walks. The NL has never had a decade when the rate of strikeouts was less than that of walks. But the AL remained in this condition from the 1920s through the 1940s.

The AL finally brought their SO/W ratios above 1.0 in the 1950s, and then they soared to record levels in the 1960s when the rules were changed in favor of pitchers in 1963. This is a clear demonstration of how dramatically poorly thought out rule changes can change the balance of power between pitchers and hitters in baseball. The adoption of the DH in 1973 brought AL SO/W ratios down from record highs, but they remained historically high for the rest of the century. The DH has effectively stabilized SO/W ratios in the AL. They have changed relatively little since the DH was adopted.

National League--Partly because of its consistent pattern of walks, the NL did not decrease in SO/W ratio as much as the AL did when strikeouts in both leagues fell in the 1920s. But the NL soared just as dramatically as the AL did when the rules were changed in the 1960s. The NL stayed ahead of the AL in SO/W ratio when the NL did not adopt the DH, and the NL was back near record highs in the 1990s when strikeouts soared in response to the big swing strategy. However, in spite of the all-time strikeout records in the 1990s, years from that decade are in the lower half of the top 10 SO/W list (Table 1-11) because of the higher level of walks in the 1990s. The recent peak SO/W year of 1996 ranks only 6th on the SO/W list.

If SO/W ratio is accepted as a key measure of pitcher quality, Figure 1-8 demonstrates that pitchers on average have never been better than they are today. Even the unique performance of the 1903-09 period in the AL is little different than that of the AL today in spite of the existence of the DH in the lineup.

Figure 1-8. AL/NL SO/W Ratio by Decade

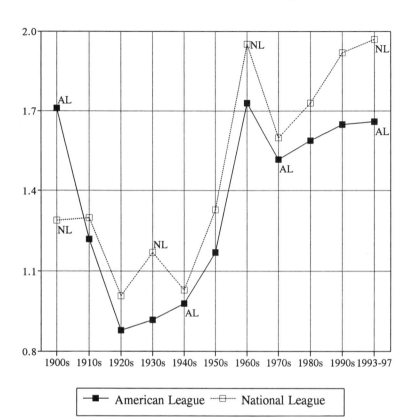

Period	AL SO/W Ratio	NL SO/W Ratio	AL/NL Ratios
1903-09	1.71	1.29	1.329
1910-19	1.22	1.30	1.059
1920-29	0.88	1.01	1.155
1930-39	0.92	1.17	1.278
1940-49	0.98	1.03	1.049
1950-59	1.17	1.33	1.142
1960-69	1.73	1.95	1.132
1970-79	1.52	1.60	1.052
1980-89	1.59	1.73	1.086
1990-97	1.65	1.92	1.162
1993-97	1.66	1.97	1.185

Part II
Team Comparisons

Team Peak Years

Table 2-1 shows peak years for runs for American League teams. Years from the 1990s are in boldface. The first part of the table shows runs peaks on a per game basis, while the second part shows runs peaks on a total year basis. The teams are listed in order of their best year in franchise history. But the table does not represent the best years ever in the league because the second or third best years for teams at the top of the list usually are better than the best year for teams farther down the list. The highest ranked years for runs regardless of how many times one team appears on the list are shown in Table 2-16.

The Yankees of the 1930s dominated both leagues in scoring runs, and they have a big lead in the rankings for both per game and total runs. This infers that the offensive level of the 1930s was dramatically better than that of the 1990s. But the record of the Yankees of the 1930s has to be put in perspective. In Table 2-16 they occupy 7 of the top 9 places on the list of the 10 highest scoring years ever in the American League. *The Evolution of Baseball* shows that the average runs per game for the Yankees in the full decade of the 1930s (6.29 runs per game over 10 years) would tie for eighth place on the list of peak *individual* years. The Yankees scored more than 1000 runs in a season four different times in the 1930s. Only the Red Sox in 1950 and the Cards in 1930 have been able to do it even once. The Mariners came close in 1996 with 993 runs, but even though the Mariners led the majors in runs in the offensive outburst of 1996, and they played a longer season, they were still 74 runs below the record 1067 runs recorded by the Yankees in 1931.

The Yankees of the 1930s were a team from another planet, overwhelming the other 15 teams in the majors. But in the 1990s many of the 28 teams reached or came close to a peak in scoring runs. Thus, although the run scoring records of the American League overall in the 1930s are being closely approached in the 1990s, the team scoring records of the Yankees in the 1930s should stand for a long time, both on the basis of runs per game and total runs in a season.

There are four teams with a different year for a peak on the basis of runs per game and a peak on the basis of total runs scored. The Yankees were almost identical in 1930 and 1931 in scoring runs, but a small difference in games played produced a per game peak in 1930 and a total runs peak in 1931. The same was true for the Twins in 1936 and 1930. The Indians, however, set their peak for runs per game in 1994 when the strike cut the number of games played to only 113. Thus, their peak for total runs was in 1996 when they had a good per game mark for a full 162 game season. The Angels also set their peak per game mark in a season shortened by the strike (1995), but their offense was not as good in 1996 and 1997, so their total runs peak reached in 1979, when they won their first division title, remains at the top of their total runs list.

Of the original 8 teams, 5 had their per game peak in the 1930s, 2 in the 1990s (Orioles and Indians), and 1 (the Red Sox) in 1950. But the Twins missed their total runs peak by only 15 runs in 1996 and the White Sox were only 22 runs short. These teams have the lowest total year peaks of the original 8 and the longer season could help them move their total year peaks to the 1990s.

Table 2-1. AL Teams Peak Years For Runs

Per Game Basis				Total Year Basis			
Team	Per Game	Total	Year	Team	Total	Per Game	Year
Yankees	6.90	1062	1930	Yankees	1067	6.88	1931
Red Sox	6.67	1027	1950	Red Sox	1027	6.67	1950
A's	6.37	981	1932	Mariners	993	6.17	**1996**
Tigers	6.22	958	1934	A's	981	6.37	1932
Mariners	6.17	993	**1996**	Tigers	958	6.22	1934
Indians	6.01	679	**1994**	Indians	952	5.91	**1996**
White Sox	6.01	920	1936	Orioles	949	5.82	**1996**
Orioles	5.82	949	**1996**	Rangers	928	5.69	**1996**
Twins	5.81	889	1936	White Sox	920	6.01	1936
Rangers	5.69	928	**1996**	Brewers	894	5.52	**1996**
Angels	5.52	801	**1995**	Twins	892	5.79	1930
Brewers	5.52	894	**1996**	Angels	866	5.35	1979
Royals	5.25	851	1979	Royals	851	5.25	1979
Blue Jays	5.23	847	**1993**	Blue Jays	847	5.23	**1993**

Of the 6 expansion teams, 5 have per game peaks and 4 have total year peaks in the 1993-97 period. Only the Royals, unable to top their 1979 marks, do not have a peak in the 1990s. The Angels, as noted above, also have their total year peak in 1979. The Mariners are by far the best expansion team in scoring runs, and they lead 4 of the original 8 teams in per game runs and all but the Yankees and Red Sox in total year runs. They only played 161 games in 1996, and this may have cost them their chance to get above the magic 1000 runs mark.

Table 2-2 shows peak years for runs for National League teams. Years from the 1990s are shown in boldface. The first part of the table shows peak runs on a per game basis, while the second part of the table shows peak runs on a total year basis. The teams are listed in order of their best year in franchise history. But the table does not represent the best years ever in the league, because the second or third best years for teams at the top of the list usually are better than the best year for teams farther down the list. The highest ranked years regardless of how many times one team appears on the list are shown in Table 2-17.

As discussed in the text accompanying Table 1-2, there was an offensive peak in the National League in 1930 that was dramatically higher than the years before and especially after. Thus, 4 of the original 8 teams set their per game and total year records in 1930 (Cards, Cubs, Giants, and Phillies). The Cards scored 1004 runs in 1930, the only time a National League team has gone over 1000 runs in a single season. The Pirates set their per game and total record in 1925 as part of the climb up to the 1930 peak, and the Dodgers did it in 1953 (the National League set its all-time home run records in the 1950s). These six teams lead the per game rankings, and in spite of the longer season they have not been able to top their records for total runs which were also set in these years.

The Reds set their per game peak in 1903, and not even the Big Red Machine of the 1970s was able to match it (in Table 1-4 1903 ranks sixth on the top ten list of the highest run scoring years for the National League). But the Reds set their total runs peak in 1976 thanks to the longer season. Similarly, the Braves set their per game peak in 1950, and the great home run teams of Aaron and Mathews and the many high scoring teams that played in the "Launching Pad" in Atlanta have unable to match it. But the longer season did permit the 1964 Braves to set a franchise peak for total runs. However, in spite of their great success in the 1990s, the Braves have been so poor in scoring runs during their history that their per game peak is ahead of only the Padres and Marlins, the two worst run scoring expansion teams in the National League.

Even though they are also an expansion team, the Rockies are the present run scoring champions of the National League. The Rockies scored 5.93 runs per game in 1996 to move past the Reds and Braves on the original teams list, and the longer season permitted the 1996 Rockies to move into third place on the total runs list, behind only the Cubs and Cards. As discussed in the Preface and the Introduction, the Rockies are the only present National League team to compete with the top American League teams in scoring runs (the Rockies were second in the majors in scoring runs in 1996). This is because playing in Coors Field in Denver compensates for the lack of a designated hitter, and the Rockies have assembled a lineup of big hitters to take advantage of that fact.

Four of the other five expansion teams set per game and season total scoring records between 1993 and 1996 during the new offensive outburst in the National

League. Only the Mets have been unable to top their peaks of 1987, when they set what were then scoring records for a National League expansion team. The Mets were so potent in 1987 that even today the 1996 Rockies are the only expansion team to score more runs in a season than the Mets did in 1987 (the peak year for total runs for the Braves is also below that of the 1987 Mets).

The 1996 Rockies caused the only change in ranking order for runs per game and total runs for the first eight teams on the list. There are more changes farther down the list because the Astros and Expos set their records for per game scoring in 1994 which was shortened by the strike. Thus, their positions for total runs do not match their positions for runs per game.

Table 2-2. NL Teams Peak Years for Runs

	Per Game Basis				Total Year Basis		
Team	Per Game	Total	Year	Team	Total	Per Game	Year
Cards	6.52	1004	1930	Cards	1004	6.52	1930
Cubs	6.40	998	1930	Cubs	998	6.40	1930
Giants	6.23	959	1930	Rockies	961	5.93	**1996**
Dodgers	6.16	955	1953	Giants	959	6.23	1930
Phillies	6.05	944	1930	Dodgers	955	6.16	1953
Pirates	5.96	912	1925	Phillies	944	6.05	1930
Rockies	5.93	961	**1996**	Pirates	912	5.96	1925
Reds	5.43	765	1903	Reds	857	5.29	1976
Astros	5.23	602	**1994**	Mets	823	5.08	1987
Expos	5.13	585	**1994**	Braves	803	4.96	1964
Mets	5.08	823	1987	Padres	795	4.91	**1997**
Braves	5.03	785	1950	Astros	777	4.80	**1997**
Padres	4.91	795	**1997**	Expos	741	4.57	87/**96**
Marlins	4.71	673	**1995**	Marlins	740	4.57	**1997**

The last six teams on the total year list trail all 14 teams on the American League list. This highlights the fact that although the National League is scoring runs on a sustained basis at its best rate in 70 years, it is still well below the peaks set in the previous period while the American League is very close to its prior peaks. The difference, again, is the designated hitter. This difference also explains why the recent peak scoring year of 1996 for the National League is only in eleventh place on the list of the league's best run scoring years.

Table 2-3 shows the peak years for home runs for American League teams. Years from the 1990s are shown in boldface. The first part of the table shows peak home runs for each team on a per game basis, while the second part of the table shows peak home runs for each team on a total year basis. The teams are listed in order of their best year in franchise history. But the table does not represent the best years ever in the league because the second or third best years for the teams near the top of the list usually are better than the best year of teams farther down the list. The top 10 years regardless of how many times one team appears on the list are shown in Table 2-18.

The impact of the offensive outburst in the 1993-97 period is shown clearly by the years in boldface in the table. On a per game basis, 8 of the 16 teams hit their peaks between 1994 and 1997, with 4 teams doing it in 1996 alone. On a total year basis, 5 of the 16 teams hit their peaks in 1996 and 2 did it in 1997. The shorter seasons of 1994 and 1995 prevented any total year records in these seasons, although the Indians and Tigers set per game peaks in 1994 and the Angels did it in 1995. With so many teams setting individual team records in 1996, the league easily set its all-time record in 1996 (Table 1-5).

The top 3 teams in 1996 (Orioles, Mariners, and A's) also became the top 3 teams in history at the time. Each broke the per game record (1.48 by the 1994 Indians) and the total year record (240 by the 1961 Yankees). The 1997 Mariners then broke the 1996 record. The 1961 Yankees and 1963 Twins have the oldest records on the list, and together with the 1977 Red Sox, they are the only teams not to set their records in the 1980s or 1990s. The two top years for the league in hitting home runs are 1996 and 1987 (Table 1-5), and this is consistent with the fact that 5 teams had their peak total year in 1996 and 3 had their peak total year in 1987. In addition, in 1996 the Red Sox fell only 4 home runs short of breaking their 1977 record for total year home runs.

Although the Yankees have the oldest record on the list, they have remained one of the top teams in home runs since they set their record in 1961. It took 35 years for their record to be broken, and since the advent of the designated hitter in 1973, the Yankees rank third in the league in home runs behind the Tigers and the Orioles. The Yankees, however, are only 10th among the 14 teams in home runs in the 1993-97 period. A far cry from their years as the "Bronx Bombers."

The story is different for the Twins, who have the second oldest record listed. Since their great years in the early 1960s, the Twins have been one of the poorest home run hitting teams in the league (in spite of the reputation of their Metrodome as a "homerdome"). Since 1973, the Twins are ahead of only the rock-bottom Royals in hitting home runs in the American League. In the 1993-97 period, the Twins are dead last in the league. To complete the pattern, the Twins not only were last in the American League in home runs in 1996 and 1997, they had the lowest total in the majors in 1996.

The Royals matched the Twins in 1996 in hitting fewer home runs than any team in the National League. Before 1996, the last time an American League team was last in the majors in home runs was in 1975 when the Angels were far behind everyone with only 55 home runs. The Royals have always hit few home runs, but they usually offset that by scoring runs with a good serial offense. However, the Royals were last in the league in scoring in 1996. In a common pattern, they added offense in 1997, but their once excellent pitching was missing (they set a team record for high ERA in 1997), and they were not competitive. Once a team drifts too far away from balance between offense and pitching, it can take a long time to get back into balance again. And balance wins.

Table 2-3. AL Teams Peak Years for Home Runs

Per Game Basis				Total Year Basis			
Team	Per Game	Total	Year	Team	Total	Per Game	Year
Mariners	1.63	264	**1997**	Mariners	264	1.63	**1997**
Orioles	1.58	257	**1996**	Orioles	257	1.58	**1996**
A's	1.50	243	**1996**	A's	243	1.50	**1996**
Indians	1.48	167	**1994**	Yankees	240	1.47	1961
Yankees	1.47	240	1961	Twins	225	1.40	1963
Tigers	1.40	161	**1994**	Tigers	225	1.39	1987
Twins	1.40	225	1963	Rangers	221	1.36	**1996**
Rangers	1.36	221	**1996**	Indians	220	1.37	**1997**
Blue Jays	1.33	215	1987	Brewers	216	1.33	1982
Brewers	1.33	216	1982	Blue Jays	215	1.33	1987
Red Sox	1.32	213	1977	Red Sox	213	1.32	1977
Angels	1.28	186	**1995**	White Sox	195	1.20	**1996**
White Sox	1.20	195	**1996**	Angels	192	1.19	**1996**
Royals	1.04	168	1987	Royals	168	1.04	1987

In confirmation of the need for balance, none of the top three teams in hitting home runs in 1996 finished first in their division in spite of their record setting performances with the long ball (the 1996 Orioles did make it to the playoffs). The 1997 Mariners won their division after finishing second in 1996. The 1996 A's did not even make it over .500 due to their poor pitching. Home runs are fun to watch, and the ability to hit it out at least gives you hope for a comeback, but pitching ultimately separates the men from the boys.

Table 2-4 shows the peak years for home runs for National League teams. Years from the 1990s are shown in boldface. The first part of the table shows peak home runs for each team on a per game basis, while the second part of the table shows peak home runs for each team on a total year basis. The teams are listed in order of their best year in franchise history. But the table does not represent the best years ever in the league because the second or third best years for the teams near the top of the list usually are better than the best year of the teams farther down the list. The top 10 years regardless of how many times one team appears on the list are shown in Table 2-19.

There is a much wider spread in the years in which teams reached their peak in the National League compared to the American League (Table 2-3). The American League teams are concentrated in the 1993-97 period, with many peaks in 1996. In the National League, 5 of 14 teams reached their per game peaks in the 1993-97 period, and 5 of 14 reached their total year peaks in the period. But the Rockies and Marlins did not exist before 1993 and thus the distinction is meaningless for them. Of the 12 other teams, only 3 reached per game peaks and total year peaks in the 1993-97 period. Of the original 8 teams, 5 reached per game peaks and 3 reached total year peaks in the 1947-57 period. The Cubs and Mets reached both peaks in 1987, the Phillies in 1977, and the Padres in 1970. The Cards split between 1994 and 1997.

This wide disparity is consistent with the fact that the National League hit its peak in home runs in 1955 (Table 1-5), and 5 of the league's top 10 years came between 1953 and 1958. That is why a majority of the original 8 teams set their per game records in the 1947-57 period. Since that period was before expansion, 4 of the 6 expansion teams set their records in the next sustained offensive peak in the National League which came in 1993 through 1997.

The Giants have by far the oldest home run peak records in the major leagues, with both their per game and total year peaks coming a half-century ago in 1947. The Reds are not far behind with peak records in 1956 (the oldest American League records are held by the 1961 Yankees). But more notable is the fact that these two team records lasted as the league records until the 1996 Rockies tied the total year record and the 1997 Rockies broke both the per game and total year record. No other National League teams have come close to the records of the 1947 Giants and 1956 Reds in the 50 years that have passed since the 1947 Giants originally set the record.

It was expected that the Rockies would eventually break the records. But the Rockies (and Coors Field) remain unique in the National League. Thus, except for the Rockies, the league home run record will start its next 50 years in 1998 while in the American League 3 different teams broke the existing records in 1996 and the Mariners broke them again in 1997. There are several contenders in the American League but the Rockies stand alone in the National League.

Excluding the Rockies, the closest approach to the records of the Giants and Reds in total home runs was made by the 1987 Cubs who were 6 percent behind in spite of the longer season. No other team is really close in per game home runs, not even the Braves of Hank Aaron. Ironically, the pitching-rich Braves were the best team behind the Rockies in 1996 and 1997. The peak for the Braves was 1.22 home runs per game for a total of 197 in 1996, still far behind the records set five decades ago by the Giants and the Reds. The outburst of home runs in the league in the 1993-97 period are due to the rise of the Rockies, and the fact that the other teams on average are hitting more home runs than they were prior to 1993 even if they are not at record levels.

Table 2-4. NL Teams Peak Years for Home Runs

	Per Game Basis				Total Year Basis		
Team	Per Game	Total	Year	Team	Total	Per Game	Year
Rockies	1.48	239	**1997**	Rockies	239	1.48	**1997**
Giants	1.43	221	1947	Giants	221	1.43	1947
Reds	1.43	221	1956	Reds	221	1.43	1956
Dodgers	1.34	208	1953	Cubs	209	1.30	1987
Cubs	1.30	209	1987	Dodgers	208	1.34	1953
Braves	1.28	199	1957	Braves	207	1.27	1966
Mets	1.19	192	1987	Mets	192	1.19	1987
Phillies	1.15	186	1977	Phillies	186	1.15	1977
Expos	1.06	172	**1997**	Expos	172	1.06	**1997**
Padres	1.06	172	1970	Padres	172	1.06	1970
Astros	1.04	120	**1994**	Pirates	158	0.98	1966
Marlins	1.01	144	**1995**	Marlins	150	0.93	**1996**
Pirates	1.00	156	1947	Cards	144	0.89	**1997**
Cards	0.94	108	**1994**	Astros	138	0.85	**1993**

Seven of the 14 National League teams have not been able to hit at least 190 home runs in one year, while only one American League team has failed to do so (the Royals at 168). Further, the average peak for total home runs on the National League list is 187 while for the American League the average is 221. This means the average number of peak home runs in the American League matches the all-time peak in the National League before the Rockies came along. This 18 percent difference is due to the designated hitter.

   Table 2-5 shows the peak years for doubles for American League teams. Years from the 1990s are shown in boldface. The first part of the table shows peaks in doubles for each team on a per game basis, while the second part of the table shows peaks in doubles for each team on a total year basis. The teams are listed in order of their best year in franchise history. But the table does not represent the best years ever in the league because the second or third best years for the teams near the top of the list usually are better than the best year of teams farther down the list. The top 10 years regardless of how many times one team appears on the list are shown in Table 2-18.

   The top years for doubles per game in the American League were from 1927 through 1936 (Table 1-6), with 8 of the 10 years in this period making the top 10 list and 4 of those years (1936, 1930, 1931, and 1932 in that order) taking the top 4 spots on the list. The other 2 places on the top 10 list are taken by 1996 and 1994 in 5th and 7th place respectively. Accordingly, 3 of the original 8 teams set their per game records in the period from 1927 through 1936 (1930 Indians, 1934 Tigers, and 1928 A's), and the 1926 White Sox and 1937 Orioles set franchise records just before and just after this period. But the Twins and Yankees set their per game records in 1994, and the Red Sox broke the American League record and tied the major league record for total doubles in 1997. The 6 expansion teams all set their per game records between 1990 and 1996.

   The 1997 Red Sox are the big story for doubles. Before 1997 it was hard to imagine a team topping the per game or total year records of the 1930 Indians. The Mariners hit 343 doubles in 1996, the most in the majors since 1934, but they were well short of the per game record although only 15 doubles short of the total year record of 358. The 1996 Mariners were on a pace to beat the record, and they might have done so if Edgar Martinez had not been injured. But the per game record still seemed out of reach. However, the 1997 Red Sox, a great hitting team, hit doubles at a blazing pace through the summer of 1997. They were ahead of the per game record as late as the last week in August, but they fell back in September. They had enough left to easily break the American League record for total doubles, and their total of 373 ties the major league record set by the 1930 Cardinals (Table 2-6).

   The Red Sox joined the Yankees and Twins as members of the original 8 teams that set peak records in the 1990s. When they were home run champs, the Yankees hit relatively few doubles (they hit them over the wall instead of against the wall). Presently ranking low in home runs, they set their per game doubles peak in the shortened strike year of 1994, then broke their 1936 record of 315 total doubles in 1997. The Twins also broke team records from the 1930s, hitting their per game peak of 2.12 in 1994 and their total year peak of 332 doubles in 1996. But of these 3 teams only the Red Sox were able to make the top ten list for the league (Table 2-20) with their record performance in 1997.

The most unusual record for doubles in the American League is that of the Angels, but it is a record of futility. They set their total year record as recently as 1997, but they are still at the bottom of both lists. They need an increase of 12 percent on the per game list to catch the Royals in 13th place, and an increase of that size would vault the Royals into 4th place. It is almost as if the Angels were in another league in doubles, and in fact the Angels not only trail all American League teams on the per game list, they would rank 13th in the National League as well (Table 2-6). The Angels are also low in the American League in runs and home runs, but at least they would be in the middle of the pack in the National League. In doubles they nearly don't exist.

Table 2-5. AL Teams Peak Years for Doubles

Per Game Basis				Total Year Basis			
Team	Per Game	Total	Year	Team	Total	Per Game	Year
Indians	2.32	358	1930	Red Sox	373	2.30	**1997**
Red Sox	2.30	373	**1997**	Indians	358	2.32	1930
Tigers	2.27	349	1934	Tigers	349	2.27	1934
Mariners	2.13	343	**1996**	Mariners	343	2.13	**1996**
Twins	2.12	239	**1994**	Twins	332	2.05	**1996**
A's	2.11	323	1928	Orioles	327	2.10	1937
Yankees	2.11	238	**1994**	Yankees	325	2.01	**1997**
Orioles	2.10	327	1937	A's	323	2.11	1928
Brewers	2.07	238	**1994**	Rangers	323	1.98	**1996**
White Sox	2.03	314	1926	Blue Jays	317	1.96	**1993**
Rangers	1.98	323	**1996**	Royals	316	1.96	**1990**
Blue Jays	1.96	317	**1993**	White Sox	314	2.03	1926
Royals	1.96	316	**1990**	Brewers	304	1.88	**1996**
Angels	1.74	252	**1995**	Angels	279	1.72	**1997**

Four teams set their records for total year doubles in 1996 (Mariners, Twins, Rangers, and Brewers). Three did it in 1997 (Red Sox, Yankees, and Angels), and the remaining 7 set their total year records in 7 different years. Three teams set per game peaks in 1994 (Twins, Yankees, and Brewers) and 2 in 1996 (Mariners and Rangers). The remaining 9 teams did it in 9 different years. It's easy to see why 1994 and 1996 made the top 10 list (Table 1-6) for doubles in the American League.

Table 2-6 shows the peak years for doubles for National League teams. Years from the 1990s are shown in boldface. The first part of the table shows peaks in doubles for each team on a per game basis, while the second part of the table shows peaks in doubles for each team on a total year basis. The teams are listed in order of their best year in franchise history. But the table does not represent the best years ever in the league because the second or third best years for the teams near the top of the list usually are better than the best year of the teams farther down the list. The top 10 years regardless of how many times one team appears on the list are shown in Table 2-19.

The Cards set major league records for doubles per game and total year when they hit 373 doubles in 1930 for an average of 2.42 per game (it takes 393 doubles over 162 games to top a per game mark of 2.42). The Cards dominate the top 10 list for doubles in the National League (Table 2-21) the same way the Indians do in the American League (Table 2-20). The Phillies and Dodgers also set team records for both measures in the National League's huge offensive peak in 1930. The Cubs set their team records in 1931 and the Giants did so in 1928. These 5 teams have never been able to top either their per game or total year marks in the more than 65 years that have passed since they set their records.

Of the remaining 3 of the original 8 teams, the Pirates set their per game record in 1925 and their total year record in 1996; the Reds set their total year record in 1990 and their per game record in 1995; and the Braves set their per game record in 1948 and their total year record in 1987. All of the expansion teams hit their per game peaks between 1994 and 1997 except for the Mets who did it in 1987 when they won the World Series. The Expos, Astros, and Marlins set their total year records in 1997 and the Rockies and Padres did so in 1996. The Mets stayed with 1987 as their peak total year.

These results give an interesting cluster of years for total year records in doubles. Four teams set their records in 1930, 3 in 1997, 3 in 1996 and 2 in 1987. This means 9 teams set their total year records between 1987 and 1996 while the remaining 5 set their records between 1928 and 1931. It is easy to identify the peak periods in doubles for the teams in the National League.

The Giants are similar to the Yankees in that the Giants were known as a leading home run team, but they never hit a lot of doubles. The Giants tended to hit them over the wall rather than against it as did the Yankees. But unlike the Yankees who became a leading doubles team in the 1990s when they stopped being a leader in home runs, the Giants been unable to match their per game or total year marks in doubles that were set seven decades ago in 1928. As a result the Giants are near the bottom of both lists in the league. They rank 13th in total year doubles, just barely above the expansion Marlins. The Giants do manage to get up to 10th place in doubles per game, but they are only 0.02 above 13th place on that list as well.

On the other hand, the expansion Astros produced the highest doubles per game mark in the league in 63 years when they averaged 2.19 doubles per game in 1994. It gave the Astros the 3rd highest team mark in Table 2-6, and it was the 4th best single season in the league as only the 1930 and 1931 Cards and the 1930 Phillies had higher marks (Table 2-21). But since 1994 was cut short by the strike, the total year mark in 1994 was only 252 rather than a projected 355 which would have been the second best total in league history. The Astros set their team record for a total year in the full season of 1997, but that mark only ranks in the middle of the total year list. It counts as another potentially great performance lost to the strike.

Table 2-6. NL Teams Peak Years for Doubles

Team	Per Game Basis			Team	Total Year Basis		
	Per Game	Total	Year		Total	Per Game	Year
Cards	2.42	373	1930	Cards	373	2.42	1930
Phillies	2.21	345	1930	Phillies	345	2.21	1930
Astros	2.19	252	**1994**	Cubs	340	2.18	1930
Cubs	2.18	340	1931	Expos	339	2.09	**1997**
Expos	2.16	246	**1994**	Pirates	319	1.97	**1996**
Pirates	2.07	316	1925	Astros	314	1.94	**1997**
Dodgers	1.97	303	1930	Dodgers	303	1.97	1930
Reds	1.92	277	**1995**	Rockies	297	1.83	**1996**
Rockies	1.83	297	**1996**	Mets	287	1.77	1987
Giants	1.78	276	1928	Padres	285	1.76	**1996**
Mets	1.77	287	1987	Braves	284	1.76	1987
Braves	1.77	272	1948	Reds	284	1.75	**1990**
Padres	1.76	285	**1996**	Giants	276	1.78	1928
Marlins	1.68	272	**1997**	Marlins	272	1.68	**1997**

Before 1997 the Marlins were far behind in last place on both lists in the same way as the Angels were in the American League (Table 2-5). The Marlins still rank last, but their 1997 team was the best ever in their short history and it carried them much closer to the rest of the league in doubles (as well as to the playoffs). The 1997 Marlins only needed four more doubles to catch the Giants on the total year list, and they made a big jump in per game doubles from their prior peak of only 1.57 in 1994.

Table 2-7 shows the peak years for batting average for American and National League teams. Years from the 1990s are shown in boldface. The teams are listed in order of their best year in franchise history. But the table does not represent the best years ever in either league because the second or third best years for teams at the top of the list are usually better than the best year for teams farther down the list. The top 10 years regardless of how many times one team appears on the list are shown in Table 2-22.

American League--With the exception of the Red Sox, who set their team batting average record in 1950 (the 1950 Red Sox are the last team in either league to top .300 for a full season), all of the original American League teams set their batting average records between 1920 and 1930 (the eight original National League teams did the same). This is because of the changes in the rules in 1920. These rules outlawed doctored pitches such as the spitball and the emery ball, putting pitchers at a sudden disadvantage. Batting averages (and runs) soared in the next decade, but pitchers slowly recovered and batting averages fell steadily from 1930 through the next four decades (Figure 2-4). In spite of the designated hitter and the offensive outburst of the 1990s, league batting averages are still 10 points below the levels reached in the 1920s.

The six American League expansion teams set their batting average records between 1979 and 1996, with the Mariners recording the highest batting average for an American League expansion team at .287 in 1996. The Rangers also set their team record in 1996, and the Brewers missed by only one percentage point. The Blue Jays set their record in 1993. Only the Angels and Royals have not approached their team records in the 1990s.

It's unlikely any of the original eight teams will come close to their prior records. The White Sox, who have the lowest record of the original eight, made the closest approach when they hit over .287 in 1994, but that is still well below their 1920 record of .295. The reduced batting averages in the present offensive outburst is another indicator that poor pitching is not the cause of the surge in runs and home runs. Opposing batting average has long been used as an indicator of pitching performance, and batting averages today are much lower than in the prior offensive peaks in spite of the presence of the designated hitter.

National League--The original eight National teams have batting average records similar to those of the original eight American League teams. The huge offensive surge in 1930 in the National League resulted in 5 of the original 8 teams setting batting average records in 1930. But all 6 expansion teams set their records between 1994 and 1997, with the 1997 Rockies topping the 1996 Mariners for the highest average ever for an expansion team. However, except for the Rockies, all of the National League expansion teams have much lower batting average peaks than their American League counterparts. This a result of the lack of the designated hitter in the National League.

Batting average is another area where the Rockies perform like an American League team. The 1997 Rockies are only .004 behind the all-time record of the Braves which was set in 1925. If the Rockies manage to catch the Braves in a future year, they would be the first (and probably only) expansion team to equal the record batting average of one of the original eight teams. But even if the Rockies do not eventually match the Braves, the Rockies have already made the closest approach of an expansion team to an original team. Further, the Rockies lead the next team by 10 percentage points and the Marlins by 22. The Mariners are ahead of the next team by only one point and the last place team by eight. The Rockies far outstrip the rest of the National League in hitting.

Table 2-7. AL/NL Teams Peak Years for Batting Average

American League			National League		
Team	BatAvg.	Year	Team	BatAvg.	Year
Tigers	.316	1921	Giants	.319	1930
Orioles	.313	1922	Phillies	.315	1930
Yankees	.309	1930	Cards	.314	1930
Indians	.308	1921	Pirates	.309	1928
A's	.307	1925	Cubs	.309	1930
Twins	.303	1925	Dodgers	.304	1930
Red Sox	.302	1950	Reds	.296	1922
White Sox	.295	1920	Braves	.292	1925
Mariners	.287	**1996**	Rockies	.288	**1997**
Royals	.286	1980	Astros	.278	**1994**
Rangers	.284	**1996**	Expos	.278	**1994**
Angels	.282	1979	Padres	.275	**1994**
Brewers	.280	1979	Mets	.270	**1996**
Blue Jays	.279	**1993**	Marlins	.266	**1994**

Much has been made of the offensive outburst of the National League in 1930 and it has been claimed that it was all due to the ball used in that year. The ball may have been a factor, but the average record batting average for the original 8 National League teams is .307, exactly the same as for the 8 original American League teams. Similarly, the top two marks of .319 and .315 for the National League in 1930 are close to the .316 and .313 marks in the American League in 1921 and 1922 respectively. The American League teams basically peaked on average about five years earlier than the National League teams.

Table 2-8 shows the peak years for ERA (earned run average) for American and National League teams. Years from the 1990s are shown in boldface. The teams are listed in order of their highest year in franchise history. But the table does not represent the highest years ever in either league because the second or third highest years for teams at the top of the list are usually higher than the highest year for teams farther down the list. The top 10 years regardless of how many times one team appears on the list are shown in Table 2-23.

American League--As discussed in the text accompanying Table 1-8, ERAs are higher today than would be expected based on the ratio of runs scored today to runs scored in the past. This is because of the much lower level of errors today (errors per game in the 1920s were nearly 90 percent higher than in the 1990s). Thus, the percentage of runs scored in the 1920s that were "unearned" was 16.1 percent compared to 9.1 percent in the 1990s. For the league, as runs scored in the 1990s approach the levels of the 1920s and 1930s, the peak years for ERA will move into the 1990s. But on a team basis such a shift requires a combination of poor pitching in a high scoring period. This is why records on a team basis often differ in time compared to records on a league basis.

Thus, ERA peaks for 5 of the 8 original teams came in the 1930s. The Orioles/Browns, Red Sox, and White Sox had their worst teams in franchise history (based on winning percentage) in the 1930s, and the A's had their second worse team. These franchises produced peak ERAs by combining bad teams with the highest scoring period in league history. The Yankees recorded their peak ERA in the high scoring year of 1930 even though they had a good team. But their pitching usually has been so good that 1930 remains their peak because they have not matched poor pitching with a high scoring year similar to 1930.

The Indians, Twins, and Tigers set their ERA records in 1987, 1994, and 1996 respectively. In each case they combined poor teams with a high scoring year. All six expansion teams set their ERA records between 1994 and 1997. These were high scoring years compared to the levels that have existed since each team was born. Thus, even though the teams of the 1990s were not necessarily among the worst in franchise history, the effect of the much higher level of runs outweighed team performance factors and produced peak ERAs.

National League--Six of the original 8 teams had peak ERAs in 1929 and 1930, the top years in league scoring. The Cards and Giants were among the best teams of that time, and they set their ERA records in 1994 and 1995 respectively when they had bad teams to accompany the league's highest scoring period since 1930. Four of the 6 expansion teams set their records in the 1990s. The Rockies and Marlins by definition had their ERA peaks in the 1990s because they were not born until 1993. The Astros, who have focused on pitching since their birth, set their peak ERA record in 1996 when they combined a high scoring year with a team that was not up to the very high pitching standards of their franchise.

The other expansion teams demonstrate why individual team records can occur in different years than when league records are being set. The Mets set their ERA peak in 1962, the year of their birth. The 1962 Mets were one of the worst teams in league history and they had no trouble producing a high ERA in what was a good scoring year in the league. Similarly, the 1970 Expos, in the year after their birth, had a pitching staff that issued the second highest number of walks per game in league history. Combining this staff with a year in which the league scored runs at the same rate it would in 1987, a year of run scoring just below the peaks in the 1993-97 period, made it easy for the 1970 Expos to set their franchise peak in ERA.

Table 2-8. AL/NL Teams Peak Years for ERA

American League			National League		
Team	ERA	Year	Team	ERA	Year
Tigers	6.38	**1996**	Phillies	6.71	1930
Orioles	6.24	1936	Rockies	5.59	**1996**
A's	6.08	1936	Pirates	5.24	1930
Twins	5.76	**1995**	Cards	5.14	**1994**
Rangers	5.45	**1994**	Braves	5.12	1929
Angels	5.42	**1994**	Reds	5.08	1930
White Sox	5.41	1934	Mets	5.04	1962
Indians	5.28	1987	Padres	4.98	**1997**
Mariners	5.21	**1996**	Dodgers	4.92	1929
Brewers	5.14	**1996**	Giants	4.86	**1995**
Red Sox	5.02	1932	Cubs	4.80	1930
Blue Jays	4.88	**1995**	Expos	4.50	1970
Yankees	4.88	1930	Marlins	4.50	**1994**
Royals	4.70	**1997**	Astros	4.37	**1996**

The 1997 Padres set the franchise peak by combining a bad pitching year with a time of high scoring. The Padres had good pitching in 1994 through 1996, but they fell apart in 1997. Their previous peak year was in 1974. The team had been terrible since their 1969 birth, and the 1974 Padres had a pitching staff that was just behind the 1970 Expos in high walk levels (Table 2-12). 1974 was not a high scoring year in the league, but the Padres were poor enough to set a franchise peak for ERA that lasted until 1997. The two peaks for the Padres are good examples of how team and league ERA peaks can combine and diverge.

Table 2-9 shows peak years for strikeouts for American League teams. Years from the 1990s are shown in boldface. The first part of the table shows peaks in strikeouts on a per game basis, while the second part shows peaks in strikeouts on a total year basis. The teams are listed in order of their best year in franchise history. But the table does not represent the best years ever in the league because the second or third best years for teams at the top of the list usually are better than the best year for teams farther down the list. The top 10 years regardless of how many times one team appears on the list are shown in Table 2-24.

The 1997 Mariners, led by Randy Johnson, set an all-time American League record for strikeouts per game and for a total year. They broke their own record set in 1994 for per game strikeouts, and they broke the total year record of the 1967 Indians. The Indians, Tigers, and Twins are the only teams that have not topped their strikeout peaks set during the 1963-68 period when the rules were changed in favor of pitchers. In spite of the addition of the designated hitter in 1973 and the modification of the 1963-68 rules in 1969, both changes which reduced strikeouts in the league at the time they were implemented, the remaining 11 teams have set their strikeout records in the last decade.

Seven teams set their strikeout peaks between 1994 and 1997 when the big swing dominated offense. The importance of the big swing in setting strikeout records was demonstrated in 1996 and then again in 1997 when the American League set its all-time strikeout records (Table 1-9). Each year in succession topped the previous record years from the 1963-68 period (1997 topped 1996 and 1994 and 1995 hold 5th and 6th place respectively on the top 10 list). The A's and Brewers set their records in 1987, the last period of high offense in the league before the 1990s.

The Rangers set their strikeout record in 1989. This was not a year of high offense. In fact, in 1989 the American League scored fewer runs per game than in any year between 1981 and 1997. But it was a year when Nolan Ryan led the majors with 301 strikeouts while pitching for the Rangers. This is a good example of how a team can set a team record due to different factors than those that control results within the league overall. The Rangers recently have had decent pitching during the big swing and high offense period from 1993 through 1997, but Nolan Ryan was unique and he was in great form in 1989. That counts for more on a team basis than the factors existing in the league. Thus, 1989 remains the peak year for strikeouts for the Rangers.

The Royals are also a good example of how a team can have a peak in a certain measure essentially independent of league trends. The Royals have focused on pitching since their birth in 1969, and they have the second lowest ERA in the American League (behind the Yankees) over the period from 1973 (the year the designated hitter was born) through 1997. But the Royals always concentrated on pitchers who got outs even if not necessarily strikeouts.

In 1990 the Royals, in spite of having a losing team, happened to have a staff that topped all prior franchise records for strikeouts. They did not produce very many strikeouts compared to the peaks of other teams, but it was a high mark for the Royals. The Royals have the lowest peak in the American League, and, except for the Rockies whose pitchers toil in the arcade atmosphere of Coors Field, the Royals have the lowest strikeout peaks in the majors in both strikeouts per game and total strikeouts. As strikeouts soared due to the big swing later in the 1990s, the Royals continued to feature pitchers with good ERAs rather than high strikeouts. More recently they have had pitchers who had both poor ERAs and low strikeouts. Thus, they have not been able to top their low 1990 peaks.

Table 2-9. AL Teams Peak Years for Strikeouts

Per Game Basis			Total Year Basis			
Team	Per Game	Total	Year	Team	Total	Per Game	Year
Mariners	7.45	1207	**1997**	Mariners	1207	7.45	**1997**
Indians	7.34	1189	1967	Indians	1189	7.34	1967
Blue Jays	7.23	832	**1994**	Red Sox	1165	7.19	**1996**
Red Sox	7.19	1165	**1996**	Yankees	1165	7.19	**1997**
Yankees	7.19	1165	**1997**	Blue Jays	1150	7.10	**1997**
Orioles	7.03	1139	**1997**	Orioles	1139	7.03	**1997**
Rangers	6.86	1112	1989	Tigers	1115	6.80	1968
Tigers	6.80	1115	1968	Rangers	1112	6.86	1989
Twins	6.74	1099	1964	Twins	1099	6.74	1964
White Sox	6.67	754	**1994**	Angels	1052	6.53	**1996**
Angels	6.53	1052	**1996**	A's	1042	6.43	1987
A's	6.43	1042	1987	Brewers	1039	6.41	1987
Brewers	6.41	1039	1987	White Sox	1039	6.41	**1996**
Royals	6.25	1006	**1990**	Royals	1006	6.25	**1990**

The Yankees led the league in strikeouts prior to 1945, but they are only an average team in strikeouts since WWII even though they continued to be the ERA leader. As of 1994 the Yankees had the lowest strikeout peak in the league. Similarly, since 1973 the Orioles are an ERA leader but are next to last in strikeouts. The Yankees soared in strikeouts in 1996 and 1997, and the Orioles followed in 1997. Both teams are now respectably high on the league strikeout list as well as 1st (Yankees) and 3rd in lowest ERA in the 1993-97 period.

Table 2-10 shows the peak years for strikeouts for National League teams. Years from the 1990s are shown in boldface. The first part of the table shows peaks in strikeouts for each team on a per game basis, while the second part of the table shows peaks in strikeouts for each team on a total year basis. The teams are listed in order of their best year in franchise history. But the table does not represent the best years ever in the league, because the second or third best years for teams at the top of the list usually are better than the best year for teams farther down the list. The top 10 years regardless of how many times one team appears on the list are shown in Table 2-25.

Table 2-10 shows that the National League is setting its strikeout records in the 1990s. In both strikeouts per game and total strikeouts, 11 of the 14 teams hit their peaks in the 1990s, with 6 teams doing it in 1997. The league set its all-time strikeout record in 1997 (Table 1-9), with 1996, 1995 and 1994 following in second, third, and fourth place respectively.

The 1996 Braves broke the record of the 1969 Astros for total strikeouts in one year. The 1996 Braves also broke the per game record set by the 1994 Braves. At the time, both the Braves and the Astros set major league records as well as the National League record. Many fans assume today that the National League has always led the American League in strikeouts. But from 1903 through 1972, the American League led the National League in strikeouts per game with an average of 3.99 compared to the National League average of 3.92. It was only after the designated hitter rule took effect in 1973 that the National League began to build a big edge over the American League in strikeouts. This is because pitchers strike out regularly when they come to bat (not to mention in such a futile way that it hardly rates as a contest between a batter and the opposing pitcher). The pitcher never bats in the American League and thus total strikeouts are lower (and much more of an equal contest between hitter and pitcher).

With the big swing greatly increasing the rate at which all hitters strike out, strikeouts per game in the National League increase literally every year. This makes it likely that all teams will eventually reach strikeout peaks in a year after 1990, and the high strikeout rates of the 1963-68 period, when the rules were changed in favor of the pitcher, will be just a memory.

Only the Giants still have their strikeout peak in the 1963-68 period. Their 1965 peak is not very high, but their generally poor pitching in the last three decades has left them unable to top it. The Pirates and Astros set their peaks in 1969 even though the rules favoring pitchers were reversed that year. The Pirates happened to have their best strikeout staff assembled that year and have not been able to top their moderate peak since. The Astros had one of the best strikeout staffs in history in 1969. The Astros have been (and are) a leader in strikeouts, but 1969 was such a great year the franchise (and most other teams) have not been able to top it.

It is likely, however, that if the Astros themselves do not top their 1969 peak, they will begin to move farther down the list. Prior to 1996, the 1969 Astros and 1990 Mets were the only major league teams to record more than 1200 strikeouts in one year. In 1996 the Braves, Dodgers, and Expos all broke the 1200 barrier, and in 1997 the Dodgers (again) and Marlins did it. Unless there is a fundamental change in the National League (such as adopting the designated hitter), more and more teams will approach and then surpass the 1969 Astros. In the same way the Pirates and Giants should replace their teams from the 1960s on the list. But regardless of the movement of teams up and down the list, it is likely the Rockies will remain in last place.

Table 2-10. NL Teams Peak Years For Strikeouts

Per Game Basis				Total Year Basis			
Team	Per Game	Total	Year	Team	Total	Per Game	Year
Braves	7.69	1245	**1996**	Braves	1245	7.69	**1996**
Dodgers	7.60	1232	**1997**	Dodgers	1232	7.60	**1997**
Astros	7.54	1221	1969	Astros	1221	7.54	1969
Mets	7.51	1217	**1990**	Mets	1217	7.51	**1990**
Phillies	7.46	1209	**1997**	Phillies	1209	7.46	**1997**
Expos	7.44	1206	**1996**	Expos	1206	7.44	**1996**
Padres	7.37	1194	**1996**	Padres	1194	7.37	**1996**
Marlins	7.33	1188	**1997**	Marlins	1188	7.33	**1997**
Reds	7.15	1159	**1997**	Reds	1159	7.15	**1997**
Cards	6.98	1130	**1997**	Cards	1130	6.98	**1997**
Pirates	6.94	1124	1969	Pirates	1124	6.94	1969
Cubs	6.62	1072	**1997**	Cubs	1072	6.62	**1997**
Giants	6.50	1060	1965	Giants	1060	6.50	1956
Rockies	6.19	891	**1995**	Rockies	932	5.75	**1996**

The reason the Rockies will probably stay last is not due completely to the fact that they play in Coors Field. The altitude there does reduce the bite on a good curve ball and makes it harder to effectively mix pitch selection and get a lot of strikeouts. But a related problem is that teams like the Rockies emphasize hitters when they spend their payroll money. Considering that few pitchers are anxious to pitch in Denver anyway, the result tends to be lots of hitters but few really good pitchers. This reduces strikeouts as well as playoff opportunities.

Table 2-11 shows the peak years for walks for American League teams. Years from the 1990s are shown in boldface. The first part of the table shows peaks in walks for each team on a per game basis, while the second part of the table shows peaks in walks for each team on a total year basis. The teams are listed in order of their highest year in franchise history. But the table does not represent the highest years ever in the league because the second or third highest years for the teams near the top of the list usually are higher than the highest year for teams farther down the list. The highest 10 years regardless of how many times one team appears on the list are shown in Table 2-26.

By far the highest year for walks in the major leagues is the record 827 issued by the 1915 A's. Their per game mark of 5.37 is also the highest in the century. To put the A's record in perspective, their 1915 mark was 58 percent higher than the league average. For comparison, the 1949 Yankees, in second place, were only 15 percent above the league average in 1949. Fifteen percent is a reasonable percentage above the league average for a leader in a particular measure. But the 1915 A's were so bad they were in a league of their own.

The reason for the A's record performance in 1915 was that Connie Mack was disassembling his great teams from the 1910-14 period. Hall of Fame pitchers Eddie Plank and Chief Bender pitched in the Federal League in 1915. Herb Pennock (also a future Hall of Famer) was sold to the Red Sox in June and Bob Shawkey was sold to the Yankees in July. What was left was not a major league staff. The A's were even worse in 1916 when they had the lowest winning percentage in the century, but at least their pitchers issued fewer walks than they did in 1915. On both a per game and total year basis, the A's record high in walks in 1915 is the oldest record in the American League for the measures being considered in this book.

The circumstances surrounding the 1949 Yankees when they set their peak for walks is completely different from that of the 1915 A's. The 1949 Yankees were a very good team and went on to win the World Series. But as discussed in the text accompanying Table 1-10, there was a huge peak in walks in both leagues in 1949. The Yankees led the league in walks that year, but their total was not dramatically high for the period, even though it was an all-time high for the franchise. Five of the 7 original teams other than the A's set per game and total year peaks for walks between 1949 and 1951 (Yankees, Orioles/Browns, Twins/Senators, Red Sox, and White Sox). The Indians had a great pitching staff in that period and didn't set their peaks in walks until they had a terrible team in 1971. The Tigers set their record in 1996 when they had an even worse team than the 1971 Indians (the 1996 Tigers also had an all-time high in ERA as shown in Table 2-8). Thus, the peak years for the original eight teams were a mix of bad teams with peaks in a low walk period, good teams with peaks in high walk periods, and bad teams with peaks in high walk periods.

Except for the 1993-97 period, the expansion teams have played in periods when walks in the league were much lower than they were for the original teams in the 1940s and 1950s. The recent rise in the 1993-97 period is not even close to the peaks in the 1949-51 period. Thus, the 8 original teams occupy the first 8 places on the per game list and the 6 expansion teams occupy the last 6 places. The same is true on the total year list except for the 1987 Rangers who beat out two original teams on the list. In time it can expected that some expansion teams will copy the 1996 Tigers in pitching futility, and with the longer schedule now these teams will move into higher positions on the total year list. But the highest per game records of 1949-51 period seem out of reach.

Table 2-11. AL Teams Peak Years for Walks

Per Game Basis				Total Year Basis			
Team	Per Game	Total	Year	Team	Total	Per Game	Year
A's	5.37	827	1915	A's	827	5.37	1915
Yankees	5.24	812	1949	Yankees	812	5.24	1949
Orioles	5.20	801	1951	Orioles	801	5.20	1951
Twins	5.06	779	1949	Tigers	784	4.84	**1996**
Red Sox	4.86	748	1950	Twins	779	5.06	1949
Tigers	4.84	784	**1996**	Indians	770	4.75	1971
Indians	4.75	770	1971	Rangers	760	4.69	1987
White Sox	4.71	734	1950	Red Sox	748	4.86	1950
Rangers	4.69	760	1987	White Sox	734	4.71	1950
Blue Jays	4.54	654	**1995**	Angels	713	4.40	1961
Angels	4.40	713	1961	Mariners	661	4.08	**1992**
Mariners	4.34	486	**1994**	Blue Jays	654	4.54	**1995**
Brewers	4.19	603	**1995**	Brewers	653	4.01	1969
Royals	3.96	641	1970	Royals	641	3.96	1970

As noted in the text accompanying Table 1-10, walks in the American League in 1996 were at their highest level in 40 years. But the 3.79 per game mark for walks in 1996 is far below the 1949 peak of 4.55. Pitchers are steadily more inclined to issue walks rather than watch the ball fly over the fence, but a dramatic increase is needed for walks to reach 1949 levels. Combining this with the fact that even the 1996 Tigers were not as inept as the 1915 A's leads to the conclusion that the highest marks on the list are unlikely to be topped.

Table 2-12 shows the peak years for walks for National League teams. Years from the 1990s are shown in boldface. The first part of the table shows peaks in walks for each team on a per game basis, while the second part of the table shows peaks in walks for each team on a total year basis. The teams are listed in order of their highest year in franchise history. But the table does not represent the highest years ever in the league because the second or third highest years for the teams near the top of the list usually are better than the highest year for the teams farther down the list. The top 10 years regardless of how many times one team appears on the list are shown in Table 2-27.

The Phillies set the National League record for walks per game in 1928. The record for the Phillies is similar to that of the A's in the American League (Table 2-11) in that it is the oldest record in the league among the measures in this book. Even the circumstances are similar for the terrible A's of 1915 and the terrible Phillies of 1928. The Phillies had the league's worst pitching staff and were 42 percent above the league average in walks. Thus, the Phillies set the league record with an average of 4.44 walks per game, just beating out the 1991 Cards by 0.004 walks per game. The 1911 Cards were a winning team, but their pitching staff issued walks at a rate 28 percent above the league average in a year when the league had a temporary peak in walks.

The National League had a sustained peak in walks from 1946 through 1954. It was similar to the American League peak described in the text accompanying Table 2-11. But the National League peak was not as high nor as sharp as that in the American League. Still, 5 of the original 8 teams had their peak in walks per game during that period (Giants, Dodgers, Reds, Cubs, and Pirates). The Phillies, who had their best pitching staffs in 35 years during the 1946-54 period, and the Cards did not top their prior peaks. The Braves set their peak in 1977 when they had a bad team during a time of high walks in the league overall.

Before 1993, when the Marlins and Rockies were born, there were only 4 expansion teams in the National League. Three of these teams (Expos, Padres, and Astros) hit their peaks for walks in the 1970s (together with the Braves as noted above) when walks in the National League hit their highest levels since the 1946-54 period (Table 1-10). The Expos did it in 1970, the second year of their existence. The 1970 Expos approached the league record as they recorded the third highest mark for walks per game in the century. The 1974 Padres also approached record levels and finished just behind the 1970 Expos on the peak list. The Astros, who normally had very good pitching staffs, hit their peak in 1975 but they were not close to record levels. The Mets did not set their record in their terrible first year of 1962, but much later when they had a bad team in 1983. Still, the record for the Mets is so favorable compared to the rest of the league that the Mets did not even lead the league in walks the year they set their franchise record.

Because of the 162 game schedule in the 1970s, the 1970 Expos and 1974 Padres easily beat out the Phillies and Cards in total walks in a year, and the 1977 Braves tied the mark of the 1911 Cards. Further, the 1974 Phillies, 1987 Cubs, and 1970 Pirates all beat out the teams that set franchise marks for walks per game when it came to total walks in a season. The only teams that hit their peaks in the 1990s are the Marlins and the Rockies, and since these franchises did not exist until 1993, the fact that they set their marks in the 1990s is essentially a "technicality." In spite of the high offensive levels in the 1993-97 period, walks in the National League have not risen to uncommonly high levels in this period as they have in the American League.

Table 2-12. NL Teams Peak Years for Walks

Per Game Basis				Total Year Basis			
Team	Per Game	Total	Year	Team	Total	Per Game	Year
Phillies	4.44	675	1928	Expos	716	4.42	1970
Cards	4.44	701	1911	Padres	715	4.41	1974
Expos	4.42	716	1970	Cards	701	4.44	1911
Padres	4.41	715	1974	Braves	701	4.33	1977
Braves	4.33	701	1977	Phillies	682	4.21	1974
Giants	4.29	660	1946	Astros	679	4.19	1975
Dodgers	4.27	671	1946	Dodgers	671	4.27	1946
Astros	4.19	679	1975	Giants	660	4.29	1946
Reds	4.10	640	1949	Reds	640	4.10	1949
Cubs	4.02	619	54/58	Marlins	639	3.94	**1997**
Pirates	4.00	616	1950	Cubs	628	3.90	1987
Marlins	3.94	639	**1997**	Pirates	625	3.86	1970
Rockies	3.85	624	**1996**	Rockies	624	3.85	**1996**
Mets	3.80	615	1983	Mets	615	3.80	1983

The reason why National League walks are not rising sharply with increasing offense as they are in the American League is due again to the designated hitter. When a pitcher bats in the National League, the probability he will draw a walk is low (as is the probability he will even make contact). The designated hitter bats in place of the pitcher in the American League, and he walks much more often because he represents a legitimate offensive threat. The only threat a pitcher presents as a hitter in the National League is to his fingers.

Table 2-13 shows the peak years for SO/W (strikeout-to-walk) ratios for American and National League teams. Years from the 1990s are shown in boldface. The teams are listed in order of their best year in franchise history. But the table does not represent the best years ever in either league because the second or third best years for teams at the top of the list usually are better than the best year for teams farther down the list. The top 10 years regardless of how many times one team appears on the list are shown in Table 2-28.

American League--For the original 8 teams, there were 2 periods when pitchers were dominant and had high SO/W ratios. The first was the 1903-04 period when 4 of the 8 teams set their franchise records (Red Sox, A's, Yankees, and Orioles/Browns). The second was the 1963-68 period when the remaining 4 original teams set their franchise records (Twins, White Sox, Indians, and Tigers). The 1963-68 period is well known as a time when pitchers dominated due to the 1963 rule change in favor of pitchers. The first period also followed a rule change in 1903 when the American League agreed to count foul balls as strikes up to the second strike. As discussed in the text accompanying Table 1-9, hitters took a few years to adapt to the 1903 rule and pitchers dominated just as they would 60 years later when the rules were changed again in their favor. SO/W ratio is an excellent example of what happens to the shift between offense and defense when rules are changed.

The 6 expansion teams set their records in various periods. The Blue Jays and Mariners hit their peak in 1997, the league's highest year for strikeouts (Table 1-9), and the Blue Jays lead 4 of the original teams in SO/W ratio. The Angels and Brewers set their franchise records in 1986 and 1987 respectively. This was the last offensive peak period in the league before the 1993-97 period, and a time when swinging for the fences helped SO/W ratios. The Rangers hit their peak in 1974 behind Hall of Famer Ferguson Jenkins whose SO/W ratio in 1974 was exactly 5.00. The Royals hit their peak in 1989 behind Bret Saberhagen who had a SO/W ratio of 4.49 that year.

Only the Blue Jays and Mariners reached their peaks in the high offense years of the 1990s because the growing level of walks in the American League is holding down SO/W ratios in spite of the big-swing hitting strategy.

National League--With no designated hitter, SO/W ratios are increasing in the National League in the 1990s in spite of a small increase in walks. Thus, 7 of the 14 teams reached peaks in the 1990s. Even without the Marlins and Rockies, who did not exist until 1993, 5 of the remaining 12 teams reached peaks in the 1990s. But 6 of the original 8 teams peaked in the 1963-68 period when the rules were changed to favor pitchers. It appeared at the time that the SO/W records set in this period would never be topped. This is true on a league basis (Table 1-11), but on a team basis the 1994 Expos, 1996 Braves, and 1990 Mets have topped all the 1963-68 records except that of the 1966 Dodgers.

The 1966 Dodgers are a special case. It was the last year for Sandy Koufax who had a SO/W ratio of 4.12 (following a 5.38 mark in 1965). Don Sutton was at 4.02, Don Drysdale at 3.93, and relief ace Phil Regan at 3.67. Koufax and Drysdale are in the Hall of Fame and Sutton should be in soon. The Dodgers led the league in strikeouts in 1966 and also had the lowest level of walks in the majors. The result was a SO/W ratio of 3.04 (it nearly rounds up to 3.05). This is the highest mark in the century, the only one above 3.00, and one still 9 percent above the second place mark of the 1994 Expos. With the ever increasing level of strikeouts in the National League, it is possible some team may yet top the 1966 Dodgers in SO/W ratio, but the record is at 31 years and holding.

Table 2-13. AL/NL Teams Peak Years for SO/W Ratios

American League			National League		
Team	SO/W	Year	Team	SO/W	Year
Twins	2.75	1967	Dodgers	3.04	1966
Red Sox	2.63	1904	Expos	2.80	**1994**
A's	2.42	1904	Braves	2.76	**1996**
White Sox	2.38	1964	Mets	2.74	**1990**
Blue Jays	2.31	**1997**	Giants	2.74	1968
Indians	2.31	1965	Cards	2.59	1968
Tigers	2.29	1968	Reds	2.57	1964
Yankees	2.20	1904	Astros	2.48	1963
Orioles	2.16	1903	Phillies	2.40	1967
Royals	2.15	1989	Padres	2.36	**1996**
Mariners	2.02	**1997**	Pirates	2.29	**1991**
Angels	2.00	1986	Cubs	2.28	1968
Brewers	1.96	1987	Marlins	1.86	**1997**
Rangers	1.94	1974	Rockies	1.74	**1995**

The lowest peak in the majors is that of the Rockies. In spite the lack of the designated hitter in the National League, all American League teams easily lead the Rockies (and the Marlins). Further, the 12th place Cubs lead the last place Rockies by 31 percent, a percentage that nearly would jump the Cubs into first place. This means the Cubs are closer to the top than the last place Rockies are to 12th place. It took very little time for the Rockies to assemble hitters who left their mark on league hitting records, but even in the era of free agency it takes a much longer time to develop a good pitching staff in the thin air of Denver.

Table 2-14 shows peak years for American League teams for each of the key measures used in this book. Years from the 1990s are shown in boldface. The peaks are shown on a per game basis and a total year basis. Thus, this table summarizes in one place the all-time American League team leaders for each key measure.

The total for the year in which a per game peak was reached and/or the per game value for a total year peak can be found in the tables preceding Table 2-14 that show peak years by team for each key measure. For the American League, the only measures for which there is a difference in the teams achieving the per game peak and the total year peak are runs (the Yankees in 1930 and 1931) and doubles (the Indians in 1930 and the Red Sox in 1997).

Runs--The Yankees set the per game peak in 1930 with 6.90 runs per game. But they "only" scored 1062 runs that year (Table 2-1), and thus the peak for total runs in one year is the 1067 runs they scored in 1931 when they played one more game than they did in 1930 (as shown in Table 2-1, their per game average in 1931 was 6.88). The Yankees hold the top three spots on the all-time major league list for scoring runs both on a per game and total basis (Table 2-16). Even with the longer season and the high offensive output of the 1990s, the run scoring records of the Yankees of the 1930s should last for many decades.

Home Runs--Until 1994, the 1961 Yankees held the per game and total home run peaks. But the Indians set a new peak on a per game basis in 1994, and the Orioles set new records for both per game and total home runs in 1996. The Mariners and A's also surpassed the prior records in 1996 (Table 2-3). But in 1997 the Mariners set brand new records for per game and total year home runs. New peaks can be expected as the league continues to set records (Table 1-5).

Doubles--The Indians set the original peaks for doubles on both a per game and total basis in 1930. The 1997 Red Sox made a good run at the per game record, which seemed unbeatable up to then, and the Red Sox set a new total year record on the way. The 1996 Mariners hit 343 doubles and may have missed a total year record due to a mid-season injury to Edgar Martinez, who was on a pace to set an individual record. Thus, the 1990s may yet bring another run at both the per game and total year peaks.

Batting Average--There is no difference in batting average (or any average) on a per game or total basis. The Tigers set the peak at .316 in 1921, the next year after the rule changes favoring hitters were put into effect in 1920. No American League team has approached the record since, and only the 1930 Giants at .319 have been able to top the 1921 Tigers. With the big-swing style of play today, there is no reason to expect any future team to top this record.

ERA--Again, with no difference on a per game or total year basis, the 1996 Tigers set the new record at 6.38. They broke the record of the 1936 Orioles (then the St. Louis Browns), who had an ERA of 6.24 in 1936. Thus the Tigers broke a record that was 60 years old. But it is hard to compare ERAs of the 1930s with the 1990s because of the much lower level of errors today. In 1936, 11.1 percent of all runs in the American League were "unearned." In 1996, the rate had fallen to 7.4 percent. Thus, for the same level of scoring, more runs were earned by definition even if pitching prowess was the same. This is why league ERA values are near record highs, and the same holds true for the teams.

Strikeouts--The 1997 Mariners broke both the per game peak of the 1995 Mariners and the total year peak of the 1967 Indians. These records will be broken regularly as batters keep taking their big swings regardless of the count and today's strong-arm pitchers keep mowing them down.

Table 2-14. AL Teams Peak Years for Key Measures

Measure	Per Game Basis			Total Year Basis		
	Team	Per Game	Year	Team	Total	Year
Runs	Yankees	6.90	1930	Yankees	1067	1931
Home Runs	Mariners	1.63	**1997**	Mariners	264	**1997**
Doubles	Indians	2.32	1930	Red Sox	373	**1997**
BatAvg.	Tigers	.316	1921	Tigers	.316	1921
ERA	Tigers	6.38	**1996**	Tigers	6.38	**1996**
Strikeouts	Mariners	7.45	**1997**	Mariners	1207	**1997**
Walks	A's	5.37	1915	A's	827	1915
SO/W Ratio	Twins	2.75	1967	Twins	2.75	1967

Walks--The Philadelphia A's won their 4th pennant in 5 years in 1914, but then Connie Mack disassembled his team. The 1915 A's were on their way to the worst winning percentage record in the century in 1916, and in 1915 their terrible pitching staff walked 827 batters for an average of 5.37 per game. In the 82 seasons since then no one has been able to top this mark. In fact, in spite of the longer season, only the 1949 Yankees and 1951 Orioles have even managed to produce more than 800 walks in a season (Table 2-26).

Strikeout Ratio--The Twins set the American League record in 1967 during the 1963-68 period when the rules were changed in favor of pitchers. In spite of the increasing strikeout levels in the 1990s, the presence of the designated hitter keeps the level of walks high enough that no team is able to challenge the record of the 1967 Twins. In fact, 6 of the top 10 years in the American League for strikeout-to-walk ratios came in the 6 seasons from 1963 through 1968 (Table 1-11). The designated hitter should keep it that way.

Table 2-15 shows peak years for National League teams for each of the key measures used in this book. Years from the 1990s are shown in boldface. The peaks are shown on a per game basis and a total year basis. Thus, this table summarizes in one place the all-time National League team leaders for each key measure.

The total for the year in which a per game peak was reached and or the per game value for a total year peak can be found in the tables preceding Table 2-15 that show peak years by team for each key measure. For the National League, the only measure for which there is a difference in the teams achieving the per game peak and the total year peak is walks (the Phillies on a per game basis in 1928 and the Expos on a total year basis in 1970).

Runs--The Cards set the per game peak in 1930 with 6.52 runs per game. They scored 1004 runs that year to set the peak for total runs, becoming the only National League to score over 1000 runs in one year. These records, set in the offensive peak year of 1930, have not been challenged since. The only National League team to average more than 6.0 runs per game since 1930 is the 1953 Dodgers who averaged 6.16 with 955 runs scored (Table 2-17). The best mark since 1953 is that of the 1996 Rockies who scored 961 runs for an average of 5.93. Neither team came close to the peaks set by the Cards.

Home Runs--The 1947 New York Giants hit 221 home runs for an average of 1.43 per game. This was at a time when it appeared home run records would be set regularly. But after the 1956 Reds tied both marks, it took 41 years and a mile of altitude before the Rockies broke the prior records in 1997. The Rockies tied the total year mark in 1996, and in 1997 the Rockies set new peaks for both per game and total home runs. It is likely the Rockies are not done setting National League home run records.

Doubles--The Cards set doubles peaks on a per game and total basis in the offensive peak of 1930 when they also set the league records for runs. Both of these doubles marks were also major league records, but the 1997 Red Sox tied the mark for total doubles in one year. With no DH in the National League, no league team is likely to top the 1930 Cards in doubles. It takes 393 doubles in one year to top the 1930 Cards on a per game basis, and the highest total in the league since the 1930s is 339 by the 1997 Expos who averaged 2.09 per game.

Batting Average--There is no difference in batting average (or any average) on a per game or total basis. The Giants set the peak at .319, not surprisingly in the National League's peak offensive year of 1930. This is only .003 ahead of the American League record of .316 by the 1921 Tigers, and, as noted in the text accompanying Table 2-14, these two records should stand indefinitely.

ERA--Again, with no difference on a per game or total year basis, the 1930 Phillies set the record at 6.71, matching the league peak for runs, doubles, and batting average in that year. Even with league ERAs tending higher today due to the much lower level of errors (see the discussion accompanying Table 2-14), the mark of the 1930 Phillies will be hard to beat. The Rockies are the present high ERA leaders in the league, as would be expected, but their highest mark is 5.59 in 1996, and that's more than one full run below the 1930 Phillies. As long as there is no designated hitter in the National League, the Phillies' record is safe.

Strikeouts--League strikeout records were set every year from 1994 through 1997, but the Braves set the records for a team in 1996 and no one could top them in 1997. It will probably happen sooner rather than later. With no designated hitter, National League strikeouts steadily increase as hitters keep taking those big swings and pitchers keep mowing them down.

Table 2-15. NL Teams Peak Years for Key Measures

Measure	Per Game Basis			Total Year Basis		
	Team	Per Game	Year	Team	Total	Year
Runs	Cards	6.52	1930	Cards	1004	1930
Home Runs	Rockies	1.48	**1997**	Rockies	239	**1997**
Doubles	Cards	2.42	1930	Cards	373	1930
Bat Avg.	Giants	.319	1930	Giants	.319	1930
ERA	Phillies	6.71	1930	Phillies	6.71	1930
Strikeouts	Braves	7.69	**1996**	Braves	1245	**1996**
Walks	Phillies	4.44	1928	Expos	716	1970
SO/W Ratio	Dodgers	3.04	1966	Dodgers	3.04	1966

Walks--The 1928 Phillies set the per game record although the 1911 Cards, who trailed the Phillies by only 0.004 walks per game, had more total walks than the Phillies (Table 2-12). But with the longer season after expansion, the 1970 Expos, a mediocre team in the year after their birth, set the league all-time record for total walks in one year. The Expos edged out the 1974 Padres by issuing one more walk than the Padres in their peak year.

Strikeout Ratio--The Braves hold 3 of the first 4 spots on the all-time National League per game strikeout list (Table 2-25), but not even their great pitching teams of the 1990s can match the 3.04 strikeout-to-walk ratio of the 1966 Dodgers. The 1966 Dodgers are the only team ever to go over 3.0, and are well ahead of the next closest ratio of 2.80 by the 1994 Expos (Table 2-28). The 1966 Dodgers had the advantage of pitching during the 1963-68 period when the rules were changed to favor pitchers, but with Sandy Koufax ending his career in a blaze of glory, they were a great pitching team in any era.

Table 2-16 shows the 15 highest years for runs by a team in one year in the American League. Years from the 1990s are shown in boldface. Only seven teams are listed (Yankees, Red Sox, A's, Tigers, Mariners, Indians and Orioles) because the peak years for the other teams in the league are below the 15th place teams listed here. The first part of the table has runs ranked on a per game basis, while the second part has runs ranked on a total year basis. The rankings for each basis are shown in the middle column of the table.

The dominance of the Yankees of the 1930s in scoring runs is shown clearly in Table 2-16. On a per game basis, the Yankees have 7 of the top 9 years in the table, and only one year (1927) was not from the 1930s. Overall, the Yankees have 10 of the top 15 years with 8 of those 10 years coming in the 1930s. On a total runs basis, the Yankees hold 8 of the top 11 years, and once again 1927 is the only year of those 8 years that is not from the 1930s.

Many fans consider the 1927 Yankees to be the best team of all time. Their average of 6.29 runs per game is 8th on the per game list, and their total of 975 runs is 9th on the total runs list. But the Yankees of the 1930s averaged 6.29 runs per game for the full decade from 1930 through 1939, even though two years (1934 and 1935) do not appear on the top 15 lists. The Yankees of the 1930s not only scored at peak levels that are unlikely to be matched, they scored at a sustained level that will almost surely never be matched.

But although the Yankees of the 1930s dominate the lists, the performance of the Red Sox in 1950 for a single year was as dominant as that of the Yankees in the 1930s. In 1950 the Red Sox scored runs at a rate 32 percent higher than the league average. The Yankees, in their three big years of 1930, 1931, and 1936, when they were scoring at a rate of 6.88 runs per game, were "only" 27 percent above the league average. In 1931, the Yankees were, however, nearly 34 percent above the league average. The Red Sox couldn't sustain their huge peak, but for that one year they dominated the rest of the league as the Yankees had done in the 1930s.

The only team from the 1990s on the per game list is the 1996 Mariners who scored the most runs per game since the 1950 Red Sox. But three teams from the 1990s appear on the total runs list due to the longer season. The Indians hit their peak for total runs in 1996, as did the Orioles. Both of these teams and the Mariners scored the most total runs in one year in the American League since the 1950 Red Sox.

The Mariners were only seven runs away from becoming the sixth team in the American League to score 1000 or more runs in a season. They were only 12 runs away from breaking the National League record of 1004 set by the Cards in 1930 (Table 2-17). No other National League team has been able to score over 1000 runs in a season, but it's likely the Mariners and some other American League teams will pass 1000 in a future year.

The effects of the designated hitter and the longer season will slowly begin to eliminate Yankee teams of the 1930s from the total runs list. The Yankee teams of 1921 and 1933, 11th and 15th on the per game list, were displaced from the total runs list in 1996 by the Indians and the Orioles. The Mariners were only 13th on the per game list, but they passed four Yankee teams (1921, 1927, 1937, and 1939) on the total runs list. The first team from the 1990s to get over 1000 runs may well displace the 1932 Yankees. But it should take a very long time to approach the top three Yankee teams (as well as the 1950 Red Sox). On a per game basis, just catching the 1932 Yankees in 5th place requires 1040 runs in the present 162 game season. That's a very tall order.

Table 2-16. AL Teams Ranked Years for Runs

Per Game Basis					Total Year Basis			
Team	Per Game	Total	Year	Rank	Team	Total	Per Game	Year
Yankees	6.90	1062	1930	1	Yankees	1067	6.88	1931
Yankees	6.88	1067	1931	2	Yankees	1065	6.87	1936
Yankees	6.87	1065	1936	3	Yankees	1062	6.90	1930
Red Sox	6.67	1027	1950	4	Red Sox	1027	6.67	1950
Yankees	6.42	1002	1932	5	Yankees	1002	6.42	1932
A's	6.37	981	1932	6	Mariners	993	6.17	**1996**
Yankees	6.36	967	1939	7	A's	981	6.37	1932
Yankees	6.29	975	1927	8	Yankees	979	6.24	1937
Yankees	6.24	979	1937	9	Yankees	975	6.29	1927
Tigers	6.22	958	1934	10	Yankees	967	6.36	1939
Yankees	6.20	948	1921	11	Yankees	966	6.15	1938
A's	6.18	951	1930	12	Tigers	958	6.22	1934
Mariners	6.17	993	**1996**	13	Indians	952	5.91	**1996**
Yankees	6.15	966	1938	14	A's	951	6.18	1930
Yankees	6.10	927	1933	15	Orioles	949	5.82	**1996**

After the above comparisons, the question that quickly arises is how many runs would a team have to score to displace the 1930 Yankees from the top of the per game list. The answer is 1118 runs in the 162 game season. Since the best total in the last 46 years is 993 runs for the 1996 Mariners, it's not likely any team is going to top 1100 runs in the next half-century (unless there is a change in the rules allowing two designated hitters).

Table 2-17 shows the 15 highest years for runs by a team in one year in the National League. Years from the 1990s are shown in boldface. Only seven teams are listed (Cards, Cubs, Giants, Dodgers, Phillies, Pirates, and Rockies) because the peak years for the other teams in the league are below the 15th place teams listed here. The first part of the table has runs ranked on a per game basis, while the second part has runs ranked on a total year basis. The rankings for each basis are shown in the middle column of the table.

Unlike the American League (Table 2-16), where the Yankees of the 1930s dominate the list, there is no single dominant team in the National League. The 1930 Cards lead both the per game and total list, but the 1930 Cubs are close behind in second place. Further, the 1929 Cubs are in third place, but the Cards do not reappear on either list at all. Similarly, the Cubs cannot be considered a dominant team because they also do not appear again on either list after taking the second and third spots.

What does dominate the list in the National League is the huge offensive peak of 1929 and 1930. Much has been made of the 1930 peak, but it followed quite logically from the results of 1929. It is the two years together that stand out in the National League. Four teams that placed both their 1929 and 1930 teams on the list account for 8 of the 15 positions (Cubs, Giants, Phillies, and Pirates). On a per game basis, 11 of the 15 teams come from 1930 and before. On the total year list, "only" 10 of the 15 teams come from 1930 and before. The difference is that the 1962 Giants scored enough runs in the longer season to get on the total runs list, even though their per game mark places them much farther down the runs per game list.

The most recent additions to the list are the 1996 and 1997 Rockies. The 1996 Rockies averaged 5.93 runs per game, the best in the National League since the Dodgers set their all-time record in 1953 (the Dodgers of 1949 and 1953 are the only other teams on the per game list to reach their peaks after 1930). The 1996 Rockies are 8th on the per game list, and their total of 961 runs puts them 4th on the total runs list. This was the highest total runs mark in the National League since 1930, in spite of the fact that the Rockies fell off in scoring near the end of the 1996 season. The 1997 Rockies finished well to rank 13th on the per game list and 8th on the total runs list.

Playing in the thin air in Denver with a team designed to score runs, the Rockies are the only present National League team with a chance to score more than 1000 runs in a year. The 1996 Rockies were 24 percent ahead of the second place National League team, and only the Mariners scored more runs in the American League. The Rockies need to average 6.21 runs per game to top the total runs record set by the Cards 67 years ago in 1930. The 1997 Rockies "only" averaged 5.70 runs per game (again only the Mariners scored more), but the 1997 Rockies did break the National League home run record (Table 2-19).

In contrast to the close approach of the Rockies to the top, the rest of the present National League teams are not likely to even get on the total runs list, let alone the per game list. The best per game mark for the other National League teams during the 1993-97 offensive outburst is the 5.41 mark recorded by the 1993 Phillies. That puts them in 16th place on the total runs list. The next best mark is 5.30 by the 1994 Reds. This would give them 859 runs in a full 162 season, which would still leave them off the total runs list (it also is not enough to match their all-time per game high of 5.43 recorded 94 years ago in 1903). The 1962 Giants made the total runs list with a per game mark of 5.32 because they played 165 games including a playoff for the league championship.

Table 2-17. NL Teams Ranked Years for Runs

Per Game Basis					Total Runs Basis			
Team	Per Game	Total	Year	Rank	Team	Total	Per Game	Year
Cards	6.52	1004	1930	1	Cards	1004	6.52	1930
Cubs	6.40	998	1930	2	Cubs	998	6.40	1930
Cubs	6.29	982	1929	3	Cubs	982	6.29	1929
Giants	6.23	959	1930	4	Rockies	961	5.93	**1996**
Dodgers	6.16	955	1953	5	Giants	959	6.23	1930
Phillies	6.05	944	1930	6	Dodgers	955	6.16	1953
Pirates	5.96	912	1925	7	Phillies	944	6.05	1930
Rockies	5.93	961	**1996**	8	Rockies	923	5.70	**1997**
Giants	5.90	897	1929	9	Pirates	912	5.96	1925
Pirates	5.87	904	1929	10	Pirates	904	5.87	1929
Phillies	5.82	897	1929	11	Giants	897	5.90	1929
Pirates	5.79	891	1930	12	Phillies	897	5.82	1929
Rockies	5.70	923	**1997**	13	Pirates	891	5.79	1930
Dodgers	5.66	871	1930	14	Dodgers	879	5.63	1949
Dodgers	5.63	879	1949	15	Giants	878	5.32	1962

In addition to being the only teams of the original 8 to make the per game list after 1930, the 1949 and 1953 Dodgers were part of an average of 5.53 runs per game for the 1949-53 period. This is the top mark for five years in league history (*The Best of Teams, the Worst of Teams*). None of the teams that can include the huge peaks of 1929 and 1930 in such an average match the 1949-53 Dodgers, and the 1993-97 Rockies at 5.33 runs per game are also well behind.

Table 2-18 shows the 10 highest years for home runs by a team in one year in the American League. Years from the 1990s are shown in boldface. Only eight teams are listed (Orioles, Mariners, A's, Indians, Yankees, Tigers, Twins, and Rangers) because the peak years for the rest of the teams in the league are below the 10th place teams listed here. The first part of the table has home runs ranked on a per game basis, while the second part has home runs ranked on a total year basis. The rankings for each basis are shown in the middle column of the table.

The domination of teams from the 1990s on the top 10 list in the American League is shown clearly in Table 2-18. On a per game basis, 7 of the top 10 years come from the 1990s. On the total year list, 6 of the top 10 teams come from the 1990s. The difference is due to the shorter season in 1994 and 1995 as a result of the strike. The 1994 and 1995 Indians and 1994 Tigers make the per game top 10 list, but they do not make the total year list because the shorter seasons in 1994 and 1995 meant low totals for all measures.

In 1996 the Orioles, Mariners, and A's all beat the per game record of the 1994 Indians who had topped the per game record of the 1961 Yankees. The three 1996 teams also easily beat the total year record of the 1961 Yankees. The 1997 Mariners then topped their 1996 marks and set the all-time league records for both per game and total year home runs. The 1996 Orioles hit 17 more home runs than the 1961 Yankees, an increase of 7 percent. This is a substantial increase over a prior record, especially one that was set 35 years ago (the 1997 Mariners topped the 1996 Orioles by less than 3 percent). With the 1996 Mariners and 1996 A's also beating the prior team record, it is no surprise the American League set its all-time home run record in 1996 (Table 1-5).

There is no precedent for the league's present home run level, but there is no reason to believe it will decline significantly. Home runs were down in 1997, but 1997 still holds 4th place on the all-time league list (Table 1-5). Home runs are the prime goal of today's big hitters, and no one complains about the record number of strikeouts that accompany the record number of home runs. As long as the designated hitter rule remains in effect, the American League will continue to hit home runs at or near its present record levels.

Since the new labor contract should insure that there will be no more strikes until at least the next century, many teams from before the 1990s will probably fall off the total home runs list over the next several years. The 1997 Mariners and 1997 Indians bumped the 1982 Brewers (and 1996 Indians) off the top 10 total year list, and if the 1997 Indians had hit just two more home runs they would have moved the 1963 Twins and 1987 Tigers farther down the list. Thus, it's likely that in several years the only team prior to 1996 on the top 10 total home run list in the American League will be the 1961 Yankees. But the 1961 Yankees were ahead of their time in hitting home runs and it will probably take a long time before they fall completely off the list.

It's not clear how far the team home run record in the American League can be advanced. The league home run record will probably keep moving up because all teams are looking for big hitters, and the difference from top to bottom in the league will probably keep shrinking. If the next team to set the record beats the 1997 Mariners by as large a percentage margin as the 1996 Orioles beat the 1961 Yankees, then the league record would jump to a total of 283 home runs for one year. That sounds like a very high number, but 257 home runs also seemed a long way off as teams kept making unsuccessful runs at the Yankee record of 240 during the last 35 years. The only sure forecast is that with the present approach to the game the American League home run record with keep climbing.

Table 2-18. AL Teams Ranked Years for Home Runs

Per Game Basis					Total Year Basis			
Team	Per Game	Total	Year	Rank	Team	Total	Per Game	Year
Mariners	1.63	264	**1997**	1	Mariners	264	1.63	**1997**
Orioles	1.58	257	**1996**	2	Orioles	257	1.58	**1996**
Mariners	1.52	245	**1996**	3	Mariners	245	1.52	**1996**
A's	1.50	243	**1996**	4	A's	243	1.50	**1996**
Indians	1.48	167	**1994**	5	Yankees	240	1.47	1961
Yankees	1.47	240	1961	6	Twins	225	1.40	1963
Indians	1.44	207	**1995**	7	Tigers	225	1.39	1987
Tigers	1.40	161	**1994**	8	Rangers	221	1.36	**1996**
Twins	1.40	225	1963	9	Twins	221	1.36	1964
Tigers	1.39	225	1987	10	Indians	220	1.37	**1997**

One final comment should be made about the Twins of 1963 and 1964, even though they may soon fall off the top 10 list. The Twins at that time were playing without the designated hitter (the DH did not come until 1973), and they were also playing in the 1963-68 period that became a graveyard for runs due to the rule changes made in 1963 in favor of pitchers. In spite of these handicaps compared to teams playing today, the 1963 and 1964 Twins hit a total of 446 home runs in back-to-back seasons as Harmon Killebrew led the way with 94. This was the last big surge in home runs in the American League until the late 1980s, when the league was on its way to its all-time home run record in 1987 (the record that was broken in 1996). The Twins' performance can be considered a tribute to Killebrew, the fifth leading home run hitter in history.

Table 2-19 shows the 10 highest years for home runs by a team in one year in the National League. Years from the 1990s are shown in boldface. Only six teams are listed (Rockies, Giants, Reds, Dodgers, Cubs, and Braves) because the peak years for the rest of the teams in the league are below the 10th place teams listed here. The first part of the table has home runs ranked on a per game basis, while the second part has home runs ranked on a total year basis. The rankings for each basis are shown in the middle column of the table.

The peak year for home runs in the National League was 1955, and 5 of the top 10 years in the league are from the 1950s (Table 1-5). Thus, it is not surprising that 5 of the top 10 teams on the ranked per game list in Table 2-19 are from 1957 or before. But only 3 of these teams are on the total year list because the longer season has permitted teams with lower per game values to climb onto the total year list. However, the rise of the Colorado Rockies has made this kind of analysis academic. It is only a matter of time before the Rockies become the only franchise listed in the table.

Because of the shorter 1995 season due to the strike, the 1995 Rockies hit "only" 200 home runs in 1995 and thus they did not make the total year list when they made their first appearance on the per game list. In 1996 the Rockies hit fewer home runs per game, but the full 162 season permitted them to appear on the total year list as well. In 1997 the Rockies set the all-time National League records for home runs on both a per game and total year basis. They presently hold 3 of the top 10 spots on the per game list, and they can be expected to appear on both lists for at least the next 8 years if there are no strikes. That may permit them to occupy all 10 places on both lists.

Some fans have complained about the home field advantage of the Rockies. But the 1947 Giants played in the Polo Grounds, and the Polo Grounds Giants over the years had higher ratios of home runs at home to home runs on the road than the Rockies presently have. Even the 1956 Reds had a park configuration that was deliberately modified to be friendly to hitters. (*The Evolution of Baseball* has much more detail on parks that were true home run havens.)

The Rockies are a new phenomenon in the National League. In the thin air of Denver, they score runs and hit home runs as if they were an American League team with a designated hitter. If the National League ever adopts the designated hitter rule, the Rockies could hold all major league home run records. The 1997 Rockies broke a league record that was originally set 50 years ago, and they also hit more home runs in 1997 than any American League team except the Mariners. Even with a poor start as an expansion team in 1993, the 1993-97 Rockies averaged 1.23 home runs per game, breaking the record of 1.20 held by the 1952-56 Dodgers for most home runs over a five year period. In just their 5th year of existence, the Rockies are already the best home run hitting team in the history of the National League on both a peak and sustained basis.

In spite of the record set by the Rockies, the National League as a whole in 1997 was not close to its prior home run records (Table 1-5). Other than the Rockies, the best single year performance in the league during the 1993-97 offensive outburst was a per game performance of 1.22 by the 1996 Braves who hit a total of 197 home runs. Neither mark can make either the per game or total year top 10 list. The best performance in the league after 1956 and before the arrival of the Rockies in 1993 is that of the 1987 Cubs who averaged 1.30 home runs per game for a total of 209. The Rockies are both the present and future National League home run champs. The 1947 Giants and 1956 Reds will be the last teams to leave the top 10 list as the Rockies fill in all the other places.

Table 2-19. NL Teams Ranked Years for Home Runs

| | Per Game Basis | | | | | Total Year Basis | | |
Team	Per Game	Total	Year	Rank	Team	Total	Per Game	Year
Rockies	1.48	239	**1997**	1	Rockies	239	1.48	**1997**
Giants	1.43	221	1947	2	Giants	221	1.43	1947
Reds	1.43	221	1956	3	Reds	221	1.43	1956
Rockies	1.39	200	**1995**	4	Rockies	221	1.36	**1996**
Rockies	1.36	221	**1996**	5	Cubs	209	1.30	1987
Dodgers	1.34	208	1953	6	Dodgers	208	1.34	1953
Dodgers	1.31	201	1955	7	Braves	207	1.27	1966
Cubs	1.30	209	1987	8	Braves	206	1.27	1973
Braves	1.28	199	1957	9	Giants	205	1.27	1987
Braves	1.27	206	1973	10	Giants	204	1.24	1962

Although the record of the 1947 Giants was eclipsed by the 1997 Rockies, the 1947 Giants retain a unique place in league history. Until 1947 the record for home runs in one year was 182 for the 1936 Yankees in the American League and 171 for the 1930 Cubs in the National League. After the Cubs hit the National League peak in 1930, no team in the league hit more than 126 home runs in a season (the 1934 Giants) until the 1947 Giants burst upon the scene. They broke their own team record by 75 percent, and they were 29 percent above the league record set by the Cubs. Their record was tied by the 1956 Reds and 1996 Rockies (on a total basis only), but otherwise it lasted 50 years. Even in the American League, only three teams had managed to hit more than 221 home runs in one year before the big surge in 1996 (Table 2-18).

Table 2-20 shows the 10 highest years for doubles by a team in one year in the American League. Years from the 1990s are shown in boldface. Only four teams are listed (Indians, Red Sox, Tigers, and Mariners) because the peak years for the rest of the teams in the league are below the 10th place team listed here. The first part of the table has doubles ranked on a per game basis, while the second part of the table has doubles ranked on a total year basis. The rankings for each basis are shown in the middle column of the table.

The Indians were the leaders in doubles in the major leagues by a wide margin from 1903 through 1945. The Indians led the second place Tigers during that period by 9 percent, which is a very high margin over such a long period of time. For example, the difference between the second place Tigers and sixth place Yankees over that period was also 9 percent. The Indians were 12 percent ahead of the Cards who led the National League (Table 2-21), the Indians were 13 percent ahead of the American League average, and the Indians were 20 percent ahead of the National League average.

As a result, in the American League, the Indians occupy 6 of the top 10 places both for most doubles per game and total doubles. Until the Red Sox had their record breaking year for total doubles in 1997, the Indians also held the top 3 places on both lists. To demonstrate the length of the period in which the Indians were league leaders in doubles, those top 3 places were held by the 1921 Indians, the 1930 Indians, and the 1936 Indians. The Indians peaked in 1930, but no other team could top even the third place mark of the Indians between 1921 and 1936, the period when the American League set most of its doubles records (Table 1-6). Tris Speaker, who holds the all-time career record for doubles, played for the Indians from 1916 through 1926, but the Indians hit doubles at a high rate even after he was gone. However, after 1945 the Indians ranked near the bottom of the league list for doubles until the offensive outburst from 1993 through 1997. This outburst added the 1994 and 1996 Indians to the top ten lists, but the most notable addition was the 1997 Red Sox and their 373 doubles. The Red Sox, however, could not match 1930 and 1921 Indians on a per game basis.

The Tigers, who were second to the Indians in doubles from 1903 through 1945, occupy 2 of the top 10 places on both lists. Ironically, the 1996 Indians helped knock the 1936 Tigers off the total year list. The 1929 and 1934 Tigers appear on both lists. The Tigers, however, did copy the Indians in that the Tigers held a high position before WWII, fell to the middle of the pack from 1946 through 1972, and then were near the bottom of the league from 1973 onward (the trend of doubles and other measures over time by team is shown in detail in *The Best of Teams, the Worst of Teams*).

The Mariners are the only other team to make the top 10 lists. But, as shown in Table 2-5, there are several teams in the American League that could soon move up. This is because, as shown in Table 1-6, 1996 was the highest year for doubles in the American League since 1936. The 1996 Mariners are in 9th place on the top 10 list for doubles per game, but because of the longer season they are in 6th place on the top 10 list for total doubles in one year. As noted in the text accompanying Table 2-5, the 1996 Mariners might have come close to the then record of 358 doubles hit by the 1930 Indians if Edgar Martinez had not been injured, but the 1997 Red Sox made that academic with their new total record. The 1994 Indians joined their other franchise teams on the per game list, but the shortened season prevented them from making the total list. To compensate, the 1996 Indians could not top their other franchise teams on the top 10 list for doubles per game, but they moved into 8th place on the total year list.

Table 2-20. AL Teams Ranked Years for Doubles

Per Game Basis					Total Year Basis			
Team	Per Game	Total	Year	Rank	Team	Total	Per Game	Year
Indians	2.32	358	1930	1	Red Sox	373	2.30	**1997**
Indians	2.31	355	1921	2	Indians	358	2.32	1930
Red Sox	2.30	373	**1997**	3	Indians	357	2.27	1936
Indians	2.27	357	1936	4	Indians	355	2.31	1921
Tigers	2.27	349	1934	5	Tigers	349	2.27	1934
Indians	2.21	340	1934	6	Mariners	343	2.13	**1996**
Tigers	2.19	339	1929	7	Indians	340	2.21	1934
Indians	2.16	333	1926	8	Tigers	339	2.19	1929
Mariners	2.13	343	**1996**	9	Indians	335	2.08	**1996**
Indians	2.12	240	**1994**	10	Indians	333	2.16	1926

The 1994 and 1996 Indians are an example of how other teams could move onto the total year list. Like the Indians, the 1994 Twins are 11th on the per game list and the 1996 Twins are 11th on the total year list. The big-swing game has led to an increase in doubles as well as home runs. It is not easy to make the per game list, but an average of just over 2.06 doubles per game results in 334 doubles in the 162 game season. Four teams (Twins, Indians, Yankees, and Brewers) exceeded the 2.06 per game level in 1994, but the strike prevented them from making the top 10 total year list. With labor peace hopefully assured for the rest of the century, teams that exceed 2.06 doubles per game can move onto the total year list, and those more like the 1997 Red Sox can move far up the total year list even if they do not get to the top of the per game list.

Table 2-21 shows the 10 highest years for doubles by a team in one year in the National League. Years from the 1990s are shown in boldface. Only six teams are listed (Cards, Phillies, Astros, Cubs, Expos, and Pirates) because the peak years for the rest of the teams in the league are below the 10th place teams listed here. The first part of the table has doubles ranked on a per game basis, while the second part has doubles ranked on a total year basis. The rankings for each basis are shown in the middle column of the table.

As far as doubles are concerned, the Cards are the National League's equivalent to the Indians in the American League (Table 2-20). Like the Indians, the Cards led the National League in the first half of the century from 1903 through 1945. The Cards peaked in 1930, as did the Indians, but the Cards topped the Indians with 373 doubles in 1930 for a per game average of 2.42, both major league records at the time. But the Cards had a much smaller margin over the rest of the league than did the Indians. Thus, the Cards "only" occupy 4 of the top 10 places on the per game and total year lists while the Indians took 6 places on each list in the American League.

Even though the leading margin was smaller, the Cards maintained their top ranking in the National League much longer than did the Indians in the American League. The Cards led the National League in doubles from 1946 through 1972 as well as from 1903 through 1945, and the Cards stayed close to the league leaders after 1973 although they did fall to 5th by the 1990s.

Until 1997 it seemed unlikely the record of the 1930 Cards could be topped in the majors, let alone in the National League. But as shown in Table 2-20, the 1997 Red Sox hit 373 doubles to set a total year record in the American League. This tied them with the Cards, but the Red Sox were on a pace to top the Cards before falling back in September. The record of the 1930 Cards is certainly vulnerable as long as the American League continues to use the designated hitter. However, no National League team has come close, although, as discussed below, the Astros might have done so in 1994 if not for the strike. The per game record of the Cards seems safe because it would take 393 doubles in the 162 game season to average 2.42 doubles per game. That's 5 percent above the record of the 1997 Red Sox, a large margin when trying to set records.

The Cards hold the top two spots on both lists in the National League. The Phillies are in 3rd place on both lists, and they and the Expos also hold two spots on the per game list. The Phillies and the Pirates hold two spots each on the total year list. The 1996 Pirates and 1997 Expos are the only teams from the 1990s to appear on the total year list. The 1996 Pirates are just ahead of the 1925 Pirates on the list, meaning the 1996 Pirates had the best total year mark for the franchise in 71 years. But the 1925 Pirates have a comfortable margin in doubles per game. The 1996 Pirates are the only team in either league to make either list while averaging less than 2.0 doubles per game.

The 1994 strike probably kept both the Astros and Expos from occupying high positions on the total year list. The 1994 Astros moved into 4th place on the per game list and the 1994 Expos took over 6th place in the same year (as shown in Table 1-6, the league had its highest average for doubles per game in 60 years in 1994). With the highest per game average since the 1931 Cards, the 1994 Astros would have hit 355 doubles in 1994 if they had maintained their average for a full 162 games. Similarly, the Expos would have hit 350. These marks would have moved the Astros into 2nd place on the total year list and the Expos into 4th place. But because of the strike, no one knows if both teams would have been able to maintain their pace over a full year.

Table 2-21. NL Teams Ranked Years for Doubles

Per Game Basis				Rank	Total Year Basis			
Team	Per Game	Total	Year		Team	Total	Per Game	Year
Cards	2.42	373	1930	1	Cards	373	2.42	1930
Cards	2.29	353	1931	2	Cards	353	2.29	1931
Phillies	2.21	345	1930	3	Phillies	345	2.21	1930
Astros	2.19	252	**1994**	4	Cubs	340	2.18	1931
Cubs	2.18	340	1931	5	Expos	339	2.09	**1997**
Expos	2.16	246	**1994**	6	Cards	332	2.14	1936
Phillies	2.14	330	1932	7	Cards	332	2.14	1939
Cards	2.14	332	1936	8	Phillies	330	2.14	1932
Cards	2.14	332	1939	9	Pirates	319	1.97	**1996**
Expos	2.09	339	**1997**	10	Pirates	316	2.07	1925

Even if the 1994 Astros and 1994 Expos had maintained their respective per game paces over a full year, they still would be well below the record of 373 doubles in one year set by the 1930 Cards. The 1997 Expos maintained a per game average of 2.08 for the full year which put them in 10th place on the per game list and 5th place on the total year list. The 339 doubles hit by the 1997 Expos was the most in the National League since 1931. But although the 1994 Astros and 1997 Expos have reached back to 1931 for per game and total year doubles marks, moving up to the 2.31 doubles per game level that is necessary in the 162 game season to break the total year record of the 1930 Cards still seems unlikely in the National League. In the century, only the 1930 Cards, 1930 Indians, and 1921 Indians have hit 2.31 doubles per game or more.

Table 2-22 shows the 10 highest years for batting average for American and National League teams. Years from the 1990s are normally shown in boldface, but there are no such years in Table 2-22 (the most recent year is 1930). Only five teams from each league (Tigers, Orioles/Browns, Yankees, Indians, and A's, and the Giants, Phillies, Cards, Pirates, and Cubs) are listed because the peak years for the rest of the teams in each league are below that of the 10th place teams listed here. The rankings are shown in the middle column of the table.

American League--As discussed in the text accompanying Table 1-7, team batting averages soared after 1920 as a result of the new rules put into place in 1920 outlawing the "doctored" pitches pitchers had used to keep runs low after the cork-centered ball was introduced in the 1910-11 period. Putting new balls into play much more often after 1920 also contributed to the hitting surge. As also happened in the 1963-68 period, sudden rule changes often produce sudden differences in the way the game is played.

Thanks primarily to George Sisler, the Orioles (then the Browns) occupy 3 of the top 10 spots on the American League list. The 3 best years for the Browns were 1922, 1920, and 1921--exactly the same 3 years in the same order that were the best of Sisler's career, including averages of .407 in 1920 and .420 in 1922. The Tigers occupy 2 of the top 10 years, and they came in 1921 and 1922 when Ty Cobb and Harry Heilman were battling with George Sisler for the top spot in batting average in the league. The 1930 and 1927 Yankees also occupy 2 spots thanks to Babe Ruth and Lou Gehrig, and the 1921 and 1930 Indians are the final team to occupy 2 spots on the top 10 list. The 1925 A's are the only team on the list to have only one spot.

Six of the top 10 years were recorded between 1920 and 1922. This is an indication that pitchers began to recover from the 1920 rule changes by the middle of the decade. The 1925 A's and the 1927 Yankees (with perhaps the most dominant team ever in baseball) recorded their marks after the midpoint of the decade, and two teams (the 1930 Yankees and 1930 Indians) got on the list during the offensive peak in 1930. The 1930 peak (which was much stronger in the National League) generally marked the beginning of the end of high batting averages as described in the text accompanying Table 1-7. Except for 1936 in the American League, 1930 was the last year in either league to make a top 10 list.

National League--The National League was a year behind the American League in building record batting averages, and the 1921 Cards were the first team in the league to record a batting average over .300 when they hit .308 for the season. The 1922 Pirates matched that mark in the following year, and the Pirates (behind the Waner brothers) led the league in batting average from 1922 through 1928, occupying 4 of the top 10 spots on the league list. Other teams had seasons over .300 during this time, but, except for the Pirates, those years were overtaken by the huge surge in offense in the league in 1929 and 1930.

The Giants set an all-time major league record with a batting average of .319 in 1930 (their only appearance on the list). The Phillies occupy 2 spots on the list with their all-time franchise highs in 1930 and 1929, and the 1930 Cards also had a franchise record giving them a 2nd spot on the list. The Cubs got their only spot on the list with a franchise record in 1930, becoming the fourth team from 1930 to make the list. No other year has more than one team on the list, a good indication of the huge surge in offense that took place in the National League in 1930. But although the .319 recorded by the Giants in 1930 seems absurdly high by today's standards, it is only three percentage points higher than the .316 recorded by the Tigers in 1921 to set the all-time American League record.

Table 2-22. AL/NL Teams Ranked Years for Batting Average

American League				National League		
Team	BatAvg.	Year	Rank	Team	BatAvg.	Year
Tigers	.316	1921	1	Giants	.319	1930
Orioles	.313	1922	2	Phillies	.315	1930
Yankees	.309	1930	3	Cards	.314	1930
Orioles	.308	1920	4	Pirates	.309	1928
Indians	.308	1921	5	Phillies	.309	1929
Yankees	.307	1927	6	Cubs	.309	1930
A's	.307	1925	7	Cards	.308	1921
Tigers	.306	1922	8	Pirates	.308	1922
Orioles	.304	1921	9	Pirates	.307	1925
Indians	.304	1930	10	Pirates	.305	1927

There was a sharper increase in the National League in 1930 than in the American League, but both leagues increased from the years preceding 1930. Looking at the league lists side-by-side does not give the impression that the 1930 surge in the National League was totally different from the surge that took place in the American League in 1920 and 1921. The National League batting average peak was essentially delayed from that of the American League. But in both leagues a dramatic upturn took place in the 1920s due to the change in the rules at the beginning of the decade. The American League had its batting average peak well before the National League, but the National League peaked in runs in 1930 and this was well before the 1936 peak in runs in the American League. Statistical peaks are not always neat and tidy, and they do not necessarily occur at the same time in the same way in both leagues.

Table 2-23 shows the 10 highest years for earned run average (ERA) for American and National League teams. Years from the 1990s are shown in boldface. Only four teams from the American League (Tigers, Orioles/Browns, A's, and Twins) and three from the National League (Phillies, Rockies, and Pirates) are listed because the peak years for the rest of the teams in each league are below that of the 10th team listed here. The rankings are shown in the middle column of the table.

American League--The top teams on the list come from two distinct periods. The Orioles (when they were the Browns) had the worst pitching staff in the league from 1936 through 1939, the highest run scoring period in American League history. The result for the Browns is 4 of the 10 highest ERAs on the list, including a mark of 6.24 in 1936 which stood as the American League record until the Tigers topped it in 1996. The team with a pitching staff nearly as bad as that of the Browns in the 1936-39 period was the A's, and they occupy 2 of the top 10 spots to give the 1936-39 period 6 of the top 10 spots.

The remaining 4 spots on the top 10 list are held by the 1994 and 1995 Twins and the 1995 and 1996 Tigers. The formula for the 1994-96 period was the same as for the 1936-39 period. Two teams with bad pitching staffs in a period of high runs. As described in the text accompanying Table 1-8, ERAs today are higher than in the 1930s for the same level of overall run scoring due to the lower level of errors. But the 1996 Tigers took over the top spot on sheer merit. They had a truly terrible pitching staff, and the fact that Tiger Stadium is a hitter's park did not help. The 1994 and 1995 Twins and the 1995 Tigers are at the bottom of the top 10 list because pitching today generally is better than that of the A's and Browns of the 1930s, and run scoring is not quite as high in the 1990s as it was in the 1930s.

Although they no longer hold the single year American League record, the 1935-39 Browns hold the major league record for highest ERA over a five year period. They averaged 5.86 over five years, and even the Phillies, who set the major league record for one year, do not have a five year mark as high as that of the 1935-39 Browns. The 1993-97 Tigers averaged "only" 5.29, well below both the 1935-39 Browns and the 1936-40 A's. For that matter, the 1993-97 Twins matched the Tigers at 5.29 for the 1993-97 period.

National League--The National League has a pattern similar to that of the American League. The Phillies hold 5 of the top 10 spots on the list, and these came when the Phillies had the worst pitching staff in the league in the worst ballpark in the league. The Phillies made the top 10 list in 1923 and then in every year from 1927 through 1930 when the National League set its all-time run scoring records. The Phillies recorded a major league high of 6.71 when the National League scored its major league high in runs in 1930. The greatest number of these runs were scored in the bandbox that was Baker Bowl.

To prove that their pitching staff was bad enough to produce high ERAs on its own, the 1939 Phillies are 11th on the list even though they played in Shibe Park (to which a 50 foot wall in right field had been added). Two other spots on the list are held by the 1930 Pirates who had a decent team but a bad pitching staff, and the 1953 Pirates who had a truly terrible team, including the pitching staff, in a high run scoring year. The remaining 3 spots on the list are held by the 1996, 1993, and 1997 Rockies. As was the case for the Phillies through the early 1930s, the Rockies play in a park that leads the league in run scoring. Coors Field is a much nicer park than the ancient Baker Bowl was, but, like Baker Bowl, Coors Field produces arcade baseball.

Table 2-23. AL/NL Teams Ranked Years for ERA

American League				National League		
Team	ERA	Year	Rank	Team	ERA	Year
Tigers	6.38	**1996**	1	Phillies	6.71	1930
Orioles	6.24	1936	2	Phillies	6.13	1929
A's	6.08	1936	3	Rockies	5.59	**1996**
Orioles	6.01	1939	4	Phillies	5.52	1928
Orioles	6.00	1937	5	Rockies	5.41	**1993**
Orioles	5.80	1938	6	Phillies	5.36	1927
A's	5.79	1939	7	Phillies	5.34	1923
Twins	5.76	**1995**	8	Rockies	5.25	**1997**
Twins	5.68	**1994**	9	Pirates	5.24	1930
Tigers	5.49	**1995**	10	Pirates	5.22	1953

The National League list has 6 teams from the 1923-30 period that was the highest scoring period in league history (Table 1-4), one very bad team that played in a year of above average scoring (1953), and 3 teams from the offensive surge of the 1990s. It can be expected that the Rockies will place more teams on the list in the future even though they are a very competitive team. In their 5 years of existence, the Rockies trail only the 1926-30 Phillies for the highest ERA in league history over a five year period. The records of the 1929 and 1930 Phillies may not be approachable due to the combination of the binge in runs during these years and the truly terrible pitching staffs of the Phillies in a truly terrible park. But the Rockies have already topped every other year in league history, and, with arcade baseball continuing in full swing in Coors Field, the forecast most definitely is for high ERAs in the Colorado Rockies.

Table 2-24 shows the 10 highest years for strikeouts by a team in one year in the American League. Years from the 1990s are shown in boldface. Only six teams are listed (Mariners, Indians, Blue Jays, Red Sox, Yankees, and Orioles) because the peak years for the other teams in the league are below the 10th place teams listed here. The first part of the table has strikeouts ranked on a per game basis, while the second part ranks strikeouts on a total year basis. The rankings for each basis are shown in the middle column of the table.

The Indians occupy 4 of the top 10 places on both lists. All 4 teams come from the 1963-68 period when the rules were changed to favor pitchers. As is common for teams setting league records in any measure, the Indians combined a period of high strikeouts with a team that featured strikeout pitchers. "Sudden Sam" McDowell was the leader with Luis Tiant and Sonny Siebert also recording high strikeout levels. The Indians were only a .500 team during the period, but they led the league in strikeouts.

As shown in Table 1-9, the highest years for strikeouts in the American League came during the 1963-68 and 1993-97 periods. Thus, the other 6 years on the top 10 per game list in Table 2-24 came between 1994 and 1997. The 1995 Mariners set an all-time American League record for strikeouts per game behind strikeout ace Randy Johnson. There was a pause in 1996 when Johnson was injured, and then the 1997 Mariners broke their 1995 record. The Yankees and Red Sox set team records in 1996, the Yankees being led by their celebrated relief tandem of Mariano Rivera and John Wetteland while the Red Sox were led by long time strikeout king Roger Clemens. Then the 1997 Yankees broke their 1996 record, although the 1996 Yankees were pushed off the per game list by the 1997 Orioles, putting 3 teams from 1997 on the per game list. The 1994 Blue Jays moved up to 4th place on the per game list with good strikeout pitchers on a staff that was part of a mediocre team. But both the 1995 Mariners and 1994 Blue Jays played too few games as a result of the 1994 strike to be able to make the total year list.

On the total year list the absence of the 1995 Mariners put the 1967 Indians in second place for most strikeouts in one year in the American League. With the 1994 Blue Jays also missing, the Indians took 3 places in a row behind the 1996 Red Sox and 1997 Yankees who tied for 3rd. The 1996 Red Sox got a great strikeout performance from Roger Clemens in his last year with the Red Sox. Clemens then went on to help the 1997 Blue Jays take over 8th place on the list. The 1996 Yankees made the total year list even though they were pushed off the per game list. The 1997 Orioles also couldn't make the per game list (they are 11th) but moved onto the total year list. The 1997 Mariners became the first American League team to record more than 1200 strikeouts in one season. Seven teams in the National League have done so (Table 2-25), but the Mariners are the first team to do it in the American League. They won't be the last.

It will probably take a very long time to completely replace the Indians on the league strikeout lists. The big swing of the 1990s will produce more and more strikeouts, and, as shown in Table 1-9, 1997 took over the top spot from 1996 on the league list, with 1994 and 1995 not far behind. This confirms that the league overall is recording more and more strikeouts, and this is why 5 of the top 6 teams on the per game list below are from the 1990s. But the 1963-68 Indians played in a time with no designated hitter and with the rules bent in favor of pitchers. The Indians happened to have a staff full of strikeout pitchers in a favorable time, and thus they produced record after record in strikeouts. Such a fortuitous combination is not likely to occur soon again.

Table 2-24. AL Teams Ranked Years for Strikeouts

	Per Game Basis				Total Year Basis			
Team	Per Game	Total	Year	Rank	Team	Total	Per Game	Year
Mariners	7.45	1207	**1997**	1	Mariners	1207	7.45	**1997**
Mariners	7.37	1068	**1995**	2	Indians	1189	7.34	1967
Indians	7.34	1189	1967	3	Red Sox	1165	7.19	**1996**
Blue Jays	7.23	832	**1994**	4	Yankees	1165	7.19	**1997**
Red Sox	7.19	1165	**1996**	5	Indians	1162	7.09	1964
Yankees	7.19	1165	**1997**	6	Indians	1157	7.14	1968
Indians	7.14	1157	1968	7	Indians	1156	7.14	1965
Indians	7.14	1156	1965	8	Blue Jays	1150	7.10	**1997**
Blue Jays	7.10	1150	**1997**	9	Orioles	1139	7.03	**1996**
Indians	7.09	1162	1964	10	Yankees	1139	7.03	**1996**

Thus, future teams will have to work their way up the strikeout list slowly. It was unfortunate from the standpoint of league records that the 1995 Mariners and 1994 Blue Jays had per game strikeout peaks in years affected by a strike. On the other hand it is fortunate than Roger Clemens did not lose his strikeout touch after leaving the Red Sox, and that the Yankees maintained their high level of strikeouts after their unusual relief combination of 1996 was broken up in 1997. Power pitchers continue to move into the league, and they will continue to accumulate high levels of strikeouts as long as the big swing strategy continues. But although the 1966 Indians were displaced from both lists in 1997, the remaining four Indian teams from the 1960s have great records that will not be surpassed easily.

Table 2-25 shows the 10 highest years for strikeouts by a team in one year in the National League. Years from the 1990s are shown in boldface. Only eight teams are listed (Braves, Dodgers, Astros, Mets, Phillies, Expos, Marlins, and Padres) because the peak years for all the other teams in the league are below the 10th place teams listed here. The first part of the table has strikeouts ranked on a per game basis, while the second part has strikeouts ranked on a total year basis. The rankings for each basis are shown in the middle column of the table.

Actually, the fact that as many as 8 teams are listed demonstrates that record levels of strikeouts have spread throughout the National League. Even the expansion Marlins, who were born in 1993, make the total year list. They have followed the lead of the Astros, Mets, and Expos as expansion teams that have put prime resources into pitching. The degree to which the Astros, Expos, and Mets chose to focus on pitching is shown clearly in my book *The Best of Teams, the Worst of Teams*. The Astros, Expos, and Mets, in that order, trailed only the Dodgers in ERA from 1973 through 1994 (the last year covered by the book), and they do so as well from 1973 through 1997. These three are nearly in a second place tie behind the Dodgers, and all three are well ahead of all other National League teams for the period.

The Dodgers have been the best pitching team in the major leagues in the second half of the century, especially since they moved to Dodger Stadium in 1962. The Braves, however, were next to last in pitching in the league until the 1990s when they moved ahead of the Dodgers as the top pitching team and had by far the most successful period in franchise history. Thus, it is not a surprise that the Braves and Dodgers play the leading role in Table 2-25 as they continually broke team and league strikeout records while the league as a whole also broke all of its previous strikeout records (Table 1-9 and Table 2-10).

The Braves are perhaps the most remarkable story. From 1903 through 1972 only the Phillies had a worse ERA than the Braves. From 1973 through 1992 the Braves were 11th out of the 12 National League teams in ERA (only the Cubs were worse), and this included the rise from last in 1990 to first in 1991 and 1992 as the Braves became the team of the 1990s. But in the 1993-97 period the Braves took over the league lead in ERA (the Dodgers are still second), and led by John Smoltz and Greg Maddux at the top of a great pitching staff, the Braves broke the major league record of the 1969 Astros for strikeouts per game in 1994. The Braves came in a little below their 1994 record in 1995 (although still ahead of the old record of the 1969 Astros), and then the Braves broke their 1994 record by a big margin in 1996. It is easily the top performance in major league history as far as strikeouts per game and total year strikeouts are concerned. Although the National League set its all-time strikeout peak in 1997, the 1997 Braves declined from their 1994, 1995, and 1996 per game strikeout levels. However, the 1997 Braves hold 10th place on both strikeout lists.

Nine of the top 10 spots in both strikeouts per game and total year strikeouts are held by teams from the 1990s. Six of the top 10 places in per game strikeouts are from 1996 and 1997 alone, and 8 of the top 10 positions in total year strikeouts are from 1996 and 1997. This is partly because the strike in 1994 reduced the number of games played in 1994 and 1995. Thus, the 1994 and 1995 Braves, who are near the top of the per game list, do not appear on the total strikeout list. The only teams not from the 1994-97 period are the 1990 Mets (whose pitchers held 4 of the top 5 spots in strikeouts in 1990 with David Cone and Dwight Gooden at the top), and the 1969 Astros. The 1969 Astros are the only team not from the 1990s, and they are a special story in themselves.

Table 2-25. NL Teams Ranked Years for Strikeouts

Per Game Basis					Total Year Basis			
	Per						Per	
Team	Game	Total	Year	Rank	Team	Total	Game	Year
Braves	7.69	1245	**1996**	1	Braves	1245	7.69	**1996**
Dodgers	7.60	1232	**1997**	2	Dodgers	1232	7.60	**1997**
Braves	7.59	865	**1994**	3	Astros	1221	7.54	1969
Braves	7.55	1087	**1995**	4	Mets	1217	7.51	**1990**
Astros	7.54	1221	1969	5	Dodgers	1212	7.48	**1996**
Mets	7.51	1217	**1990**	6	Phillies	1209	7.46	**1997**
Dodgers	7.48	1212	**1996**	7	Expos	1206	7.44	**1996**
Phillies	7.46	1209	**1997**	8	Braves	1196	7.38	**1997**
Expos	7.44	1206	**1996**	9	Padres	1194	7.37	**1996**
Braves	7.38	1196	**1997**	10	Marlins	1188	7.33	**1997**

The 1969 Astros, who held the major league strikeout record for 25 years, were not a team that one would expect to set such a record. As mentioned, the franchise focused on pitching, and they are second to the Dodgers in ERA from 1973 through 1997. But 1969 marked the reversal of the 1963 rule changes that permitted pitchers to dominate the 1963-68 period. Also, the 1969 Astros did not have a great strikeout pitcher on their staff, or even a pitcher that many fans would remember today. Tom Griffin and Don Wilson held the first two spots in strikeouts per game that year, and both of these pitchers plus Larry Dierker had the best year for total strikeouts in their careers in 1969. Wilson had 235, Dierker 232, and Griffin 200. The result was an all-time strikeout record for a .500 team with a blue collar pitching staff. Sometimes it happens that way.

Table 2-26 shows the 10 highest years for walks by a team in one year in the American League. Years from the 1990s are shown in boldface. Only eight teams are listed (A's, Yankees, Orioles, Twins, Red Sox, Tigers, Indians, and Rangers) because the peak years for the rest of the teams in the league are below the 10th place teams listed here. The first part of the table has walks ranked on a per game basis, while the second part of the table has walks ranked on a total year basis. The rankings for each basis are shown in the middle column of the table.

As described in the text accompanying Table 1-10 and Table 2-11, there was a huge spike in walks in the American League in 1949 with the years just before and just after 1949 also far above the average for the preceding and following decades. This is why 7 of the top 10 years in walks per game in the league occurred in the period from 1948 through 1951, with 3 of the top 10 years occurring in 1949 alone. Since 6 of the 8 original teams had peaks at or near franchise records in this period (Table 2-11), no one team dominates the list. The A's appear twice because their 1915 team was so terrible it set the major league record for walks in 1915 when walks were generally low in the league. Thus, when the 1949 team had a "normal" peak for the franchise in the 1948-51 period, it marked the second appearance on the list. The worst teams in the league in the 1948-51 period were the Orioles/Browns and Twins/Senators. As a result, each of these teams also appear twice on the per game list because the general trend in the league towards high walks reinforced the tendency of these teams to be among the league leaders in issuing walks.

The 1949 Yankees, winners of the World Series in 1949, and the 1950 Red Sox, one of the best teams in the league in 1950, both appear on the list essentially as a result of playing in the league at a time when it had a surge in walks that was dramatically higher than at any other time in the century. The 1971 Indians make the list because they had great pitching in the 1948-51 period and thus did not set their franchise record in walks until they had a very bad team in 1971. The 1996 Tigers had a similar pattern in that they had good pitching in the 1948-51 period, and although they had some bad teams only a few years later, they had their worst pitching staff in franchise history in 1996 and thus set their record for issuing walks in that year.

Because of the shorter season before expansion in 1961, it would be expected that the total walk list would differ substantially from the per game list. But walks were so high in the 1948-51 period, and the 1915 A's were so bad, that there are relatively few changes between the two lists. The top 3 teams are the same on both lists, and the 1949 Twins move down only one spot from 4th to 5th as the longer season moves the 1996 Tigers up. One new team on the total year list is the 1939 Orioles/Browns. The Browns played 2 extra games in 1939 (which was still during a high walk period), and the 1939 Browns essentially displaced their 1948 team from the total year list.

The other new team on the total year list is the 1987 Rangers. They moved into 7th place thanks to the longer season and a pitching staff that issued lots of walks. The Rangers tied for last in their division, but still had 75 wins. Their leading pitcher was Charlie Hough who was a knuckleball pitcher and who led the league in innings pitched. Knuckleball pitchers get lots of strikeouts but also issue lots of walks and Hough was no exception. Bobby Witt on the other hand was a very hard thrower who also recorded lots of strikeouts, but he led the league in walks with 140 while only pitching 143 innings. The result was that the 1987 Rangers rank 10th in most strikeouts in one year (Table 2-24) and 7th in most walks in one year. Their SO/W ratio was only 1.45 for the season.

Table 2-26. AL Teams Ranked Years for Walks

| | Per Game Basis | | | | Total Year Basis | | | |
Team	Per Game	Total	Year	Rank	Team	Total	Per Game	Year
A's	5.37	827	1915	1	A's	827	5.37	1915
Yankees	5.24	812	1949	2	Yankees	812	5.24	1949
Orioles	5.20	801	1951	3	Orioles	801	5.20	1951
Twins	5.06	779	1949	4	Tigers	784	4.84	**1996**
A's	4.92	758	1949	5	Twins	779	5.06	1949
Red Sox	4.86	748	1950	6	Indians	770	4.75	1971
Tigers	4.84	784	**1996**	7	Rangers	760	4.69	1987
Twins	4.77	734	1948	8	A's	758	4.92	1949
Orioles	4.75	737	1948	9	Red Sox	748	4.86	1950
Indians	4.75	770	1971	10	Orioles	739	4.74	1939

Table 2-26 is unusual in that it only has one team from the 1990s on either list. But as noted in the text accompanying Table 2-11, walks in the American League were at their highest level in 40 years in 1996 as pitchers became steadily more inclined to issue walks in preference to watching the ball disappear over the fence. Combining this effect with a staff as bad as that of the 1996 Tigers could easily move new teams onto the high walk list. It is not a desirable list to make, but, as the World Champion 1949 Yankees demonstrated, issuing a high number of walks (even the second highest in league history) is not necessarily a bad thing per se. But a team has to have a lot going for it elsewhere if it leads the league in walks. The most likely future additions to the list will be teams like the 1996 Tigers who unfortunately had absolutely nothing else going for them.

Table 2-27 shows the 10 highest years for walks by a team in one year in the National League. Years from the 1990s are normally shown in boldface, but the most recent year in Table 2-27 is 1977. Only eight teams are listed (Phillies, Cards, Expos, Padres, Braves, Giants, Dodgers, and Astros) because the peak years for the rest of the teams in the league are below the 10th place teams listed here. The first part of the table has walks ranked on a per game basis, while the second part has walks ranked on a total year basis. The rankings for each basis are shown in the middle column of the table.

The National League pattern for walks during the century is quite different from that of the American League (Figure 1-7). As discussed in the text accompanying Tables 1-10 and 2-12, both leagues had a sharp rise in walks around 1950, but the National League rise was not as sharp or as high as that in the American League even though the National League set its all-time records for walks in this period. Further, although walks in the American League declined substantially after the peaks around 1950 and remained at reduced levels until the second half of the 1990s, National League walks climbed sharply after expansion in 1969 and into the 1970s, approaching their peaks of 1950 even though league walks had declined sharply in the 20 years after the peak near 1950. The 1970s were the first decade in which the National League topped the American League in walks since the 1903-09 period. National League walks in the 1990s are not as high as the previous peak periods for walks: 1911 (when offense jumped due to the cork-centered ball), the late 1940s and early 1950s, and the early 1970s.

The result is that the top ranked years in the National League are widely scattered. They include 1911, 1928, the 1940s, and the 1969 expansion and the following 1970s. There is a substantial difference between the per game list and the total year list because the early peak periods had seasons with fewer games than the peak period in the 1970s. The per game list has 2 teams from 1911, 3 from the 1940s, 4 from 1969 through 1977, and 1 straggler (the leading Phillies) from 1928. The total year list has one team from 1911 and 1928 (both farther down than on the per game list) and 8 teams from 1969 through 1977.

The 1928 Phillies just barely beat out the 1911 Cards for the per game league record for most walks with both teams at 4.44 to the second decimal point. The 1911 Braves also make the top 10 list, but while the 1911 Cards were an above average team with a pitching staff inclined to issue walks, the Braves were like the 1928 Phillies: Both were the worst team in the league, and the Braves had one of the worse years of any team in the century. The 1970 Expos were 3rd on a per game basis, but the Expos top the total walks list due to the longer season in 1970. The Expos were born in 1969 and in their first 2 years they claimed 2 of the top 3 places on the top 10 list for total walks. From 1969 through 1973 the Expos also set the still existing league record for average walks over a five year period. It was part of a bad start overall for the franchise.

The Padres, also born in 1969, nearly topped the Expos later in the 1970s. The 1974 Padres hold 4th on the per game list and 2nd on the total walks list, issuing just one walk less than the 1970 Expos. The 1977 Padres also are 10th on the total walks list. The 1911 Cards issued enough walks per game to appear on both the per game and total walks list. The 1911 Cards tie for 4th because they played 158 games even though the schedule only called for 154 games. In the early years of the century without lights and artificial surfaces, tie games suspended by rain or darkness or both often extended the season. The 1977 Braves appear on each list because the 1977 Braves had nearly as bad a pitching staff as their 1911 team. The 1911 Braves just miss the total year list.

Table 2-27. NL Teams Ranked Years for Walks

| | Per Game Basis | | | | | Total Year Basis | | |
Team	Per Game	Total	Year	Rank	Team	Total	Per Game	Year
Phillies	4.44	675	1928	1	Expos	716	4.42	1970
Cards	4.44	701	1911	2	Padres	715	4.41	1974
Expos	4.42	716	1970	3	Expos	702	4.33	1969
Padres	4.41	715	1974	4	Cards	701	4.44	1911
Expos	4.33	702	1969	5	Braves	701	4.33	1977
Braves	4.33	701	1977	6	Phillies	682	4.21	1974
Braves	4.31	672	1911	7	Expos	681	4.20	1973
Giants	4.29	660	1946	8	Astros	679	4.19	1975
Dodgers	4.27	671	1946	9	Phillies	675	4.44	1928
Dodgers	4.26	660	1944	10	Padres	673	4.15	1977

The 1928 Phillies are on the per game and total year list because they had a terrible team. The 1974 Phillies, also on the total year list, were a much better team, but they issued an above average number of walks in a high walk period. The only teams from the high walk period near 1950 are the 1944 and 1946 Dodgers, and the 1946 Giants. Because they are at the bottom of the per game list, they did not issue enough walks to make the total walk list. Five of the teams in positions 5 through 10 on the total walks list played between 1973 and 1977. Their prime common feature is that they played in a very high walk period in the league. This is primarily why they made the top 10 list. As noted previously in this book, the period in which a team plays can often have much to do with its appearance on a top 10 list.

Table 2-28 shows the 10 highest years for strikeout-to-walk (SO/W) ratio for American and National League teams. Years from the 1990s are shown in boldface. Only 7 teams (Twins, Red Sox, A's, White Sox, Indians, Tigers, and Blue Jays) from the American League and 5 (Dodgers, Expos, Braves, Mets, and Giants) from the National League are listed because the peak years for the rest of the teams in each league are below that of the 10th place teams listed here. The rankings are shown in the middle column of the table.

American League--As discussed in the text accompanying Tables 1-11 and 2-13, the best SO/W ratio periods in the American League came after rule changes favoring pitchers. The first was the 1903-04 period after foul balls were first counted as strikes in 1903. The second was the 1963-68 period after the strike zone was expanded in 1963. Thus, 3 of the top 10 years for SO/W ratio came in the 1903-04 period, and 6 of the top 10 places came in the 1963-68 period. The 1997 Blue Jays are the only team from the 1990s to make the list as strikeouts hit their peak in the American League in 1997.

The SO/W ratio has long been an indicator of good performance for pitchers. But it also is an indicator of team performance. A team with a good SO/W ratio has a good pitching staff, and most teams with good pitching will be winners in spite of the recent emphasis on offense. For example, 8 of the top 10 teams on the American League list had a winning percentage above .500, and 6 of the top 10 teams finished first or second in their division in the year they were on the list (as discussed below, in the National League the connection is much stronger as all of the top 10 teams finished first or second in their division, with 6 of the 10 finishing first).

The only exceptions in the American League are the 1997 Blue Jays (.469) and the 1968 Twins (.488). The Twins hold 3 of the top 10 spots on the American League list, hitting an all-time high in 1967 when they finished one game behind the Red Sox. The Twins also finished 2nd in 1966. The Red Sox had their best year in 1903 when they also won the pennant. None of these Twins or Red Sox teams are on the top 10 strikeout list (Table 2-24). Their best SO/W years came when they issued very few walks relative to their level of strikeouts (the Twins led the league in fewest walks issued in all three years they were on the list). The designated hitter in 1973 stopped this trend, and the DH is the basic reason only the 1997 Blue Jays have made the list since 1968.

National League--In the National League 5 of the top 10 spots came in years since 1968, including 3 of the top 4 places. The 1966 Dodgers set the all-time major league high at 3.04, the only time a team exceeded 3.00 for the season. The 1966 Dodgers (with Sandy Koufax, Don Drysdale, and Don Sutton) were a unique team in this respect as discussed in the text accompanying Table 2-13. Their strikeout marks have long been surpassed (Table 2-25), but their SO/W ratio record may stand for a long time.

As noted above, the National League demonstrates very well how closely a good team SO/W ratio is tied to team performance. All of the teams on the top 10 list finished either first or second in the year they appeared on the list. Equally impressive is the fact that 6 of the 10 finished in first place. The reason for this closer connection in the National League than in the American League is once again the designated hitter. Serial offense is more important in the National League because with one less big hitter in the lineup you can't wait around for a big inning (except in Coors Field). A team with a high SO/W ratio is putting fewer runners on base via walks, and that hinders the serial offense of their opponents. Hence a good SO/W ratio ties closely to a winning record.

Table 2-28. AL/NL Teams Ranked Years for SO/W Ratio

| American League | | | | National League | | |
Team	SO/W	Year	Rank	Team	SO/W	Year
Twins	2.75	1967	1	Dodgers	3.04	1966
Red Sox	2.63	1904	2	Expos	2.80	**1994**
Twins	2.59	1966	3	Braves	2.76	**1996**
A's	2.42	1904	4	Mets	2.74	**1990**
Twins	2.41	1968	5	Giants	2.74	1968
White Sox	2.38	1964	6	Dodgers	2.72	1963
Blue Jays	2.31	**1997**	7	Mets	2.72	1988
Indians	2.31	1965	8	Giants	2.71	1966
A's	2.31	1903	9	Braves	2.66	**1997**
Tigers	2.29	1968	10	Giants	2.60	1965

As in the American League, few National League teams on the SO/W ratio list appear on the top strikeout list (Table 2-25). Only the 1996 and 1997 Braves and 1990 Mets appear on both lists. But the reason is quite different in the two leagues. The National League is in the midst of such a strikeout frenzy that all prior strikeout records are being eliminated (the 1969 Astros are the only team before the 1990s to appear on the National League strikeout list). Although National League walks are higher now than in the 1963-68 period, walks are not especially high in the 1990s relative to the surge in offense. Thus, the 1990s already occupy 4 of the top 10 years for SO/W ratio (Table 1-11) in the league. We can expect other teams from the 1990s to be added to the 1994 Expos, 1996 and 1997 Braves, and 1990 Mets on the SO/W list. With the designated hitter, such expectations are much lower in the American League.

Part III
Team Summaries

A's Team Summary

Table 3-1 shows a summary of the key measures for the A's. Years from the 1990s are shown in boldface. Peak values and the years in which they occurred are shown on a per game and total year basis in the first two sets of columns in the table. The per game averages for each of the key measures from 1993 through 1997 are shown in the last column. The leaders for each measure from 1993 through 1997 are shown in Table 3-29.

Runs--The A's set their peak for runs per game in 1932 at 6.37 and they also set their total year record in 1932 with 981 runs. They rank 6th in the American League on the per game list and 7th on the total year list for runs (Table 2-16). The A's finished second in 1932, but they still had the great players who won three straight pennants from 1929 through 1931. They had poor teams in the 1993-97 period and their average of 4.87 runs per game was 10th in the league.

Home Runs--In 1996 the A's broke the existing American League records for home runs per game and total home runs when they averaged 1.50 home runs per game while hitting 243 home runs. But the Orioles and Mariners also broke both records in 1996, and the A's finished third in the league that year. The 1996 A's rank 4th all-time in the majors in home runs (Table 2-18). With their outstanding average of 1.50 in 1996, the A's averaged 1.17 home runs per game during the 1993-97 period, ranking 5th in the league.

Doubles--The A's best year for doubles was 1928 when they averaged 2.11 per game for a total of 323. They rank 5th on the per game list and 7th on the total year list (Table 2-20). They were 13th in the league with an average of 1.64 doubles per game in the 1993-97 period.

Batting Average--The A's set their batting average record at .307 in 1925, ranking 6th on the American League top 10 list (Table 2-22). As is the case for most of the original 16 teams, the A's have not come close to their record since the end of the 1920s. Their .265 average in 1996 was their best since they hit .268 in 1941, but they still were 13th in the league in the 1993-97 period.

ERA--The team record of 6.08 for the A's in 1936 is the 3rd highest ever in the American League (Table 2-23). Their ERA of 5.48 in 1997 is their highest since 1955, and their 5.06 average from 1993 through 1997 is the 3rd highest in the league for that period. The A's have won 14 pennants since 1903 (2nd to the Yankees), and they always had one of the best pitching staffs in the league when they won. But they have the highest ERA of the 8 original teams since 1903.

Strikeouts--The A's are not close to the top ten list in either strikeouts per game or for the total year with their 1987 team records (Table 2-24). Their average of 5.85 per game for the 1993-97 period ranked 11th in the league.

Walks--The A's set the all-time major league record in 1915 for highest walks per game and for one year (Table 2-26). This is the oldest league record on the books for the eight key measures. The A's mark of 4.09 walks per game in the 1993-97 period was also the highest (worst) in the league for the period.

Strikeout-to-Walk Ratio--The A's set their team record in 1904 when league walks were very low and the A's had a great pitching staff. But they have the worst ratio in the league since 1903 and ranked 13th in the 1993-97 period.

Table 3-1. Key Measures Summary for the A's

	Per Game Peaks		Total Year Peaks		1993-97
	Per Game	Year	Total	Year	Per Game
Runs	6.37	1932	981	1932	4.87
Home Runs	1.50	**1996**	243	**1996**	1.17
Doubles	2.11	1928	323	1928	1.64
Bat Avg.	.307	1925	.307	1925	.260
ERA	6.08	1936	6.08	1936	5.06
Strikeouts	6.43	1987	1042	1987	5.85
Walks	5.37	1915	827	1915	4.09
SO/W Ratio	2.42	1904	2.42	1904	1.43

The A's have a long history of being very good when they are good, and being absolutely terrible when they are bad. They rank second in the league to the Yankees in pennants won, and they are the only team other than the Yankees to win three World Series titles in a row. They also set a league record by winning five division titles in a row from 1971 through 1975. But they fielded the league's worst teams in history in 1915-19, and they have finished last twice as many times as any other team in the league.

The A's were 13th in winning percentage in the 1993-97 period, but they had a great home run outburst in 1996. Their best home run hitter, Mark McGwire, missed 32 games due to injuries but still hit 52 home runs in 423 at bats. This was a home run percentage of 12.3 percent, a mark that broke Babe Ruth's record of 11.8 percent in 1920. Terry Steinbach had a total of 35 home runs, and 34 of these were as a catcher which was the most for that position in history. As usual, even when they're bad, the A's can be very good.

Table 3-2 shows a summary of the key measures for the Angels. Years from the 1990s are shown in boldface. Peak values and the years in which they occurred are shown on a per game and total year basis in the first two sets of columns in the table. The per game averages for each of the key measures from 1993 through 1997 are shown in the last column. The leaders for each measure from 1993 through 1997 are shown in Table 3-29.

Runs--The Angels set their team record for runs per game in 1995 with an average of 5.52. But because of the shorter season in 1995 due to the strike, their peak in total runs (866) remains in 1979, the year they won their first division title. Neither mark is close to the top 15 list in the league (Table 2-16). In spite of their franchise record in 1995, the Angels averaged only 4.86 runs per game for the 1993-97 period which placed them 11th in the league. The Angels have rarely been a high scoring team, and they rank last in the league in runs per game from 1973 through 1997 with an average of 4.41.

Home Runs--The Angels also set their home runs per game record in 1995, with 1996 becoming their total year record due to the shortened 1995 season. The Angels had previously set both records in their first year of 1961, when they played in tiny Wrigley Field in Los Angeles and loaded up with home run hitters accordingly. They left Wrigley Field for Dodger Stadium after that first year, and they were unable to top their 1961 record in the next 34 seasons. But the offensive outburst of the 1993-97 period did the trick. However, the Angels did not join the outburst until 1995 and their 1.04 home runs per game average during the 1993-97 period ranks only 9th in the league.

Doubles--The Angels set their total year peak in 1997, but they could not beat out the per game peak they set in 1995. However, the Angels have never hit many doubles for some reason. Their 1.64 average for the 1993-97 period ranks 12th in the league, and their per game and total year peaks rank last in the league and are far behind those of the 13th place team (Table 2-5).

Batting Average--The 1979 Angels set the franchise record at .282 on their way to the division title. Their average of .277 in 1995 was the best the Angels have recorded since their 1979 peak, but their overall average of .270 for the 1993-97 period ranked only 8th in the league. Consistent with their bottom ranking in runs, the Angels rank 13th in the league in batting average from 1973 through 1997.

ERA--Until the offensive outburst of the 1990s, the Angels typically featured teams with good pitching. As a result, they tie for 4th in the league in lowest ERA from 1973 through 1997. But they had their highest ERA ever in 1994 when they finished last in their division. The Angels were almost as bad in 1996, and their average of 4.82 for the 1993-97 period was the 4th highest in the league. As is often the case, when the Angels tried to improve their offensive performance in 1995 and after, their pitching suffered accordingly.

Strikeouts--The Angels set both their per game and total year records in 1996, but are not close to being on the top ten list (Table 2-24). Their average of 6.07 for the 1993-97 period ranked 8th in the league.

Walks--As is the case for many expansion teams, the Angels set their per game and total year peaks for walks in their first year of existence (1961). Their per game average of 3.68 for the 1993-97 period ranked 7th in the league, one place better than their ranking for strikeouts.

Strikeout-to-Walk Ratio--The Angels had their best ratio in 1986 when they just missed going to the World Series when they couldn't get one more out in the 9th inning. Their 1.65 ratio in the 1993-97 period was 10th in the league.

Table 3-2. Key Measures Summary for the Angels

	Per Game Peaks		Total Year Peaks		1993-97
	Per Game	Year	Total	Year	Per Game
Runs	5.52	**1995**	866	1979	4.86
Home Runs	1.28	**1995**	192	**1996**	1.04
Doubles	1.74	**1995**	279	**1997**	1.64
Bat Avg.	.282	1979	.282	1979	.270
ERA	5.42	**1994**	5.42	**1994**	4.82
Strikeouts	6.53	**1996**	1052	**1996**	6.07
Walks	4.40	1961	713	1961	3.68
SO/W Ratio	2.00	1986	2.00	1986	1.65

The Angels were founded in 1961 but they have yet to make it to the World Series in 37 seasons of trying. Their best sustained period was from 1982 through 1986, when they won two division titles. But in 1982, when the pennant playoffs were five games, they won the first two games at home and then lost three straight in Milwaukee. In 1986, when the pennant playoffs were seven games, they led the Red Sox three games to one at home and were ahead 5-4 in the top of the ninth with two out and still couldn't win the clincher. They lost the final two games at Boston and the pennant as well.

The Angels usually are never too good or too bad. They have never finished below .400, but their best year is only .574 in 1982. They had a great offensive team in 1995 but blew a big lead and finished behind the Mariners in a playoff. They flopped in 1996 and were outscored by 1.12 runs per game, the worst such deficit in their existence. In 1997 they were overachievers most of the season, but declined at the end and missed the playoffs for the 11th straight year.

Table 3-3 shows a summary of the key measures for the Blue Jays. Years from the 1990s are shown in boldface. Peak values and the years in which they occurred are shown on a per game and total year basis in the first two sets of columns in the table. The per game averages for each of the key measures from 1993 through 1997 are shown in the last column. The leaders for each measure from 1993 through 1997 are shown in Table 3-29.

Runs--The Blue Jays set their team record for runs in 1993 with a mark of 5.23 runs per game. They also set their total year record in 1993 with 847 runs. Both values rank last in the American League for per game and total year peaks (Table 2-1). The Blue Jays won the World Series for the second straight year in 1993, and in that year they were second in the league in runs. But they won with a combination of hitting and pitching and they have never been near the top of the league in peak values for runs. Accordingly, their average of 4.67 runs per game from 1993 through 1997 ranks 13th in the American League for the period, well behind the leading 5.60 per game average of the Indians (Table 3-29).

Home Runs--In the high offense year of 1987 the Blue Jays were second only to the Tigers in the major leagues in hitting home runs. The American League set an all-time home run record that year (subsequently broken in 1996), and the Blue Jays also set their all-time records for home runs per game (1.33) and total year (215). George Bell led the way with 47 home runs, second in the league and third in the majors for the year. But neither Bell nor the Blue Jays ever came close to those totals again. The Blue Jays ranked 11th in the league in home runs from 1993 through 1997 with an average of 0.99.

Doubles--The Blue Jays set their record for doubles per game (1.96) and total year (317) in 1993, the same year they set their records for runs and won their second straight World Series title. But their ranking on the doubles list (Table 2-5) is better than their last place ranking on the runs list (Table 2-1). They ranked sixth in the league with an average of 1.85 doubles per game from 1993 through 1997.

Batting Average--The championship year of 1993 was also the peak year for batting average for the Blue Jays. But just as in runs, the Blue Jays rank last in the league in peak batting average (Table 2-7). The Blue Jays fell 20 percentage points from their peak by 1996, and they were 36 points down by 1997. They were 12th in the league for batting average in the 1993-97 period.

ERA--The Blue Jays also rank near the bottom of the league list for peak ERA (Table 2-8), but that is the position teams prefer to find themselves in on this list. The Blue Jays are tied with the Yankees for 12th place on the list, and only the Royals have a lower peak ERA than the Blue Jays. The Blue Jays set their peak in 1995 and the Royals in 1996, both teams falling on hard times just as the league went on a scoring binge. But the Blue Jays still had the 6th lowest ERA in the league from 1993 through 1997.

Strikeouts--The Blue Jays hit their peak for per game strikeouts in 1994 when they had the 4th best year in league history with 7.23 strikeouts per game (Table 2-24). With the addition of Roger Clemens they set their peak in total strikeouts in 1997. This put them 2nd in the league in the 1993-97 period.

Walks--The Blue Jays set their peaks for walks in 1995 when they had a very bad year overall, but once again they rank relatively low on a list (Table 2-11) where it is preferable to have a low ranking.

Strikeout-to-Walk Ratio--With Roger Clemens leading the way, the Blue Jays set their franchise record in 1997 with a 2.31 mark that makes the top 10 list in the league (Table 2-28). Clemens had a ratio of 4.27.

Table 3-3. Key Measures Summary for the Blue Jays

	Per Game Peaks		Total Year Peaks		1993-97
	Per Game	Year	Total	Year	Per Game
Runs	5.23	**1993**	847	**1993**	4.67
Home Runs	1.33	1987	215	1987	0.99
Doubles	1.96	**1993**	317	**1993**	1.85
Bat Avg.	.279	**1993**	.279	**1993**	.262
ERA	4.88	**1995**	4.88	**1995**	4.46
Strikeouts	7.23	**1994**	1150	**1997**	6.65
Walks	4.54	**1995**	654	**1995**	3.88
SO/W Ratio	2.31	**1997**	2.31	**1997**	1.71

The Blue Jays were born in 1977 and had the worst first five years (based on winning percentage) of all American League expansion teams. Only the Mets had a poorer five year start among the 12 major league expansion teams. But the Blue Jays had 11 straight winning seasons from 1983 through 1993, capping off the streak with back-to-back World Series wins in 1992 and 1993 (the first team to do it since the 1977-78 Yankees). Free agency essentially broke up the 1993 team and the Blue Jays have not had even a winning season since.

The Blue Jays ranked 2nd in strikeouts and 6th in ERA, doubles, and SO/W ratio for the 1993-97 period. They were near the bottom of the league in the other key measures. The addition of Roger Clemens in 1997 assured they would continue to rank high in strikeouts, but as usual the cost of improving their pitching was the 2nd lowest batting average in franchise history. The Blue Jays are a long way from balance in rebuilding the team that began the 1993-97 period so well with the second of their back-to-back championships.

Table 3-4 shows a summary of the key measures for the Brewers. Years from the 1990s are shown in boldface. Peak values and the years in which they occurred are shown on a per game and total year basis in the first two sets of columns in the table. The per game averages for each of the key measures from 1993 through 1997 are shown in the last column. The leaders for each measure from 1993 through 1997 are shown in Table 3-29.

Runs--The Brewers hit their runs peak in 1996 with 5.52 runs per game. They also set their total year record in 1996 with 894 runs. The Brewers' prior record for runs per game was set in 1982 when they won their only pennant as "Harvey's Wallbangers." This nickname was in honor of their manager Harvey Kuenn and the fact that the Brewers were a great offensive team in 1982. Up to 1995 the Brewers led all league expansion teams in peak runs. But after 1996 they led only the Royals and Blue Jays (Table 2-1) in spite of the fact that the Brewers broke their own record that year. The league surge in runs has passed the Wallbangers by. The Brewers ranked 12th in runs for the 1993-97 period.

Home Runs--The Wallbangers of 1982 also set franchise peaks for home runs per game (1.33) and total home runs (216). Before 1996, the 1982 Brewers were in the top 5 teams in the league with their 216 home runs. But 5 teams passed them in 1996 alone, and the 1982 Brewers are no longer on the top 10 list for home runs (Table 2-18). Further, the Brewers only ranked 12th in the league in home runs per game from 1993 through 1997 with an average of 0.89. Only 3 teams other than the Brewers averaged below 1.00 home runs per game.

Doubles--The Brewers set their peak for doubles per game in the short season of 1994, so their record for total doubles did not come until 1996. Although their peak for doubles per game is 9th in the league, the Brewer's peak mark for total doubles ranks 13th. This means the only team with a lower total than the Brewers are the Angels who rank 27th among the 28 teams in the majors (Table 2-5). The Brewers ranked 8th in the league with an average of 1.80 doubles per game from 1993 through 1997.

Batting Average--The Brewers set their batting average peak in 1979 when they were assembling the team that would win the 1982 pennant. It is the lowest peak in the league except for that of the Blue Jays (Table 2-7). The Brewers ranked 10th in the league for batting average from 1993 through 1997.

ERA--The Brewers were born in 1969 and after one disastrous year in Seattle they moved to Milwaukee. Their ERA in that first year was 4.35, but they were generally a good pitching team and did not exceed their 1969 ERA until 1985 when the league was starting an offensive uptick. The Brewers hit a new record peak of 4.62 in the high scoring year of 1987, recovered, then tied their record in 1994, broke it at 4.82 in 1995, and soared to a peak of 5.14 in 1996. But in spite of these sharp increases in franchise ERA, they still were 7th in ERA from 1993 through 1997 because ERAs climbed throughout the league.

Strikeouts--In spite of their generally good pitching during their franchise history, the Brewers are near the bottom of the league in peaks for per game and total year strikeouts (Table 2-9). This is consistent with their dead last ranking in the major leagues in strikeouts from 1993 through 1997.

Walks--The Brewers have the best (lowest) peaks in walks in the league except for the Royals (Table 2-11) who lead the league in fewest walks from 1973 through 1997. The Brewers were 7th in the 1993-97 period.

Strikeout-to-Walk Ratio--Because of their poor strikeout record, the Brewers rank 13th in the league for best SO/W ratio (Table 2-13). They also rank 12th for the 1993-97 period, just ahead of the A's and Tigers.

Table 3-4. Key Measures Summary for the Brewers

	Per Game Peaks		Total Year Peaks		1993-97
	Per Game	Year	Total	Year	Per Game
Runs	5.52	**1996**	894	**1996**	4.83
Home Runs	1.33	1982	216	1982	0.89
Doubles	2.07	**1994**	304	**1996**	1.80
Bat Avg.	.280	1979	.280	1979	.265
ERA	5.14	**1996**	5.14	**1996**	4.65
Strikeouts	6.41	1987	1039	1987	5.28
Walks	4.19	**1995**	653	1969	3.67
SO/W Ratio	1.96	1987	1.96	1987	1.44

The Brewers have not won even a division title since winning the pennant in 1982, but they did have 11 seasons at .500 or better in the 15 years from 1978 through 1992. They started poorly in the 1993-97 period (1993 was their worse year since 1984), then climbed to 80-82 in 1996. But they finally won only 78 games in 1997 after being in the division title race for a few months. They were below the league average in the 1993-97 period in every key measure.

Probably the most "notable" thing about the Brewers in the 1993-97 period was their overall SO/W ratio of 1.44. This is extremely low (the league average was 1.66), and only the A's and the Tigers, who set the all-time league high for ERA in 1996, were worse. Further, in a period when the league average for strikeouts per game was 6.06, the Brewers averaged only 5.28. Even the Tigers were higher at 5.40, and the next lowest mark was 5.58 for the Twins. No one else was below 5.85. There's more to pitching than strikeouts, but the record of the Brewers gives little sign of young strong arms.

Table 3-5 shows a summary of the key measures for the Indians. Years from the 1990s are shown in boldface. Peak values and the years in which they occurred are shown on a per game and total year basis in the first two sets of columns in the table. The per game averages for each of the key measures from 1993 through 1997 are shown in the last column. The leaders for each measure from 1993 through 1997 are shown in Table 3-29.

Runs--The Indians hit their franchise peak of 6.01 runs per game in the short season of 1994. Their peak for total runs (952) came in 1996. Both marks are sixth on the league list of peak years (Table 2-1), but only the total of 952 runs makes the list of the best years ever in the league where it claims 13th place (Table 2-16). The Indians had their best run scoring teams ever in the 1990s, and they led the league in runs per game for the 1993-97 period (Table 3-29).

Home Runs--The prime reason the Indians led the league in runs in the 1993-97 period was that they also set their franchise records in home runs. Their per game peak came in 1994 at 1.48 home runs per game which was a new major league record at the time. But the short season kept the Indians from setting a total year record, and after the 1996 season 3 teams had surpassed the per game record the Indians set in 1994 (Table 2-18). The Indians set their total year record (220) in 1997, and this total ranks 10th on the list of the top 10 years for total home runs. The Indians were 2nd to the Mariners for home runs per game from 1993 through 1997 with an average of 1.30.

Doubles--The 1930 Indians hold the all-time American League record for doubles per game, but the 1997 Red Sox passed the 1930 Indians in total doubles (Table 2-20). The Indians also hit doubles at a high level in the 1990s and they ranked 3rd in the league for the 1993-97 period. But the 335 doubles the Indians hit in 1996 rank only 5th on their own franchise list and 9th on the top 10 list for the league (Table 2-20). The Indians of the 1930s set marks that are hard for any franchise to top, let alone future editions of their own franchise.

Batting Average--The Indians have the oldest record for peak batting average in the major leagues. They hit .308 in 1921 and have not been able to top it since (Table 2-7). But few other teams have been able to top it either, and the 1921 Indians rank 3rd all-time in batting average in the league (Table 2-22). The Indians led the majors in batting average in the 1993-97 period, and their .293 average in 1996 was their best since 1936.

ERA--With good pitching teams in the years of high offense in the 1930s and 1990s, the Indians set their peak ERA in the high offense year of 1987 during the time the Indians had truly terrible pitching teams. The Indians are the only American League team not to set their ERA peak in either the 1930s or 1990s (Table 2-8). To emphasize how well balanced the Indians were in the 1993-97 period, the Indians had the 3rd best ERA in the period to go with their league leads in batting average and runs scored.

Strikeouts--The 1967 Indians held the league record for strikeouts per game and total year until the 1995 and 1997 Mariners in sequence broke the per game record and the total year record (Table 2-9). But even with their good pitching now, the Indians were only 7th in strikeouts in the 1993-97 period.

Walks--With historically good pitching until the 1960s, the Indians did not hit their peak in walks until 1971 when they had very poor pitching. The 1971 Indians rank 6th in the league for most walks given up in one year (Table 2-26).

Strikeout-to-Walk Ratio--Thanks to their high strikeout rates in the 1960s, the Indians set their peak SO/W ratio in 1965. It ranks 7th all-time in the league (Table 2-28). The Indians also had the league's best ratio in the 1993-97 period.

Table 3-5. Key Measures Summary for the Indians

| | Per Game Peaks | | Total Year Peaks | | 1993-97 |
	Per Game	Year	Total	Year	Per Game
Runs	6.01	**1994**	952	**1996**	5.60
Home Runs	1.48	**1994**	220	**1997**	1.30
Doubles	2.32	1930	358	1930	1.93
Bat Avg.	.308	1921	.308	1921	.287
ERA	5.28	1987	5.28	1987	4.37
Strikeouts	7.34	1967	1189	1967	6.13
Walks	4.75	1971	770	1971	3.38
SO/W Ratio	2.31	1965	2.31	1965	1.81

From 1903 through 1959 the Indians were second in the league to the Yankees in winning percentage, and the 1954 Indians set the league's all-time record at .721 (equivalent to 117 wins in 162 games). But after being swept in the 1954 World Series the Indians declined steadily, and from 1973 through 1993 they had the worst winning percentage in the majors except for the Mariners. But after a seventh straight losing season in 1993, the Indians emerged as one of the best teams in the league in 1994, and they went to the World Series for the first time in 41 years in 1995. They also made the playoffs in 1996 and 1997.

The Indians confirmed their return to the elite level by finishing in the top 3 teams in all of the key positive measures except strikeouts from 1993 through 1997, even though the 1993 team had a losing record. They broke their franchise records for total runs and home runs, but to prove this was not just due to the longer season, they also broke the franchise record for runs per game (set in 1921) as well as the per game record for home runs (set in 1987).

   Table 3-6 shows a summary of the key measures for the Mariners. Years from the 1990s are shown in boldface. Peak values and the years in which they occurred are shown on a per game and total year basis in the first two sets of columns in the table. The per game averages for each of the key measures from 1993 through 1997 are shown in the last column. The leaders for each measure from 1993 through 1997 are shown in Table 3-29.

   Runs--The Mariners set franchise records for runs per game (6.17) and total runs (993) in 1996. The 1996 Mariners are the only team in the league on the top 15 list for runs per game (Table 2-16) that hit their peak after 1950. They also scored the most runs in one year since 1950, and they rank 6th on the top 15 list. But the Mariners are 3rd in the league in runs for the 1993-97 period because they did not establish themselves as a great run scoring team until 1995.

   Home Runs--The 1996 Mariners also set franchise records for home runs per game (1.52) and total home runs (245), but they broke both records in 1997 and now stand at the top of the all-time home run list (Table 2-18). The 1997 Mariners broke the record set the year before by the 1996 Orioles. The Mariners did not begin to hit home runs at a high rate until 1994, but they still rank first in the majors in the 1993-97 period. Their average of 1.35 home runs per game over the five year period is the highest in major league history, breaking the record of the 1960-64 Yankees that had stood until the 1993-97 period (the Indians and Orioles also broke the old record of the Yankees in the period).

   Doubles--The 1996 Mariners rank 9th on the all-time league list for per game doubles and they rank 6th on the list for total doubles in one year (Table 2-20). It appeared the Mariners had a chance to set an all-time doubles record in 1996, but injuries removed that possibility and the 1997 Red Sox made it academic by setting a new all-time record themselves. The Mariners are only 5th in the league in doubles in the 1993-97 period because of their slow start in the period.

   Batting Average--The Mariners set their batting average record in their big offensive year of 1996. This is the highest batting average for any expansion team except the Rockies, but the Mariners were only 6th in the league for batting average for the full 1993-97 period.

   ERA--The ERA marks for the Mariners explain why their high rankings for offense translated only into a 5th place ranking for winning percentage in the 1993-97 period. The Mariners won their first division title in 1995, reaching the playoffs for the first time that year. But they did not make the playoffs in 1996 even though they play in the weak Western Division. They got back into the playoffs in 1997, but pitching still continues to be their weakness. They set their all-time team record for peak ERA in 1996, breaking the record they had set in 1994. Their pitching improved in 1997, but they still had the 6th highest ERA in the league for the 1993-97 period. As for most teams, the key to the future of the Mariners is improving their pitching.

Strikeouts--Behind Randy Johnson, the Mariners set the league record for strikeouts per game in 1995 (Table 2-24). After he was injured for most of 1996, Johnson returned in 1997 to lead the Mariners to all-time records for per game and total year strikeouts (the Mariners are the first AL team to pass 1200).

Walks--Lots of strikeouts often means lots of walks, and the Mariners had the 2nd highest average in the league for walks per game in the 1993-97 period. This helps explain their high ERA mark for the period.

Strikeout-to-Walk Ratio--The Mariners cut back on their walks in 1997 while they were setting their strikeout records, and thus gave them their best SO/W ratio in their history. This placed them 5th in the 1993-97 period.

Table 3-6. Key Measures Summary for the Mariners

	Per Game Peaks		Total Year Peaks		1993-97
	Per Game	Year	Total	Year	Per Game
Runs	6.17	**1996**	993	**1996**	5.40
Home Runs	1.63	**1997**	264	**1997**	1.35
Doubles	2.13	**1996**	343	**1996**	1.90
Bat Avg.	.287	**1996**	.287	**1996**	.274
ERA	5.21	**1996**	5.21	**1996**	4.74
Strikeouts	7.45	**1997**	1207	**1997**	6.90
Walks	4.34	**1994**	661	**1992**	3.92
SO/W Ratio	2.02	**1997**	2.02	**1997**	1.76

The Mariners, born in 1977, had by far their best teams in franchise history during the 1993-97 period. The Mariners were easily the worst team in baseball from their birth in 1977 through most of the 1980s. They began to assemble a competitive team in 1989, and they had their first winning season in 1991. They were winners again in 1993, had a relapse in 1994, and then made a strong run late in the season to win their first division title in 1995. They fell off in 1996 when Randy Johnson was injured, but they came back in 1997 to win the division title and advance to the playoffs again.

The Mariners have a legitimate candidate for the Hall of Fame in Ken Griffey, Jr., and they have one of the most powerful offensive teams in the major leagues. If they can assemble a pitching staff capable of supporting Randy Johnson without breaking up their offense, they could be a contending team for years to come. But this is a challenge that faces several teams in the American League, and with expansion in 1998 it will be a hard challenge to meet.

Table 3-7 shows a summary of the key measures for the Orioles (the Browns until 1954). Years from the 1990s are shown in boldface. Peak values and the years in which they occurred are shown on a per game and total year basis in the first two sets of columns in the table. The per game averages for each of the key measures from 1993 through 1997 are shown in the last column. The leaders for each measure from 1993 through 1997 are shown in Table 3-29.

Runs--The Orioles set a franchise peak of 5.82 runs per game in 1996, the same year they set their peak for total runs (949). The Orioles and the Twins are the only original teams never to exceed 6.00 runs per game (Table 2-1). Thanks to the longer season, the 1996 Orioles just make the list of the 15 highest years for runs in one season (Table 2-16). The Orioles were 6th in the league in scoring runs from 1993 through 1997.

Home Runs--Earl Weaver said the strategy for winning was good pitching and three-run homers, and the Orioles hit lots of home runs in 1996. They set the all-time major league record for home runs per game and in a season when they hit 257 home runs for an average of 1.58 per game. They soared well past both prior records as did the Mariners and A's who finished behind them in 1996 and on the all-time list (Table 2-18). But the 1997 Mariners topped the records of the 1996 Orioles, and the Orioles only ranked 3rd in the league in home runs for the 1993-97 period behind the Mariners and Indians. The 1993-97 period was obviously a time for three-run homers for nearly everybody.

Doubles--The St. Louis Browns, the forerunners of the Orioles, set the franchise peak for doubles in 1937 just as the league's peak years for doubles were coming to an end (Table 1-6). The 1937 peaks rank in the middle of the league list for peaks in doubles (Table 2-5), but don't make the list of the top ten years (Table 2-20). The Orioles ranked 10th in doubles for the 1993-97 period.

Batting Average--With George Sisler hitting .420, the 1922 Browns, who just missed winning the pennant, set the franchise record at .313 in 1922. It still is the second best year in league history behind the 1921 Tigers (Table 2-22). The Browns hit over .300 in three different years, but the Orioles, playing in a different era, had their best year ever at .274 in 1996. The Orioles ranked only 9th in the league in batting average from 1993 through 1997.

ERA--The Browns had some good hitting teams but never had good pitching. The Orioles made their reputation as one of the best teams in the league over a long period with great pitching. Thus, the Browns set the franchise record for the highest ERA. They peaked at 6.24 in 1936, and this was the all-time league high until the Tigers topped it in 1996 (Table 2-23). The Browns, however, still hold 4 of the top 10 positions on the high ERA list and clearly can make a case that their pitching staffs from 1935 through 1939 were the worst in major league history. The Orioles record is exactly the opposite. They had the 4th lowest ERA in the league in the 1993-97 period, and were only 0.05 behind the leader.

Strikeouts--In spite of their good ERA record during their part of franchise history, the Orioles did not have great strikeout pitchers. But in 1997 they had their best staff for strikeouts in history, and they moved onto the top 10 list (Table 2-24). They were 5th in strikeouts in the 1993-97 period.

Walks--The Browns set the franchise peaks in 1951. They were bad enough to rank 3rd on the all-time league list for high walks (Table 2-26). In contrast, the Orioles had the 5th best mark for fewest walks in the 1993-97 period.

Strikeout-to-Walk Ratio--The Browns set the franchise record in 1903 when the league had a very low level of walks. The text accompanying Table 2-13 explains why. The Orioles were 3rd best in the league in the 1993-97 period.

Table 3-7. Key Measures Summary for the Orioles

| | Per Game Peaks | | Total Year Peaks | | 1993-97 |
	Per Game	Year	Total	Year	Per Game
Runs	5.82	**1996**	949	**1996**	5.17
Home Runs	1.58	**1996**	257	**1996**	1.24
Doubles	2.10	1937	327	1937	1.70
Bat Avg.	.313	1922	.313	1922	.268
ERA	6.24	1936	6.24	1936	4.40
Strikeouts	7.03	**1997**	1139	**1997**	6.28
Walks	5.20	1951	801	1951	3.50
SO/W Ratio	2.16	1903	2.16	1903	1.80

The Browns won only one pennant from 1903 through 1953, and that came in 1944 when "replacement" teams played during WWII. The Orioles won 6 pennants from 1966 through 1983, and won the World Series 3 times during that period. But the Orioles had losing seasons in 5 of the 6 years from 1986 through 1991 before becoming a consistent winner again in 1992. They made the playoffs in 1996 and 1997 and were one of the league's best teams in the 1993-97 period.

The most notable record for the Orioles from 1993 through 1997 was their outburst of runs and home runs in 1996. But, as noted above, the Orioles ranked only 6th in the league in runs and 3rd in home runs. The Orioles were successful in the 1993-97 period because of their balance. They upgraded their pitching in 1997 at the expense of their great 1996 offense and had a better team in 1997. They also had, as they have had for many years, very good defense. It is this balance between pitching, hitting, and defense that has kept the Orioles successful since the 1960s during their part of franchise history.

Table 3-8 shows a summary of the key measures for the Rangers (who were the second version of the Washington Senators from 1961 through 1971 before moving to Texas for the 1972 season). Years from the 1990s are shown in boldface. Peak values and the years in which they occurred are shown on a per game and total year basis in the first two sets of columns in the table. The per game averages for each of the key measures from 1993 through 1997 are shown in the last column. The leaders for each measure from 1993 through 1997 are shown in Table 3-29.

Runs--The Rangers set a franchise peak of 5.69 runs per game in 1996, the same year they set their peak for total runs (928). The Rangers had their best offensive team in franchise history in 1996, but they were not able to make the league's top 15 list for either per game or total runs (although they did so for home runs as noted below). The Rangers were 5th in the league in scoring runs from 1993 through 1997.

Home Runs--The Rangers set franchise records for home runs per game (1.36) and total home runs (221) in 1996. Their total of 221 home runs put the Rangers in a tie with the 1964 Twins for 9th place on the all-time American League list for total home runs (Table 2-18). But the American League hit home runs at such a high rate from 1993 through 1997 that the Rangers only ranked 6th in the league in home runs during the period, averaging 1.13 home runs per game compared to the league average of 1.08.

Doubles--The Rangers set the franchise record for doubles per game (1.98) and total doubles (323) in 1996. Neither of these marks could make the league's top ten list for doubles (Table 2-20). The Rangers, in fact, are one of only four American League teams who have yet to average at least 2.00 doubles per game (Table 2-5) in one season. The Rangers ranked 7th in doubles for the 1993-97 period.

Batting Average--Consistent with their franchise highs in runs, home runs, and doubles in 1996, the Rangers also set their franchise record for batting average in 1996 with a mark of .284. Only three American League teams have a lower peak batting average (Table 2-7). The Rangers ranked 7th in the league in batting average for the 1993-97 period, averaging three percentage points higher than the overall league average.

ERA--The Rangers reached their franchise peak in ERA in 1994 with a mark of 5.45. This highlights a major problem for the franchise in the 1990s when they generally had good offense but poor pitching. They were able to reduce their ERA substantially in 1996 while generating a great offense, and this is why they won their first division title in 1996 and made the playoffs for the first time in franchise history. They were only a little above their 1996 ERA level in 1997, but they had hoped for an improvement that did not materialize. The Rangers had the 5th highest ERA in the league for the full 1993-97 period.

Strikeouts--The Rangers set franchise records for strikeouts when they had Nolan Ryan on their staff in 1989. This put the Rangers on the all-time league list for per game and total year strikeouts at the time, but the surge in strikeouts in the 1990s pushed them off the list in 1997 (Table 2-24).

Walks--The Rangers also had high strikeouts in 1987, and the high level of walks that accompany high strikeouts created the franchise record for walks in that year. The 1987 Rangers make the top ten list for total walks (Table 2-26).

Strikeout-to-Walk Ratio--The best SO/W ratio for the Rangers came in 1974 when their staff was led by Hall-of-Famer Ferguson Jenkins who was unique in ranking high in strikeouts and low in walks.

Table 3-8. Key Measures Summary for the Rangers

	Per Game Peaks		Total Year Peaks		1993-97
	Per Game	Year	Total	Year	Per Game
Runs	5.69	**1996**	928	**1996**	5.20
Home Runs	1.36	**1996**	221	**1996**	1.13
Doubles	1.98	**1996**	323	**1996**	1.82
Bat Avg.	.284	**1996**	.284	**1996**	.274
ERA	5.45	**1994**	5.45	**1994**	4.75
Strikeouts	6.86	1989	1112	1989	5.88
Walks	4.69	1987	760	1987	3.48
SO/W Ratio	1.94	1974	1.94	1974	1.69

The franchise started as the replacement for the old Washington Senators who became the Twins when they moved to Minnesota in 1961. The new Washington Senators were as bad as their predecessors had been since WWII, and they had only one winning season in 11 years before being reborn as the Texas Rangers in 1972. The Rangers had some good years in the 1970s, and in 1977 they had a winning percentage of .580 and finished 2nd to the Royals in the division. A winning percentage of .580 would have won the division in 1976, 1978, and 1979, but it was not good enough in 1977.

The Rangers became competitive again in the late 1980s, and they finally broke through with their first division title in 1996 (not counting the strike year of 1994 when they were in first place with a losing record at the time of the strike). Their pitching potential appeared to be much better in 1997, but the potential did not become reality. Offense declined from the 1996 peak and the result was another losing season in 1997.

Table 3-9 shows a summary of the key measures for the Red Sox. Years from the 1990s are shown in boldface. Peak values and the years in which they occurred are shown on a per game and total year basis in the first two sets of columns in the table. The per game averages for each of the key measures from 1993 through 1997 are shown in the last column. The leaders for each measure from 1993 through 1997 are shown in Table 3-29.

Runs--The Red Sox set their franchise peaks for runs per game (6.67) and total runs (1027) in 1950. Both marks rank 4th on the all-time league list for runs (Table 2-16). The 1950 Red Sox are the last team in the majors to score over 1000 runs in one season. In the 162 game season of today, the Mariners and Rockies have come close to scoring 1000 runs. But neither team has come close to the average of 6.34 runs per game it would take to match the 1027 runs scored by the 1950 Red Sox. Other than the Red Sox, the last team to reach that level was the 1939 Yankees. However, during the 1993-97 period the Red Sox ranked only 7th in the league in scoring runs.

Home Runs--The 1977 Red Sox set franchise highs in home runs per game (1.32) and total home runs (213). Neither mark is high enough to make the top ten league list (Table 2-18). The 1996 Red Sox came close to setting a franchise record, missing by only 4 home runs. They fell back a little in 1997, but they averaged 1.08 home runs per game during the 1993-97 period, just missing their peak for over five years that was set in the 1976-80 period. But they still ranked only 7th in the league from 1993 through 1997.

Doubles--The Red Sox have the best doubles average in the majors since 1946, and they also lead since 1973, the year the designated hitter was born. They capped this performance in 1997 with an all-time league high for total doubles, although they were only 3rd on the all-time league per game list (Table 2-20). Fittingly, the Red Sox led the majors in doubles in the 1993-97 period and were the only team to average more than 2.0 doubles per game.

Batting Average--Consistent with their huge outburst in runs in 1950, the Red Sox also set their franchise record for batting average in 1950 with a mark of .302. This makes the 1950 Red Sox the last team in the majors to average over .300 for a full season. The last year prior to 1950 with a team hitting .300 or better was 1936, so the 1950 Red Sox represent the best in the last 61 years. With a great year in 1997, the Red Sox were 4th for the 1993-97 period.

ERA--The Red Sox set their franchise high for ERA with a mark of 5.02 in 1932, when they had a bad team and the league was in a period of high offense. The Red Sox threatened the 1932 mark in 1997, but a recovery late in the year avoided this dubious honor. Red Sox pitching has rarely matched their hitting, but they had better pitching before 1997, and thus they ranked 7th in ERA in the league during the 1993-97 period. Their mark of 4.58 for the period was at least well below the overall league average of 4.68.

Strikeouts--Roger Clemens bid farewell to the Red Sox in 1996 by leading them to franchise peaks in strikeouts. The 1996 Red Sox are tied for 4th in per game and 3rd in total year strikeouts on the all-time league list (Table 2-24). The Red Sox finished 3rd in the league in strikeouts for the 1993-97 period.

Walks--The Red Sox peaked in walks in 1950 as the league also peaked in walks in the 1948-50 period. The 1950 Red Sox make both the per game and total year top 10 list for walks (Table 2-26).

Strikeout-to-Walk Ratio--The franchise peak of 2.63 in 1904 ranks 2nd on the all-time league list (Table 2-28). But Red Sox pitching after 1918 was never as effective as it was in the 1903-18 period when they won six pennants.

Table 3-9. Key Measures Summary for the Red Sox

	Per Game Peaks		Total Year Peaks		1993-97
	Per Game	Year	Total	Year	Per Game
Runs	6.67	1950	1027	1950	5.10
Home Runs	1.32	1977	213	1977	1.08
Doubles	2.30	**1997**	373	**1997**	2.02
Bat Avg.	.302	1950	.302	1950	.276
ERA	5.02	1932	5.02	1932	4.58
Strikeouts	7.19	**1996**	1165	**1996**	6.39
Walks	4.86	1950	748	1950	3.77
SO/W Ratio	2.63	1904	2.63	1904	1.69

The Red Sox peaked early as a franchise, winning pennants in 1903 and 1904 as well as the first World Series ever played in 1903 (the Giants refused to play in 1904). The Red Sox won 4 pennants in 7 years from 1912 through 1918, and won the World Series each time. By 1918 the Red Sox had won 6 pennants and every World Series (5) they played. They have not won the World Series since, and have won only 4 pennants in the 79 seasons from 1919 through 1997.

In all of those 79 seasons the Red Sox have usually been stuck in the same rut of good hitting and mediocre pitching. Ironically, when Babe Ruth played for the Red Sox from 1914 through 1918, he was primarily a pitcher until 1918. He was a big hitter in 1919, but the Red Sox had a losing record that year and in 1920 the Babe was gone. It was 20 years before the Red Sox assembled enough big hitters to be competitive again, and they have primarily stuck with the "big hitters, little pitchers" approach since. The Red Sox led often in runs, but never in ERA. Even the Roger Clemens era couldn't turn things around.

Table 3-10 shows a summary of the key measures for the Royals. Years from the 1990s are shown in boldface. Peak values and the years in which they occurred are shown on a per game and total year basis in the first two sets of columns in the table. The per game averages for each of the key measures from 1993 through 1997 are shown in the last column. The leaders for each measure from 1993 through 1997 are shown in Table 3-29.

Runs--The Royals set their franchise peaks for runs per game (5.25) and total runs (851) in 1979, during a period when they had their best teams in franchise history. The Royals have always concentrated on pitching, and with some poor hitting teams in the 1990s, the offensive peak of the 1990s has not been able to lift the Royals run production past the levels they set in the 1976-85 period when they had good hitting teams to go along with their good pitching. Only the Blue Jays have lower runs peaks than the Royals (Table 2-1), and the Royals have been in existence 18 more years than the Blue Jays. The Royals ranked last in the league in runs during the 1993-97 period.

Home Runs--The Royals set their home run peaks in 1987, the year the league set what was then a record for home runs and a year that still ranks 2nd on the all-time league list (Table 1-5). The Royals have the lowest home run peaks in the league (Table 2-3), and only the Twins ranked below the Royals in home runs during the 1993-97 period.

Doubles--The Royals set their doubles peaks in 1990, but once again they are near the bottom of the list for peak years in doubles (Table 2-5), and they were 9th in the league in doubles for the 1993-97 period. But the Royals have had a lot of speedy line drive hitters since they came into the league in 1969, and since the DH was born in 1973, the Royals rank 2nd behind the Red Sox in average doubles per year (the Royals are 1st in triples over that period).

Batting Average--In spite of their limited run production, the Royals have been one of the better teams in batting average over the last few decades (George Brett was a big help in this respect). Their 1980 peak of .286 trails only the Mariners and Rockies among the 12 expansion teams (Table 2-7). It is a mark of the poorer teams they have had recently that the Royals are only 11th in batting average in the league for the 1993-97 period.

ERA--The Royals have had great pitching since their birth in 1969. From 1973 through 1997 the Royals are only 0.01 behind the Yankees for lowest ERA, and their peak ERA is the lowest (best) in the league. They peaked in 1996 when they finished last for the only time in their (now) 29 years in the league, but they set a new peak in 1997 when they finished last again. The Royals have never had a winning percentage below .400 (only the Angels can say the same), and they were consistent winners until 1995 through 1997 when they had three losing seasons in a row for the first time. In spite of this low point in franchise history, the Royals had the league's 5th lowest ERA in the 1993-97 period.

Strikeouts--The Royals have concentrated on getting batters out rather than striking them out, and their 1990 peak is easily the lowest on the league strikeout list (Table 2-9). Accordingly, the Royals ranked 10th in the league in strikeouts for the 1993-97 period.

Walks--A pitching staff with a good ERA and low strikeouts infers a very low walks level. The Royals have the lowest (best) mark on the peak walks list (Table 2-11), and issued the fewest walks in the league for the 1993-97 period.

Strikeout-to-Walk Ratio--Low walks gave the Royals the best SO/W peak among expansion teams on the league list (Table 2-13) until the 1997 Blue Jays topped them. The Royals were 4th in the league during the 1993-97 period.

Table 3-10. Key Measures Summary for the Royals

	Per Game Peaks		Total Year Peaks		1993-97
	Per Game	Year	Total	Year	Per Game
Runs	5.25	1979	851	1979	4.56
Home Runs	1.04	1987	168	1987	0.84
Doubles	1.96	**1990**	316	**1990**	1.74
Bat Avg.	.286	1980	.286	1980	.265
ERA	4.70	**1997**	4.70	**1997**	4.40
Strikeouts	6.25	**1990**	1006	**1990**	5.87
Walks	3.96	1970	641	1970	3.32
SO/W Ratio	2.15	1989	2.15	1989	1.77

In terms of lifetime winning percentage the Royals are the most successful expansion franchise. They are still the only expansion team in the majors to have a lifetime winning percentage over .500, and their mark of .512 puts them in 3rd place in the American League. Even for a lifetime of only 29 years, this is an impressive achievement. The Royals have also won 6 division titles, 2 pennants, and a World Series title. Among the other 11 expansion teams, only the Blue Jays and the Mets can claim World Series wins.

The main negative note for the Royals is that all these titles came in the 10 year period from 1976 through 1985. They had an unusually consistent lineup with the same key players staying together for most of those 10 years. They have not been in the playoffs since 1985, and their overall winning percentage has regularly declined through 1997. Even their normally good pitching has declined sharply recently, and with their typical lack of offense they are far from putting together a balanced team that can get them back into the playoffs.

Table 3-11 shows a summary of the key measures for the Tigers. Years from the 1990s are shown in boldface. Peak values and the years in which they occurred are shown on a per game and total year basis in the first two sets of columns in the table. The per game averages for each of the key measures from 1993 through 1997 are shown in the last column. The leaders for each measure from 1993 through 1997 are shown in Table 3-29.

Runs--The Tigers set their franchise peaks for runs per game (6.22) and total runs (958) in 1934, when they had a great hitting team that won their first pennant since 1909. The 1934 Tigers are the franchise's only entry on the top 15 runs list (Table 2-16), ranking 10th in per game runs and 12th in total runs. But this is a good showing since the domination of the Yankees means there are only 5 franchises on the per game list and 6 on the total runs list. The Tigers ranked 8th in runs during the 1993-97 period, a low ranking for a franchise that has consistently battled the Yankees and Red Sox for the top position in run scoring during the entire century.

Home Runs--The Tigers set their per game home run peak in 1994 when they had a poor team but lots of home run hitters. They set their total year record in 1987 when they had a good team that won the division but lost in the first round of the playoffs. Both marks make the top ten league list (Table 2-18). The Tigers rank 4th in home runs for the 1993-97 period, again a low ranking for a team that led the major leagues in home runs from 1973 through 1997.

Doubles--The 1934 Tigers set franchise peaks in doubles as well as in runs. The 1934 Tigers make the league's top 10 list for doubles (Table 2-20), ranking 5th on both the per game and total year lists. The 1929 Tigers also appear on the list, showing that the Tigers of the 1920s and 1930s hit a lot of doubles. But the Tigers hit fewer and fewer doubles as they hit more and more home runs (a common occurrence in both leagues), and they ranked only 11th in the league in doubles for the 1993-97 period.

Batting Average--The Tigers set the all-time league record for batting average when they hit .316 in 1921 (Table 2-22). Led by Ty Cobb, they also hit .306 in 1922 to rank 8th on the list. But after leading the league in batting average from 1903-72, the Tigers fell to 10th place from 1973 onward. They were last in batting average for the 1993-97 period.

ERA--After WWII the Tigers rarely had pitching that matched their ability to score runs. The Tigers initially had their worst ERA year in 1953 when they had a series of bad teams. They broke that mark in 1994, broke the 1994 mark in 1995, and then set the all-time league record for highest ERA in 1996 with a mark of 6.38 (Table 2-23). Only the terrible 1930 Phillies, playing in tiny Baker Bowl, had a higher mark in the majors. The Tigers had much better pitching (for them) in 1997, but they stayed last in the league with the highest ERA for the 1993-97 period, a position they assumed after their terrible year in 1996.

Strikeouts--The Tigers set their strikeout peak in 1968 when their pitching matched their hitting and they won the World Series (while Denny McLain won 31 games). But the strikeout peaks do not make the top ten list (Table 2-24), and the Tigers ranked 13th in strikeouts for the 1993-97 period.

Walks--The terrible 1996 team set the franchise peak in walks. They are the only team from the 1990s on the top 10 list for most walks (Table 2-26). The Tigers issued more walks than all but three teams during the 1993-97 period.

Strikeout-to-Walk Ratio--The Tigers set their peak in 1968 when they set their strikeout peak, and they made the top ten list (Table 2-28). But high walks and low strikeouts put the Tigers last in SO/W ratio in the 1993-97 period.

Table 3-11. Key Measures Summary for the Tigers

| | Per Game Peaks | | Total Year Peaks | | 1993-97 |
	Per Game	Year	Total	Year	Per Game
Runs	6.22	1934	958	1934	5.09
Home Runs	1.40	**1994**	225	1987	1.19
Doubles	2.27	1934	349	1934	1.69
Bat Avg.	.316	1921	.316	1921	.260
ERA	6.38	**1996**	6.38	**1996**	5.29
Strikeouts	6.80	1968	1115	1968	5.40
Walks	4.84	**1996**	784	**1996**	3.84
SO/W Ratio	2.29	1968	2.29	1968	1.41

The Tigers are a great franchise that has recently fallen on very hard times. The Tigers are second to the Yankees in lifetime winning percentage in the American League, and the Tigers have won 9 pennants and 4 World Series titles. But since 1945 they have only won 2 pennants (1968 and 1984), although they did win the World Series both times. Their last division title came in 1987, and they very nearly had their worst year ever in 1996. They were a much better team in 1997 and nearly got back to the .500 level.

A team that reflected the slashing style of Ty Cobb in thc first quarter of the century, the Tigers became primarily a team of big hitters in the 1930s. Since WWII Tiger Stadium has consistently been the true "homerdome" in the league. The Tigers and the Red Sox have been quite similar in the last 60 years. They hit lots of home runs and produce many winning seasons, but they rarely have the pitching to match their hitting. The result is lots of entertaining wins, but very few playoff wins and even fewer entries into the World Series.

Table 3-12 shows a summary of the key measures for the Twins (who were the Washington Senators before moving to Minnesota for the 1961 season). Years from the 1990s are shown in boldface. Peak values and the years in which they occurred are shown on a per game and total year basis in the first two sets of columns in the table. The per game averages for each of the key measures from 1993 through 1997 are shown in the last column. The leaders for each measure from 1993 through 1997 are shown in Table 3-29.

Runs--The franchise per game peak (5.81) came in 1936 and the total runs peak (892) in 1930. These are the lowest peaks of the original 8 teams, and 3 expansion teams are higher as well (Table 2-1). The Washington Senators had their last good teams in the 1930s (they won the pennant in 1933), and they were scoring more after having been primarily a pitching team in huge Griffith Stadium. But the 1930s were a time of high runs, and the peaks of the Senators were relatively low. Still, the great home run hitters in Minnesota and the high runs environment of the Metrodome have not produced higher peaks than those of the 1930s. The Twins ranked 9th in runs scored in the 1993-97 period.

Home Runs--In home runs the Washington Senators were mostly notable for having the stadium with the fewest home runs in the league. But in Minnesota Harmon Killebrew and friends put the Twins on the top 10 list for home runs in 1963 and 1964 (Table 2-18). However, this was a short-lived surge. The Twins rank next to last in the league in home runs since 1973, and the Twins were dead last in home runs during the 1993-97 period.

Doubles--The Senators ranked next to last in the league in doubles from 1903 through 1945, but the Twins reversed the trend. The 1994 Twins set the per game peak for the franchise, and the 1996 Twins set the total year peak. Both teams are 11th on the per game and total year top 10 list (Table 2-20). The Twins were 4th in the league in doubles for the 1993-97 period.

Batting Average--Except for the Red Sox (who did it in 1950), the original 16 teams set their batting average peaks between 1920 and 1930, and all 16 teams have higher peaks than any expansion team (Table 2-7). The Senators set the franchise high in 1925, but the Senators/Twins were 8th in the league from 1903 through 1972 while the Twins were 2nd in the league from 1973 through 1977. The Twins were 5th in the league for the 1993-97 period.

ERA--The Senators won the first franchise pennants in 1924 and 1925 by leading the league in ERA behind the great Walter Johnson. The Twins had good years in Minneapolis between 1965 and 1970 with good pitching and Harmon Killebrew, and they won the World Series in the Metrodome in 1987 and 1991 with a mix of just enough pitching and hitting and some mirrors. Otherwise they are next to last in the league in ERA since 1973. They set the franchise peak in 1994, broke that record in 1995, and had the 2nd highest ERA in the league for the 1993-97 period just behind the terrible Tigers.

Strikeouts--The Twins set the franchise strikeout peaks in 1964. The peaks are in the middle of the league list (Table 2-9) and do not make the top ten list. The Twins were 12th in the league in strikeouts for the 1993-97 period.

Walks--The 1949 Senators set the franchise peak with terrible pitching during the league's peak year in walks, and they rank in the middle of the top ten list (Table 2-26). But the Twins were 3rd in fewest walks for the 1993-97 period.

Strikeout-to-Walk Ratio--Issuing very few walks enabled the 1967 Twins to set the all-time league high for SO/W ratio (Table 2-28). The 1966 and 1968 Twins also make the top ten list, and no team has since even come close to any of these three Twin teams. This record should last as long as the DH does.

Table 3-12. Key Measures Summary for the Twins

	Per Game Peaks		Total Year Peaks		1993-97
	Per Game	Year	Total	Year	Per Game
Runs	5.81	1936	892	1930	4.92
Home Runs	1.40	1963	225	1963	0.81
Doubles	2.12	**1994**	332	**1996**	1.91
Bat Avg.	.303	1925	.303	1925	.276
ERA	5.76	**1995**	5.76	**1995**	5.29
Strikeouts	6.74	1964	1099	1964	5.58
Walks	5.06	1949	779	1949	3.39
SO/W Ratio	2.75	1967	2.75	1967	1.65

Of the 16 original teams, only the Braves and Phillies have lower lifetime winning percentages than the Senators/Twins. Since 1973, only the Cubs, Padres, and Mariners have lower winning percentages. But at least the Twins have won two World Series titles since 1973, and only the Yankees, A's, and Reds have been able to win as many as three. The Senators were typically a winning team between the early teens and the early 1930s, but they were horrible before and after. After moving to Minneapolis for the 1961 season and becoming the Twins, the franchise usually had winning records for much of the 1960s and 1970s. But they primarily have been losers since then except for surges in 1987 and 1991 that brought them the two World Series titles.

The Twins are in a small market and an unattractive stadium. It will be hard to attract large crowds and revenues until they become winners, but it will be hard to become winners until they have the large crowds and revenues to acquire the players they need. It's a cycle several teams find themselves in today.

Table 3-13 shows a summary of the key measures for the White Sox. Years from the 1990s are shown in boldface. Peak values and the years in which they occurred are shown on a per game and total year basis in the first two sets of columns in the table. The per game averages for each of the key measures from 1993 through 1997 are shown in the last column. The leaders for each measure from 1993 through 1997 are shown in Table 3-29.

Runs--The White Sox set their peaks for runs per game (6.01) and total runs (920) in 1936, the peak year for runs in the American League. Playing in huge Comiskey Park, the White Sox typically featured pitching and were next to last in the league in runs from 1903 through 1972. They are, however, one of the seven franchises in the league to have a peak over 6.0 runs per game (Table 2-1). With the move into the new Comiskey Park and the acquisition of hitters like Frank Thomas, the White Sox are now a higher scoring team. They were 4th in the league in scoring for the 1993-97 period, and in 1996 they were only 22 runs (0.14 per game) away from matching their all-time high in total runs.

Home Runs--The White Sox were last in the league in home runs from 1903 through 1972, and Comiskey Park was the only stadium close to Griffith Stadium for fewest home runs. It's not surprising that the White Sox set peaks for home runs in 1996. However, only the Royals have a lower per game peak and only the Royals and Angels have fewer total home runs peaks (Table 2-3). The White Sox were 8th in the league in home runs during the 1993-97 period.

Doubles--The peak for the White Sox in doubles came in 1926, but their total year peak is 12th on the league peak list (Table 2-5). The White Sox were last in the league in doubles from 1903 though 1972, and they were last in the league during the 1993-97 period.

Batting Average--The White Sox set their peak for batting average in 1920, when they still had the same team that won the pennant in 1919. It was after the 1920 season that several of the White Sox were banned for throwing the 1919 World Series to the Reds. But the White Sox have the lowest peak among the original 8 teams, and they are the only one of the original 8 never to hit over .300 as a team (Table 2-7). However, led by Frank Thomas, the White Sox were 3rd in the league in batting average for the 1993-97 period.

ERA--The 5.41 peak ERA for the White Sox in 1934 was partly due to moving home plate in Comiskey Park closer to the fences to increase the home run output of Al Simmons who had been acquired in 1933. But visitors took much more advantage than Simmons and the White Sox led the league in ERA (home place was moved back again in 1935). Overall, the White Sox were 2nd to the Yankees in lowest ERA from 1903 through 1972. They are tied for 6th in lowest ERA since 1973, and they had the 2nd lowest ERA in the league during the 1993-97 period. They moved down the peak ERA list (Table 2-8) and fell off the top 10 list (Table 2-23) as other teams set their peak ERAs in the 1990s.

Strikeouts--Like the Royals, the White Sox from 1903 through 1972 were near the bottom of the league in strikeouts but near the top in low ERA. The White Sox peaked in strikeouts in the 1990s, but rank near the bottom of the peak list (Table 2-9). They were 6th in strikeouts for the 1993-97 period.

Walks--The White Sox led the league in fewest walks in the 1903-72 period, and peaked in walks when the league did. They are near the middle of the peak list (Table 2-11), but were 6th in issuing the most walks in the 1993-97 period.

Strikeout-to-Walk Ratio--The White Sox led in SO/W ratio as well as low walks in the 1903-72 period. Their 1964 peak makes the top ten list (Table 2-28). But they are far down the list since 1973, and were 8th in the 1993-97 period.

Table 3-13. Key Measures Summary for the White Sox

	Per Game Peaks		Total Year Peaks		1993-97
	Per Game	Year	Total	Year	Per Game
Runs	6.01	1936	920	1936	5.20
Home Runs	1.20	**1996**	195	**1996**	1.05
Doubles	2.03	1926	314	1926	1.61
Bat Avg.	.295	1920	.295	1920	.277
ERA	5.41	1934	5.41	1934	4.35
Strikeouts	6.67	**1994**	1039	**1996**	6.24
Walks	4.71	1950	734	1950	3.69
SO/W Ratio	2.38	1964	2.38	1964	1.69

The White Sox were one of the best teams in baseball in the 1903-20 period, and they won 3 pennants and 2 World Series titles during that time (the missing title is 1919). But they were losers for the next 3 decades after their key players were banned. They had 17 straight winning seasons from 1951 through 1967, the third best such streak ever in the American League. But they were able to win the pennant only in 1959, and they have not won one since. The White Sox won division titles in 1983 and 1993, and they were leading in 1994 when the strike came. They had a very good team in 1994 and might have gone all the way, but the strike suggests that the curse of the "Black Sox" has a very long reach.

Since their championship in 1917, the White Sox have gone longer than any of the 8 original American League teams without a World Series win. Of the original 16 teams, only the Cubs, who last won in 1908, have waited a longer time. The White Sox have a lifetime winning percentage just over .500, but they have little to show for it, especially since the debacle of 1919.

Table 3-14 shows a summary of the key measures for the Yankees. Years from the 1990s are shown in boldface. Peak values and the years in which they occurred are shown on a per game and total year basis in the first two sets of columns in the table. The per game averages for each of the key measures from 1993 through 1997 are shown in the last column. The leaders for each measure from 1993 through 1997 are shown in Table 3-29.

Runs--The Yankees set their peak for runs per game (6.90) in 1930 and their peak for total runs (1067) in 1931. Both marks are the best ever in the league (Table 2-16), and the best ever in the majors. The Yankees have 7 of the top 10 spots (including the top 3), and 10 of the top 15 spots for runs per game. They have the same ranking in the total runs list except that they have "only" 8 of the top 15 spots because the longer season enabled other teams to move into the bottom rungs of the top 10 list. The Yankees are the lifetime leader in runs per game in the majors, and although they no longer dominate the rest of the teams in scoring runs, they were 2nd in the league in runs for the 1993-97 period.

Home Runs--The Yankees also are the lifetime leaders in home runs, although they only rank 3rd in the majors since 1973 (behind the Orioles and Tigers). Their 1961 peaks for per game and total year home runs were finally surpassed in the 1990s, but the Yankees are still on the top 10 list (Table 2-18). However, the Yankees were only 10th in home runs for the 1993-97 period as they had unusually few home run hitters when the offensive outburst began.

Doubles--The Yankees typically never hit many doubles (they hit them over the fence rather than against it), but in the 1990s they began to hit more as their home run pace declined. They set their per game peak in 1994 and their total year peak in 1997 (beating a record set in 1936). The Yankees ranked 2nd in the 1993-97 period, a much higher ranking than they usually have for doubles.

Batting Average--The peak of .309 recorded by the Yankees in 1930 is the 3rd highest ever in the league (Table 2-22). As is the case for many measures other than runs, the Yankees were not necessarily the league leader in batting average over various periods, but they were always close to the top and are the leader among teams playing for the full century. The Yankees were 2nd to the Indians in batting average for the 1993-97 period.

ERA--With nicknames like the "Bronx Bombers," the Yankees are associated with home runs and big innings. But the real edge for the Yankees over the years was pitching and defense. The Yankees are the league's lifetime leader in low ERA for the century, and they also are the best in the league since 1973. The peak ERA for the Yankees came in 1930, the league's 2nd highest scoring year ever. Only the Royals have a lower peak ERA than the Yankees, and the Yankees, Royals, and Blue Jays are the only franchises in the league to have a peak ERA below 5.00 (Table 2-8). Accordingly, the Yankees had the lowest ERA in the league for the 1993-97 period.

Strikeouts--The Yankees led the league in strikeouts in the 1903-45 period. They slid down the list afterwards, but they set peaks in strikeouts in 1996 and then again in 1997 with both years making the top 10 list (Table 2-24). The Yankees were 4th in the league in strikeouts in the 1993-97 period.

Walks--The Yankees were always near the top in fewest walks, but their 1949 peak is the 2nd highest in league history (Table 2-26). Still, the Yankees won the pennant in 1949. They were 6th in fewest walks in the 1993-97 period.

Strikeout-to-Walk Ratio--Although their peak was back in 1904 and ranks only in the middle of the list (Table 2-13), the Yankees are the league's lifetime leader in SO/W ratio. They were 2nd in SO/W ratio in the 1993-97 period.

Table 3-14. Key Measures Summary for the Yankees

	Per Game Peaks		Total Year Peaks		1993-97
	Per Game	Year	Total	Year	Per Game
Runs	6.90	1930	1067	1931	5.41
Home Runs	1.47	1961	240	1961	1.03
Doubles	2.11	**1994**	325	**1997**	1.93
Bat Avg.	.309	1930	.309	1930	.284
ERA	4.88	1930	4.88	1930	4.35
Strikeouts	7.19	**1997**	1165	**1997**	6.37
Walks	5.24	1949	812	1949	3.53
SO/W Ratio	2.20	1904	2.20	1904	1.80

The Yankees were one of baseball's best teams during the 33 seasons from 1903 through 1935, but they did not dominate baseball. The Giants, Cubs, and A's won more pennants during that period, and the A's and Red Sox won five World Series titles while the Giants and Yankees won four. But during the next 29 seasons from 1936 through 1964, the Yankees absolutely dominated baseball. They won 22 pennants (76 percent) and 16 World Series titles (73 percent). In terms of the World Series, the Yankees were even more dominant from 1927 through 1953 when they won 15 of the 16 World Series they appeared in. The Yankees also had 39 straight winning seasons from 1926 through 1964.

In the 33 seasons from 1965 through 1997, the Yankees were once again just one of baseball's best teams. But they stayed near the top in pennants and World Series titles, and they had the best winning percentage in the majors from 1973 through 1997 after claiming the same distinction by a much wider margin from 1903 through 1972. The Yankees are clearly the best franchise of the century.

Table 3-15 shows a summary of the key measures for the Astros. Years from the 1990s are shown in boldface. Peak values and the years in which they occurred are shown on a per game and total year basis in the first two sets of columns in the table. The per game averages for each of the key measures from 1993 through 1997 are shown in the last column. The leaders for each measure from 1993 through 1997 are shown in Table 3-29.

Runs--As is the case for most of the expansion teams, the Astros set their franchise peaks for offensive measures in the 1990s. They set their per game runs peak (5.23) in 1994, but because of the short season due to the strike in 1994 the Astros set their total runs peak (770) in 1997. Playing in the pitching friendly environment of the Astrodome, the Astros rank third from the bottom in the league in runs scored since 1973. But with the modification of the Astrodome and the development of such players as Jeff Bagwell, the Astros became a higher scoring team just as the offensive peak of the 1993-97 period began. The per game runs peak for the Astros is only 9th on the peak list (Table 2-2), but the Astros rank ahead of all the expansion teams in the league except the Rockies, and the Astros even rank ahead of the Braves. The Astros ranked 2nd to the Rockies in scoring runs during the 1993-97 period.

Home Runs--The Astros set their per game home run peak in 1994 and their total home runs peak in 1993. Their per game mark is 11th on the peak list (Table 2-4), and their total year mark is last on the list. The Astros rank next to last in the league in home runs since 1973, and this is why their home run peaks are still low compared to most other teams. The Astros confirmed this with a ranking of 10th in the league in home runs for the 1993-97 period.

Doubles--The Astros, however, became a great doubles hitting team in the 1990s. Their 1994 per game peak of 2.19 ranks 4th on the all-time league list (Table 2-21), and they were 2nd in the league in doubles for the 1993-97 period. The Expos at 1.92 and the Astros at 1.91 were far ahead of the rest of the league for the 1993-97 period (the Pirates were 3rd with an average of 1.77).

Batting Average--The Astros also recorded their peak year in batting average in 1994 with a mark of .278. This ranks 10th on the league list (Table 2-7), but once again is higher than the peaks of all the expansion teams in the league except the Rockies. Consistent with their higher runs scoring level, the Astros ranked 2nd in the league in batting average for the 1993-97 period.

ERA--The Astros, Expos, and Mets cluster together just behind the Dodgers for lowest ERA in the league since 1973. Until the 1993-97 period, the best teams in franchise history for the Astros always had outstanding pitching. The new emphasis on offense moved the Astros towards higher ERAs, and they had the highest ERA in franchise history in 1996. But this is still the lowest (best) peak in the league (Table 2-8). Accordingly, the Astros had the 4th lowest ERA in the league during the 1993-97 period.

Strikeouts--The 1969 Astros held the all-time major league strikeout records until the Braves and Dodgers passed them between 1994 and 1997 (Table 2-25) as the league topped all its previous strikeout records (Table 1-9). The Astros still finished 3rd in strikeouts for the 1993-97 period.

Walks--Their hard throwing pitchers kept the Astros near the top of the league in issuing walks, and their 1975 peak of 679 walks makes the league's top 10 list (Table 2-27). But they were 5th in fewest walks in the 1993-97 period.

Strikeout-to-Walk Ratio--Their high walk level put the Astros 8th on the peak SO/W list (Table 2-13), and not near the top 10 list. But their recent drop in walks puts them 3rd in the league in SO/W ratio in the 1993-97 period.

Table 3-15. Key Measures Summary for the Astros

	Per Game Peaks		Total Year Peaks		1993-97
	Per Game	Year	Total	Year	Per Game
Runs	5.23	**1994**	777	**1997**	4.86
Home Runs	1.04	**1994**	138	**1993**	0.85
Doubles	2.19	**1994**	314	**1997**	1.91
Bat Avg.	.278	**1994**	.278	**1994**	.268
ERA	4.37	**1996**	4.37	**1996**	3.91
Strikeouts	7.54	1969	1221	1969	6.90
Walks	4.19	1975	679	1975	3.16
SO/W Ratio	2.48	1963	2.48	1963	2.18

The Astros were one of the National League's first expansion teams, being born with the Mets in 1962. They have generally been competitive, and only once did they have a winning percentage below .400 (.398 in 1975). But the only titles for the franchise were divisional titles in 1980 and 1986 which did not translate into pennants. Until the offensive outburst in the 1993-97 period, the Astros were a good example of a team that excels in only one part of the game (pitching). Their pitching has been good enough to make them consistent winners, but not good enough to overcome their weakness at the plate when it comes to "winning time."

The Astros were a much stronger offensive team in the 1993-97 period. But although they play in the weak Central Division, they won the division title only in 1997 and once again it did not translate into a pennant. They had a winning percentage of only .519 when they won the division, and they clearly had not yet put together the kind of balanced team that can win it all.

Table 3-16 shows a summary of the key measures for the Braves. Years from the 1990s are shown in boldface. Peak values and the years in which they occurred are shown on a per game and total year basis in the first two sets of columns in the table. The per game averages for each of the key measures from 1993 through 1997 are shown in the last column. The leaders for each measure from 1993 through 1997 are shown in Table 3-29.

Runs--The Braves played in the high offense 1920s and 1930s, but their per game runs peak is 12th in the National League (Table 2-2) and 26th in the majors. One problem for the Braves was playing in huge Braves Field, and another was that they usually had bad teams before WWII. The Braves were last in the majors in runs from 1903 through 1972, and they only moved up 5th in the league after 1973 in spite of moving to the top in home runs. The 1947-51 period was the best for the Braves in scoring runs on a per game basis (they won the pennant in 1948). Their total year peak came in the longer season of 1964 when they were in Milwaukee and were a great home run team behind Hank Aaron and company. The Braves became a pitching team in the 1990s, but still ranked 4th in the league in runs during the 1993-97 period. That excellent balance explains why the Braves were the top team in the league in the 1990s.

Home Runs--The Braves were next to last in the league in home runs before WWII. But the ascent of Hank Aaron and Eddie Mathews put the Braves 2nd in the majors (behind the Giants) for the 1946-72 period, and the Braves also broke records for home runs on the road in that period (contrary to most perceptions Milwaukee Stadium was not a good home run park). The Braves moved to the top of the league home run list after 1973, and the per game and total year peaks for the Braves moved to the top 10 league list (Table 2-19). However, the Braves are moving down the list as the Rockies take over the top spots and displace teams below them. The Braves ranked 2nd to the Rockies in home runs for the 1993-97 period, confirming again the great balance of the Braves in the 1990s.

Doubles--The Braves usually ranked low in doubles except in the 1947-51 period when they set their per game peak. They are near the bottom of the league peak list (Table 2-6), and they ranked 10th in doubles in the 1993-97 period.

Batting Average--The original 16 teams set their batting average peaks between 1920 and 1930, and no expansion teams have yet matched those marks. But the Braves have the lowest peak of the 16 teams (Table 2-7), although they were 5th in the league in batting average in the 1993-97 period.

ERA--The Braves' 1929 ERA peak combined a bad team with the league's 2nd highest scoring year. The Braves are high on the peak list (Table 2-8), but they miss the top 10 list. Pitching for the Braves has been so bad that only the Phillies were worse in the 1903-72 period, and only the Cubs were worse in the 1973-90 period. But the Braves came from worst to first in ERA between 1990 and 1992, and they easily had the lowest ERA in the 1993-97 period.

Strikeouts--Although last in the league for the century, the Braves broke all major league strikeout records in the 1990s. They hold 3 of the top 4 places on the per game list, and are also first in total year strikeouts (Table 2-25). They led the majors in strikeouts by a wide margin during the 1993-97 period.

Walks--The 1977 peak which ranks 5th on the top 10 list (Table 2-27) was typical of Braves pitching in the 1973-90 period when they among the leaders in issuing walks. But they issued the 2nd fewest walks in the 1993-97 period.

Strikeout-to-Walk Ratio--Last in the league from 1903 through 1990, the Braves had the 3rd best SO/W ratio ever in 1996 (Table 2-28). The Braves easily led the majors in SO/W ratio during the 1993-97 period.

Table 3-16. Key Measures Summary for the Braves

	Per Game Peaks		Total Year Peaks		1993-97
	Per Game	Year	Total	Year	Per Game
Runs	5.03	1950	803	1964	4.72
Home Runs	1.28	1957	207	1966	1.14
Doubles	1.77	1948	284	1987	1.59
Bat Avg.	.292	1925	.292	1925	.264
ERA	5.12	1929	5.12	1929	3.37
Strikeouts	7.69	**1996**	1245	**1996**	7.32
Walks	4.33	1977	701	1977	2.97
SO/W Ratio	2.76	**1996**	2.76	**1996**	2.46

The Braves had 34 losing seasons in 45 years between 1903 and 1945 and were grouped with the Phillies and Browns as the worst franchises in baseball. Their one success was the "miracle" of 1914 when they won the World Series over the world champion A's in 4 games. The Braves became competitive in 1946, won the 1948 pennant, and moved to Milwaukee in 1953 where they had 13 straight winning seasons. They won the 1957 pennant and the 1958 World Series, but moved to Atlanta in 1966. They won their division in 1969 and 1982, but in the 1985-89 period they had the worst winning percentage in the majors.

Then came the miracle of the 1990s. The Braves went from last in 1990 to first in 1991, and became the best pitching team in baseball with good balance in scoring runs. Excluding the 1994 strike year, the Braves won a record 6 straight division titles in the 1991-97 period. They also advanced to the league championship round every year. The Braves of the 1990s are by far the best teams in franchise history as well as the best in baseball for the decade.

Table 3-17 shows a summary of the key measures for the Cardinals. Years from the 1990s are shown in boldface. Peak values and the years in which they occurred are shown on a per game and total year basis in the first two sets of columns in the table. The per game averages for each of the key measures from 1993 through 1997 are shown in the last column. The leaders for each measure from 1993 through 1997 are shown in Table 3-29.

Runs--The 1930 Cards were the league's best scoring team in the league's best scoring year, and as a result they hold the all-time league record for per game (6.52) and total year (1004) runs (Table 2-17). In spite of the longer season now, no other National League team has scored more than 1000 runs in a year, and since 1930 only the Rockies have even come close. In the American League the Yankees did it 4 times and the Red Sox once (Table 2-16). The Cards were only 4th in the league for most runs over selected 5 year periods between 1926 and 1931, but they had the highest peak when it counted. The Cards are 2nd in the league for runs from 1903 through 1972, but only 7th since 1973. They have continued to decline and were only 11th in the 1993-97 period.

Home Runs--The Cards were 4th in the league in home runs for the 1903-45 period, but since 1946 they have been by far the worst home run team in the league. The Cards featured good contact hitters and lots of speed on the bases to remain a reasonable run scoring team, but they did not hit home runs. They have been last both in home runs at home and on the road, so it is not a stadium issue. It is simply a choice of offensive strategy. The Cards have had a few more big hitters recently and they hit their per game home run peak in 1994, but it is the lowest peak in the league (Table 2-4). The Cards' best year for total home runs was in 1997 and only the weak hitting Astros have a lower peak. The Cards were 11th in the league in home runs in the 1993-97 period.

Doubles--Just as good home run teams often hit few doubles, the Cards hit a lot of doubles to compensate for low home runs. They led the league in doubles from 1903 through 1990, but have declined recently. They set the all-time major league record for doubles in 1930 both on a per game and total year basis (the 1997 Red Sox tied the total year mark), and they place 4 teams on the top 10 list (Table 2-21). But the Cards were only 7th in doubles in the 1993-97 period.

Batting Average--Further compensating for their lack of power, the Cards led the league in batting average from 1903 through 1997. They have 2 teams on the top 10 list (Table 2-22), but they were only 11th in the 1993-97 period.

ERA--The Cards had terrible pitching in the early years of the century, and they rank only in the middle of the league for ERA over the century. But they have had great pitching in their pennant winning periods. Their all-time peak in 1994 was reflective of the bad teams they had in 1994 and 1995. They are high on the peak list (Table 2-8), but they did avoid the top 10 list. The Cards had the 7th highest ERA during the 1993-97 period.

Strikeouts--The Cards were in the top part of the league for strikeouts in the 1903-72 period, but they have been dead last since 1973. They set their peaks in 1997 when the league set its record (Table 1-9). The peaks for the Cards rank low (Table 2-10), and they were 12th in strikeouts during the 1993-97 period.

Walks--As part of the terrible pitching for the franchise early in the century, the 1911 Cards set the 2nd highest peak in issuing walks (Table 2-27). But the Cards are 2nd in fewest walks since 1973 and ranked 4th in the 1993-97 period.

Strikeout-to-Walk Ratio--Low strikeouts puts the Cards at the bottom of the SO/W ratio list since 1973 and in 8th place in the 1993-97 period. They peaked with Bob Gibson in 1968, but fell off the top 10 list in 1997 (Table 2-28).

Table 3-17. Key Measures Summary for the Cards

| | Per Game Peaks | | Total Year Peaks | | 1993-97 |
	Per Game	Year	Total	Year	Per Game
Runs	6.52	1930	1004	1930	4.44
Home Runs	0.94	**1994**	144	**1997**	0.84
Doubles	2.42	1930	373	1930	1.71
Bat Avg.	.314	1930	.314	1930	.261
ERA	5.14	**1994**	5.14	**1994**	4.23
Strikeouts	6.98	**1997**	1130	**1997**	5.92
Walks	4.44	1911	701	1911	3.04
SO/W Ratio	2.59	1968	2.59	1968	1.95

The Cards were one of the worst teams in baseball up to 1920, recording only 3 winning seasons in the 18 years of the 1903-20 period. But they started to improve in the early 1920s and they had 30 winning seasons in the 33 years of the 1921-53 period. They won 9 pennants and 6 World Series titles between 1926 and 1946 and were regularly one of the best teams in baseball during that time. They peaked every 20 years after 1946, winning 3 pennants and 2 World Series titles between 1964 and 1968, and winning 3 pennants and 1 World Series title between 1982 and 1987. They won another division title in 1996, but just missed winning the pennant in a tough playoff series with the Braves.

The Cards had mixed success in the 1993-97 period with an overall winning percentage of only .486. They alternated between trying to feature a little more power than usual and improving their pitching. Except for their near success in 1996, they are a franchise with a great history that is struggling hard to get back among the top teams in the baseball world.

Table 3-18 shows a summary of the key measures for the Cubs. Years from the 1990s are shown in boldface. Peak values and the years in which they occurred are shown on a per game and total year basis in the first two sets of columns in the table. The per game averages for each of the key measures from 1993 through 1997 are shown in the last column. The leaders for each measure from 1993 through 1997 are shown in Table 3-29.

Runs--The 1930 Cubs were just behind the Cards in the league's best scoring year, and as a result they are just behind the Cards for the all-time league record for per game (6.40) and total year (998) runs (Table 2-17). The Cubs led the league in scoring in 1929, the league's 2nd best year, and thus the Cubs hold both the 2nd and 3rd best marks in the league. For the century, the Cubs have consistently ranked 4th in the league in scoring. But before WWII they had good pitching as well and were one of baseball's best teams. After WWII they kept scoring at a similar rate, but their pitching disappeared. Recently their scoring also fell and they ranked only 7th in the league in runs for the 1993-97 period.

Home Runs--Typically the Cubs have ranked 4th in home runs during the century. They set their peak in 1987, a top 10 year for the league (Table 1-5), and the 1987 Cubs make the team top 10 list with the total year mark ranking 5th (Table 2-19). Home runs in Wrigley Field vary with the degree to which the wind blows out, but it has become a popular place to hit home runs in the last few decades. This is because the Cubs assembled teams that hit lots of home runs at home (but not always on the road), while opposing teams feasted on the poor pitching of the Cubs. The Cubs ranked 5th in home runs in the 1993-97 period.

Doubles--The Cubs peaked in doubles in 1931 and the 1931 Cubs rank 4th on the total year top 10 list (Table 2-21). Before WWII the Cubs were 2nd in the league to the Cards, the all-time leaders. But after WWII the Cubs drifted down to 7th in the league in hitting doubles. They were 8th in the league in doubles in the 1993-97 period.

Batting Average--The Cubs hit their peak in 1930 as did 4 of the original 8 teams. The 1930 Cubs rank 6th on the top 10 league list (Table 2-22). The Cubs typically ranked 5th in batting average during the century, but they ranked 9th in batting average in the 1993-97 period.

ERA--The Cubs look like two completely different franchises in pitching. In 1907 they set the all-time major league low for ERA, and they also set the five year low from 1905 through 1909. In every decade before 1945 the Cubs had an average ERA well below the league average. But in every decade after 1945 the team ERA has been well above the league average. Since 1973 the Cubs are dead last in ERA (they are the only league team with an average above 4.00). Their 1930 peak is low on the peak list (Table 2-8), but their average ERA is the problem. They tried recently to improve their pitching, but they had the 3rd highest ERA in the 1993-97 period (2nd highest excluding the Rockies).

Strikeouts--The Cubs led the league in strikeouts in the 1903-45 period, but fell off after 1945. They set their peak in the league's peak year of 1997, but only two teams are lower on the peak list including the Rockies (Table 2-10). The Cubs ranked 9th in strikeouts during the 1993-97 period.

Walks--The Cubs set per game peaks in 1954 and 1958 and a total year peak in the longer season of 1987. The Cubs are low on the peak list (Table 2-12), but the Cubs issued the 5th highest number of walks in the 1993-97 period.

Strikeout-to-Walk Ratio--The Cubs ranked high in SO/W ratio before 1945 and low after. They peaked in 1968 but only the Marlins and Rockies have lower peaks (Table 2-13). The Cubs ranked 11th in SO/W ratio in the 1993-97 period.

Table 3-18. Key Measures Summary for the Cubs

	Per Game Peaks		Total Year Peaks		1993-97
	Per Game	Year	Total	Year	Per Game
Runs	6.40	1930	998	1930	4.55
Home Runs	1.30	1987	209	1987	0.98
Doubles	2.18	1931	340	1931	1.68
Bat Avg.	.309	1930	.309	1930	.262
ERA	4.80	1930	4.80	1930	4.32
Strikeouts	6.62	**1997**	1072	**1997**	6.26
Walks	4.02	54/58	628	1987	3.39
SO/W Ratio	2.28	1968	2.29	1968	1.84

As the key measures demonstrate, the Cubs are two different franchises before and after WWII. The 1906 Cubs hold major league records for most wins (116) and best winning percentage (.763), and the 1906-10 Cubs hold the major league record with a .693 percentage over 5 years. Between 1906 and 1938, the Cubs won 9 pennants. But they won the World Series only in 1907 and 1908, making the Cubs the franchise with the longest wait for a World Series title as well as a pennant. In spite of their lack of success in the World Series, the Cubs were easily one of the best franchises in baseball between 1903 and 1938. They won their last pennant in 1945 as teams were returning from WWII, but they have been one of the least successful franchises in baseball since then.

The Cubs had great pitching in the 1906-10 period, and good pitching in the 1929-38 period when they won 4 pennants. Their pitching declined after 1945, and they have the worst ERA in the league since then. The problem is obvious, but the solution, while maintaining some offense, is seemingly not achievable.

Table 3-19 shows a summary of the key measures for the Dodgers. Years from the 1990s are shown in boldface. Peak values and the years in which they occurred are shown on a per game and total year basis in the first two sets of columns in the table. The per game averages for each of the key measures from 1993 through 1997 are shown in the last column. The leaders for each measure from 1993 through 1997 are shown in Table 3-29.

Runs--The Dodgers had good pitching but little hitting before 1940, then great hitting and decent pitching through the 1950s, then great pitching and little hitting after they moved to Dodger Stadium in 1962. Accordingly, the Dodgers set their peak in runs in 1953. They are the only original team not to do it between 1925 and 1930. In addition, the 1949-53 Dodgers hold the league record for most runs over 5 years, a mark not even the Rockies have been able to match. The 1953 Dodgers rank 6th on the top 15 per game list (Table 2-17). But with Dodger pitching challenging the mighty Braves for the best in the league, the Dodgers ranked 12th in scoring in the 1993-97 period. Only the Pirates (who were last in winning percentage) and expansion Marlins were worse.

Home Runs--Before 1973 the Dodgers were 5th in the league in home runs, and are essentially tied for 3rd with 2 teams since then. The Dodgers have been able to hit home runs, but their ability to generate the serial offense that keeps run scoring high has steadily declined in the last decade. The Dodger home run peak came in their high scoring year of 1953, and the 1953 Dodgers rank 6th on the top 10 list (Table 2-19). The 1955 Dodgers are also 7th on a per game basis. The Dodgers ranked 6th in the league in home runs in the 1993-97 period.

Doubles--Through 1945 the Dodgers were 5th in the league in doubles, but since then the Dodgers are just barely above the Giants who are in last place. The Dodgers peaked in the league's peak year of 1930, and the 1930 Dodgers are in the middle of the peak list (Table 2-6), but not on the top 10 list. The Dodgers were absolutely dead last in doubles for the 1993-97 period.

Batting Average--The Dodgers hit their peak in 1930 as did 4 of the original 8 teams. The 1930 Dodgers rank 6th on peak list (Table 2-7), but are not on the top 10 list. The Dodgers are 6th in the league for batting average over the century, and were 6th in batting average in the 1993-97 period.

ERA--The Dodgers have always had good pitching. They were below the league average in ERA in every decade except the 1930s and the 1903-09 period. They had the lowest ERA in the league in the 1960s, 1970s, 1980s, and they are a close second to the Braves in the 1990s. Since 1973 the Dodgers are far ahead of every team in the majors in lowest ERA and fewest runs allowed. They had their peak in 1929, the league's second highest scoring year ever. Their peak is only 8th on the peak list (Table 2-8), and not near the top 10 list. The Dodgers are behind only the Braves in ERA for the 1993-97 period, but the nearly 7 percent edge the Braves have in scoring gives the Braves many more wins.

Strikeouts--The Dodgers lead the majors in strikeouts since 1946, including the 1973-97 period. The Braves of the 1990s hold the top spots on the top 10 list, but the 1997 Dodgers are close behind (Table 2-25). The Braves (7.32) and Dodgers (7.06) are the only teams to average over 7.0 in the 1993-97 period.

Walks--The Dodgers easily lead the majors in fewest walks since 1973. But the 1946 peak in the high walk years of the 1940s makes the top 10 list (Table 2-27), and the Dodgers only ranked 8th for fewest walks in the 1993-97 period.

Strikeout-to-Walk Ratio--The Dodgers lead the majors in SO/W ratio since 1973, and their 1966 peak is the highest in major league history (Table 2-28). But high walks limited the Dodgers to 4th place in the 1993-97 period.

Table 3-19. Key Measures Summary for the Dodgers

	Per Game Peaks		Total Year Peaks		1993-97
	Per Game	Year	Total	Year	Per Game
Runs	6.16	1953	955	1953	4.43
Home Runs	1.34	1953	208	1953	0.96
Doubles	1.97	1930	303	1901	1.40
Bat Avg.	.304	1930	.304	1930	.263
ERA	4.92	1929	4.92	1929	3.68
Strikeouts	7.60	**1997**	1232	**1997**	7.06
Walks	4.27	1946	671	1946	3.30
SO/W Ratio	3.04	1966	3.04	1966	2.14

The Dodgers were a mediocre franchise before 1940. They won pennants in 1916 and 1920 with great pitching, but except for that period they lost far more often than they won. After 6 straight losing seasons between 1933 and 1938, the Dodgers suddenly came to life. They won the pennant in 1941, paused for WWII, started a revolution in 1947 with Jackie Robinson, and went on to become the most successful franchise in the league since WWII. They won 16 pennants between 1941 and 1988 and won 6 World Series titles after losing the first 7 times. They had 35 winning seasons in 40 years between 1939 and 1978, and they won 10 pennants and 4 Series titles in 20 years between 1947 and 1966.

The Dodgers had one of the best scoring teams in history between 1947 and 1956, and they won 6 pennants in 10 years. Since 1962 they have had the best pitching in the league, but their inability to score runs, especially since the early 1980s, has held them to one division title (1995) since 1988. Good pitching does always give you a chance to win, and their winning percentage remains high.

Table 3-20 shows a summary of the key measures for the Expos. Years from the 1990s are shown in boldface. Peak values and the years in which they occurred are shown on a per game and total year basis in the first two sets of columns in the table. The per game averages for each of the key measures from 1993 through 1997 are shown in the last column. The leaders for each measure from 1993 through 1997 are shown in Table 3-29.

Runs--Like most expansion teams, the Expos set their offensive peaks in the 1993-97 period. They peaked in runs per game (5.13) in 1994 when they had their best team in franchise history on a winning percentage basis. The Expos led the majors in winning percentage in 1994 and might have won their first division title outright if not for the strike. In the longer season of 1996 they tied their peak total runs mark from 1987. But they are near the bottom of the total year peak list (Table 2-2). The Expos ranked 6th in runs in the 1993-97 period.

Home Runs--The 1997 Expos soared above their previous per game peak in home runs, set only 3 years ago in their great year of 1994, and they climbed past 4 teams on the peak list (Table 2-4). Now in 9th place on the list, the Expos rank above 3 expansion teams and 2 original teams (Pirates and Cards). The 1997 Expos also topped their previous total year peak set in 1996. The Expos ranked only 8th in home runs in the 1993-97 period, but in 1997 they tied the Giants for 4th place in an unusual (for them) demonstration of power.

Doubles--In 1994 the Expos were just behind the 1994 Astros in hitting the most doubles per game in the National League since 1931 (Table 2-21). In the longer season of 1997, the Expos set their peak total year mark, becoming the only expansion team on the total year top 10 list and once again hitting the most total doubles in the league since 1931 (Table 2-21). The Expos led the National League in doubles during the 1993-97 period, as they and the Astros finished far ahead of all the other teams in the league. The Expos are nearly in a tie with the Pirates and Reds for first place in the league from 1973 through 1997.

Batting Average--The Expos set their peak batting average in their best winning percentage year of 1994, but all expansion teams except the Rockies rank well behind the original 8 teams on the peak list (Table 2-7) because the expansion teams did not play in the league's top batting average years between 1921 and 1930 (Table 1-7). The Expos were 8th in batting average in the league in the 1993-97 period.

ERA--The Expos, Astros, and Mets cluster just behind the Dodgers in lowest ERA and fewest runs allowed since 1973. The Expos peaked in ERA in their 2nd year of existence when they were still developing a pitching staff, and they are near the bottom (lowest peak) of the peak ERA list (Table 2-8). The Expos were 3rd in lowest ERA in the 1993-97 period behind the Braves and Dodgers. The Expos had some of their best pitching teams in this period, and that means they had exceptional pitching because they have a history of good pitching.

Strikeouts--The Expos set their per game and total year peaks in 1996. Both years make the top 10 league list for strikeouts (Table 2-25). The Expos ranked 5th in the league in strikeouts in the 1993-97 period.

Walks--As in ERA, the Expos peaked in walks in 1970, their 2nd year of existence. The 1970 Expos hold the all-time league record for total walks in a year (Table 2-27), but in the 1993-97 period the Expos issued the 3rd fewest walks in the league.

Strikeout-to-Walk Ratio--The 1994 Expos rank just behind the Dodgers for the best SO/W ratio in major league history (Table 2-28). The Expos were also 2nd behind the Braves for the highest SO/W ratio in the 1993-97 period.

Table 3-20. Key Measures Summary for the Expos

	Per Game Peaks		Total Year Peaks		1993-97
	Per Game	Year	Total	Year	Per Game
Runs	5.13	**1994**	741	87/**96**	4.55
Home Runs	1.06	**1997**	172	**1997**	0.90
Doubles	2.16	**1994**	339	**1997**	1.92
Bat Avg.	.278	**1994**	.278	**1994**	.262
ERA	4.50	1970	4.50	1970	3.83
Strikeouts	7.44	**1996**	1206	**1996**	6.77
Walks	4.42	1970	716	1970	3.01
SO/W Ratio	2.80	**1994**	2.89	**1994**	2.25

The Expos were born in 1969 in the second wave of expansion. They had poor teams in their first few years, but soon became competitive. They won a division title in the split season of 1981 even though they did not finish first overall. They beat the Phillies in a playoff for the division, and had a 2 games to none lead over the Dodgers in the best of 5 for the pennant. But the Dodgers won the 5th game 2-1 in snow flurries in Montreal. The Expos finally had another chance in 1994. They were 6 games ahead of the Braves at the time of the strike, and the Expos had a winning percentage of .649, the best in their history and the best in the major leagues that year. But the strike killed any opportunity for what was the franchise's best team to win a pennant.

The Expos did not (or could not) pay enough to keep the 1994 team together, and they finished last in the division in 1995. Their stubborn overachievers in 1996 finished 2nd to the powerful Braves, but the loss of more free agents produced a reality check in 1997 as they finished far back with a losing record.

Table 3-21 shows a summary of the key measures for the Giants. Years from the 1990s are shown in boldface. Peak values and the years in which they occurred are shown on a per game and total year basis in the first two sets of columns in the table. The per game averages for each of the key measures from 1993 through 1997 are shown in the last column. The leaders for each measure from 1993 through 1997 are shown in Table 3-29.

Runs--The prime years of dominance for the Giants came before 1954, and their prime offensive records were set before then as well. They set their runs peak in 1930 together with the league, and their per game peak (6.23) ranks 4th on the top 15 list while their total runs peak (959) ranks 6th (Table 2-17). The Giants led the National League in runs by a wide margin in the 1903-72 period, but they only rank 6th in the league since 1973. The Giants are the only one of the original 16 teams to score runs at a rate higher than the league average in every decade from 1903 through the 1980s, and although the Giants were only 5th in runs in the 1993-97 period, they are still 0.01 runs ahead of the league average for the decade of the 1990s from 1990 through 1997.

Home Runs--The 1947 Giants set the then all-time major league record for home runs on a per game and total year basis. This record was tied by the 1956 Reds as the league broke its records in the 1950s (Table 1-5). The 1961 Yankees set a new major league record, and the American League buried all its team and league records in the 1993-97 home run barrage. But the National League did not do the same. The 1947 Giants stayed at the top of the league list until the 1997 Rockies set new records (Table 2-19) 50 years later (and one mile higher). No other team has come close. The Giants led the league by a wide margin in home runs in the 1903-72 period, and are in a 3 way tie for 3rd in the 1973-97 period. The Giants were also 3rd in the league in home runs in the 1993-97 period.

Doubles--Unlike runs and home runs, the Giants were always near the bottom in doubles. Their 1928 peaks also are near the bottom on the league peak list (Table 2-6), and the Giants were 11th in doubles in the 1993-97 period.

Batting Average--The 1930 Giants had the highest batting average in major league history (Table 2-7). They were 3rd in the 1903-72 period, but tied for last from 1973 through 1997. They were also last in the 1993-97 period.

ERA--In addition to leading in runs and home runs in the National League in the 1903-72 period, the Giants had the lowest ERA in the major leagues during that time. It's not hard to understand why they were such a dominant team earlier in the century. But as in other measures, the Giants got worse in ERA as the century progressed, and they are 7th in the league from 1973 through 1997. Their peak ERA came in 1995 because in all other periods of high offense in league history the Giants had great pitching. Their peak is not high on the league list (Table 2-8), but in spite of their surprisingly good pitching (for them) in 1997, the Giants had the 4th highest ERA in the league in the 1993-97 period.

Strikeouts--The Giants were 2nd in strikeouts for the 1903-72 period, but they fell to 10th after 1973. Their 1965 peak is only 13th on the league list (Table 2-10), and they were 11th in the league in the 1993-97 period.

Walks--The 1946 Giants make the top 10 list for most walks per game (Table 2-27). They issued the 2nd fewest walks through 1945, but they fell to 6th place from 1946 through 1997. They were 9th in the 1993-97 period.

Strikeout-to-Walk Ratio--The Giants led the majors in SO/W ratio in the 1903-72 period, and the 1968 Giants rank 5th on the top 10 list for SO/W ratio (Table 2-28). But, following a familiar pattern, the Giants are 10th in the league from 1973 through 1997 and they ranked 12th in the 1993-97 period.

Table 3-21. Key Measures Summary for the Giants

	Per Game Peaks		Total Year Peaks		1993-97
	Per Game	Year	Total	Year	Per Game
Runs	6.23	1930	959	1930	4.68
Home Runs	1.43	1947	221	1947	1.03
Doubles	1.78	1928	276	1928	1.56
Bat Avg.	.319	1930	.319	1930	.258
ERA	4.86	**1995**	4.86	**1995**	4.31
Strikeouts	6.50	1965	1060	1965	5.98
Walks	4.29	1946	660	1946	3.31
SO/W Ratio	2.74	1968	2.74	1968	1.81

The Giants were the top franchise in baseball early in the century. They had 34 winning seasons in the 37 years from 1903 through 1939, the best record in baseball at the time, and they won 13 pennants and 4 Series titles during that period. They were passed by the Yankees as baseball's top franchise in the 1940s, and the Dodgers began to displace them in the league after WWII, but the Giants remained a top team until the 1970s. The Giants still lead the National League in lifetime winning percentage by a wide margin, but by 1981 the Dodgers had surpassed them in pennants and World Series wins.

The Giants won 3 pennants between 1951 and 1962, and they set a major league record with 5 straight 2nd place finishes between 1965 and 1969. But in the 1970s they became a mediocre franchise, and since 1973 their overall winning percentage is below .500. They revived in the 1986-90 period and won the 1989 pennant, and they had a great year in 1993 finishing 2nd to the Braves. New players in 1997 won a division title and may mark a new revival.

Table 3-22 shows a summary of the key measures for the Marlins. Years from the 1990s are shown in boldface. Peak values and the years in which they occurred are shown on a per game and total year basis in the first two sets of columns in the table. The per game averages for each of the key measures from 1993 through 1997 are shown in the last column. The leaders for each measure from 1993 through 1997 are shown in Table 3-29.

Runs--Because the Marlins were born in 1993, all of their peaks were set in the 1993-97 period. Also, two of their five years of existence (1994 and 1995) were shortened by the 1994 strike, so many of their per game and total year peaks are in different years. Their per game runs peak (4.71) was set in 1995 and their total year peak (740) in 1997. Both their per game and total year marks are last in the league peak list (Table 2-2). The Marlins were last in the league in runs by a wide margin in the 1993-97 period.

Home Runs--Although they are unable to score runs, the per game home run peak for the Marlins ranks ahead of the best the Pirates and Cards could do in the 95 years these two original teams have been in the league (Table 2-4). This is not because the Marlins hit a lot of home runs. This highlights the fact that the Pirates and Cards never were good home run teams. The Pirates did hit more total home runs than the Marlins, but two teams (Astros and Cards) rank below the low mark of the Marlins for this measure as well. The Marlins finished ahead of only the Phillies and Pirates in home runs in the 1993-97 period.

Doubles--The Marlins are dead last on the peak doubles list even though they set their peaks in 1997, the best year in their short history (Table 2-6). At least the 1997 Marlins were 7th in the league in doubles so they have a reasonable mark compared to other teams on the list. The Marlins were 13th in the league in doubles in the 1993-97 period, their peak in 1997 keeping them ahead of the Dodgers.

Batting Average--An inability to score runs usually infers a low team batting average, especially in the National League where there is no designated hitter to make up for a low batting average by bringing extra power to the lineup. The Marlins fit this scenario exactly. They are last on the league peak batting average list (Table 2-7) and were 13th in batting average in the 1993-97 period. The Giants were last, but both teams made the playoffs in 1997 with batting averages near their 1993-97 averages. So much for the importance of batting average.

ERA--The Marlins initially traded power for pitching in putting together their expansion team in 1993, and then they went for both when they spent heavily for free agents in assembling their best team in their World Series-winning team in 1997. Their peak ERA is next to last (best) in the league peak list (Table 2-8), and the 1997 Marlins had the 4th lowest ERA in the league as they moved into the playoffs for the first time. Overall, the Marlins had the 6th lowest ERA in the league in the 1993-97 period.

Strikeouts--The 1997 Marlins set the franchise peak for strikeouts, but they only ranked 8th on the league's peak list (Table 2-10) and the team only ranked 8th in the 1993-97 period. The 1997 Marlins did, however, make the top 10 list for total year strikeouts (Table 2-25).

Walks--The Marlins issued the highest number of walks in the league in the 1993-97 period, but they are low on the peak list (Table 2-12) because prior periods had much higher levels of walks in the league overall.

Strikeout-to-Walk Ratio--Because of their high walks, the Marlins are next to last on the league peak list for SO/W ratio (Table 2-13), and are next to last for the 1993-97 period. Only the Rockies were worse (much worse).

Table 3-22. Key Measures Summary for the Marlins

	Per Game Peaks		Total Year Peaks		1993-97
	Per Game	Year	Total	Year	Per Game
Runs	4.71	**1995**	740	**1997**	4.24
Home Runs	1.01	**1995**	150	**1996**	0.83
Doubles	1.68	**1997**	272	**1997**	1.49
Bat Avg.	.266	**1994**	.266	**1994**	.258
ERA	4.50	**1994**	4.50	**1994**	4.14
Strikeouts	7.33	**1997**	1188	**1997**	6.45
Walks	3.94	**1997**	639	**1997**	3.80
SO/W Ratio	1.86	**1997**	1.86	**1997**	1.70

The Marlins were born in 1993 at the beginning of the offensive explosion of the 1993-97 period. But their prime contribution to the offensive peak was to dilute a little further the pitching talent in the majors. In the 1993-97 period, the Marlins were worse than the league average in all the key measures except ERA. In all offensive measures the Marlins were not only below average, they were at or near the bottom of the league. But the Marlins were close to .500 in 1996, and by spending freely in the free agent market they assembled one of the best teams in the league in 1997. They won the World Series as a wild card, and they are no longer an "expansion team" in terms of performance on the field.

The Marlins confirmed that it is not necessary to wait many years to become competitive in today's baseball world if you are willing to spend enough money. The key question now is whether the franchise will continue to spend enough to keep their key players together and or replace them with players of equal talent who can keep the team competitive over the long term.

Table 3-23 shows a summary of the key measures for the Mets. Years from the 1990s are shown in boldface. Peak values and the years in which they occurred are shown on a per game and total year basis in the first two sets of columns in the table. The per game averages for each of the key measures from 1993 through 1997 are shown in the last column. The leaders for each measure from 1993 through 1997 are shown in Table 3-29.

Runs--The Mets were known primarily for pitching until the late 1980s when they had the best teams in franchise history in the 1985-89 period. These teams had good hitting as well as pitching, and the Mets set most of their offensive peaks in 1987, a year which at the time was the league's highest season for offense in nearly two decades. The per game runs peak (5.08) and the total runs peak (823) for the 1987 Mets rank 11th and 9th respectively on the league peak runs list (Table 2-2) because, as noted, the Mets generally have not been a high scoring team. This makes their peaks low compared to the other teams in the league. The Mets ranked 9th in the league in runs in the 1993-97 period.

Home Runs--The 1987 Mets also set franchise peaks for home runs. The Mets had good home run hitters in 1987 and their peaks rank 7th on the league peak list (Table 2-4), even though they are not near the top 10 list. But except for the Rockies, the 1987 Mets lead all of the league's expansion teams in peak home runs as well as 3 of the original 8 teams (Phillies, Pirates, and Cards). The Mets ranked 7th in home runs in the league in the 1993-97 period.

Doubles--The 1987 Mets also set franchise peaks in doubles. But the Mets have always ranked low in the league in doubles, and their peaks are 11th and 9th on the league peak list (Table 2-6), matching exactly their runs peaks. Not surprisingly, the Mets ranked 11th in the league in doubles in the 1993-97 period. This is even worse than it sounds because the last 4 teams in the league (Mets, Giants, Marlins, and Dodgers) were far below the league average and also far behind the first 10 teams in doubles.

Batting Average--The 1987 Mets also set the then franchise record for batting average at .268, which is a very low peak (the Mets are last in the league in batting average since 1973). The 1996 Mets set a new franchise peak at .270, but this average is still 13th on the league peak list (Table 2-7). The Mets were 12th in the league in batting average in the 1993-97 period.

ERA--The Mets peaked in their first year of existence while playing in the old Polo Grounds and setting the all-time major league record for losses (120). But this peak is only 7th on the league's peak list (Table 2-8), and 7 years later the 1969 Mets won the World Series behind Tom Seaver who won the league's MVP and Cy Young awards. Pitching remained the primary strength for the Mets, and the Mets, Astros, and Expos cluster behind the Dodgers for fewest runs allowed and lowest ERA since 1973. The Mets had the 5th lowest ERA in the league in the 1993-97 period.

Strikeouts--The Mets trail only the Dodgers and Astros for most strikeouts since 1973, and the 1990 Mets make the top 10 list (Table 2-25). But the Mets were 13th in the league in the 1993-97 period with a staff of control pitchers.

Walks--The Mets peaked with a bad team in 1983, but they are last (best) on the league peak list (Table 2-12). They are 3rd in fewest walks since 1973 and they led the league in fewest walks in the 1993-97 period.

Strikeout-to-Walk Ratio--The Mets are 2nd to the Dodgers in SO/W ratio since 1973, and their 1990 peak is 4th on the top 10 list (Table 2-28). But they ranked only 7th in the league in the 1993-97 period because their low level of walks couldn't make up for their greatly reduced level of strikeouts.

Table 3-23. Key Measures Summary for the Mets

	Per Game Peaks		Total Year Peaks		1993-97
	Per Game	Year	Total	Year	Per Game
Runs	5.08	1987	823	1987	4.52
Home Runs	1.19	1987	192	1987	0.95
Doubles	1.77	1987	287	1987	1.54
Bat Avg.	.270	**1996**	.270	**1996**	.259
ERA	5.04	1962	5.04	1962	4.05
Strikeouts	7.51	**1990**	1217	**1990**	5.90
Walks	3.80	1983	615	1983	2.96
SO/W Ratio	2.74	**1990**	2.74	**1990**	1.99

The Mets and Astros were born in 1962 as the first two expansion teams in the National League. The 1962 Mets proceeded to tarnish the term "expansion team." They set a major league record with 120 losses, had the league's 2nd lowest winning percentage in the century, and in their first 5 years they also had the league's 2nd lowest winning percentage for a 5 year period. Their first winning season was 1969, but the "Miracle Mets" went on to win the pennant and the World Series that year. They also won the pennant in 1973, but then they had another decade as a big loser before becoming the best team in baseball in the 1985-89 period with another pennant and World Series title in 1986.

But after winning their division in 1988, the Mets began another slide down to mediocrity. By 1991 they had a losing record, and they had the worst winning percentage in the major leagues in 1993. The Mets primarily have been an "all or nothing" team since their birth, but their 1990s dip to the bottom may be one of their briefest if their 1997 improvement means they are on the way back up.

Table 3-24 shows a summary of the key measures for the Padres. Years from the 1990s are shown in boldface. Peak values and the years in which they occurred are shown on a per game and total year basis in the first two sets of columns in the table. The per game averages for each of the key measures from 1993 through 1997 are shown in the last column. The leaders for each measure from 1993 through 1997 are shown in Table 3-29.

Runs--In spite of the pennant they won in 1984, the Padres were consistent losers from their birth in 1969 through the early 1990s, and they were easily the worst team in the league over that period. New ownership and new players gave them a division title in 1996, and many of their positive peaks came in 1996. They set runs peaks in 1996, but then broke them in 1997. Their per game runs peak (4.96) ranks 13th and their total runs peak (804) ranks 11th on the league list (Table 2-2) because the Padres were so bad for so long (the Padres are last in the league in runs since 1973). Thanks to their better offense in 1996 and 1997, the Padres ranked 8th in the league in runs in the 1993-97 period.

Home Runs--The 1970 Padres, in their 2nd year, finished dead last in what would become their usual spot. But in a high offense year (the next year as high for the league would be 1987), the Padres finished 3rd in the league in home runs behind big Nate Colbert (a potential twin to Cecil Fielder). This peak is 10th on the league peak list (Table 2-4). The Padres are also 10th in the league in home runs since 1973, but they moved up to 9th in the 1993-97 period.

Doubles--The only reason the Padres are not last on the league list since 1973 is because no team in baseball hits as few doubles as do the Dodgers. But the peak year of the 1996 Padres ranks 13th on the league per game peak list (Table 2-6) because the Dodgers hit their peak in 1930. Once again, in spite of their past history at the bottom, the Padres ranked 9th in the league in doubles in the 1993-97 period.

Batting Average--The 1994 Padres set the franchise peak at .275, a mark the much better 1996 team could not match. The Padres are 9th in batting average since 1973, and their batting average peak ranks 12th on the league peak list (Table 2-7). But as the Padres improved their offense in the 1993-97 period, their team batting average improved substantially. They ranked 3rd in the league in batting average during that time (Table 3-29).

ERA--The Padres set their original peak in 1974, a year not long after their birth, and a year in which their pitching staff just missed issuing a league record number of walks. But the 1997 Padres fell on hard times after their division title in 1996, and the hard times were due mainly to their pitching. Thus, the 1997 Padres topped the 1974 staff for peak ERA. Their peak ranks 8th on the league peak list (Table 2-8), but it is still well below the top 10 list. In spite of their 1997 peak, the Padres were exactly in the middle of the league in 7th place for ERA in the 1993-97 period.

Strikeouts--The Padres were next to last in strikeouts since 1973 when they assembled a staff of strikeout pitchers in 1974. The 1996 Padres just edged the 1974 Padres for the franchise peak, and the 1996 Padres made the top 10 list (Table 2-25). Thus, the Padres were 4th in strikeouts in the 1993-97 period.

Walks--The 1974 Padres rank 4th in most walks per game and 2nd in total walks on the top 10 list (Table 2-27). The Padres continued the trend in the 1990s by issuing the 4th highest number of walks in the 1993-97 period.

Strikeout-to-Walk Ratio--The Padres are next to last in SO/W ratio since 1973, but their 1996 SO/W ratio peak moved them up to 10th on the league peak list (Table 2-13), and they were 6th in the league in the 1993-97 period.

Table 3-24. Key Measures Summary for the Padres

	Per Game Peaks		Total Year Peaks		1993-97
	Per Game	Year	Total	Year	Per Game
Runs	4.91	**1997**	795	**1997**	4.52
Home Runs	1.06	1970	172	1970	0.88
Doubles	1.76	**1996**	285	**1996**	1.65
Bat Avg.	.275	**1994**	.275	**1994**	.267
ERA	4.98	**1997**	4.98	**1997**	4.23
Strikeouts	7.37	**1996**	1194	**1996**	6.89
Walks	4.41	1974	715	1974	3.43
SO/W Ratio	2.36	**1996**	2.36	**1996**	2.01

The Padres were born in 1969 and even for an expansion team they had very poor winning percentages from the start. They have the lowest lifetime winning percentage in the league, including the Marlins and the Rockies. The Padres had only one winning season in their first 13 years, and it was not until the 1982-86 period that they were able to sustain an average winning percentage above .500 over a 5 year period (they averaged .507 in the period). But they won a division title and converted it into a pennant in 1984, a claim only 4 of the other 11 expansion teams can make. Unfortunately, the only thing the Padres have won since 1984 is a division title in 1996 that they did not convert to a pennant.

The Padres have been both an artistic and financial failure since they were born, but with new ownership and better (more expensive) players they hoped their division title in 1996 marked a new start towards respectability. However, the Padres had a winning percentage of only .469 in 1997. Winning consistently over a period of years is still a goal for the future.

Table 3-25 shows a summary of the key measures for the Phillies. Years from the 1990s are shown in boldface. Peak values and the years in which they occurred are shown on a per game and total year basis in the first two sets of columns in the table. The per game averages for each of the key measures from 1993 through 1997 are shown in the last column. The leaders for each measure from 1993 through 1997 are shown in Table 3-29.

Runs--The Phillies played in tiny Baker Bowl during the peak offensive year of 1930, and although they gave up runs at a much higher rate than they scored them, they had big hitters who could produce lots of runs. Their per game runs peak (6.05) and total year peak (944) both make the top 15 list (Table 2-17). The 1929 Phillies also make the list. In spite of the 1930 big bang, for much of the century the Phillies had terrible teams and they were next to last in the league in scoring runs from 1903 through 1972. When Mike Schmidt and company arrived later in the 1970s, the Phillies became league leaders in scoring runs and they now rank second in the league in runs since 1973. They had a great scoring team when they won the 1993 pennant, but 1996 was ugly and 1997 was nearly much worse until a second half turnaround got 1997 a little above the poor 1996 level. As a result, the Phillies were 10th in runs in the 1993-97 period.

Home Runs--The Phillies were second in home runs before WWII in Baker Bowl, and they rank 6th in the league since 1973. But between WWII and 1972 they were next to last. They set their peak behind Mike Schmidt in 1976 when they won the first of 3 straight division titles. They rank 8th on the league peak list (Table 2-4), and are far from the top 10 list. With their bad years in 1996 and 1997, they fell to last in the league in home runs in the 1993-97 period.

Doubles--The 1930 Phillies hit enough doubles off the short right field wall in Baker Bowl to rank 3rd on the top 10 list (Table 2-21). The 1932 Phillies also make the list. The Phillies ranked 3rd in the league in doubles before WWI, and they rank 4th thereafter including the period since 1973. The Phillies were close to form by ranking 4th in the league in doubles in the 1993-97 period.

Batting Average--The most amazing thing about the 1930 Phillies is that they had a batting average of .315 for the season and still finished second to the Giants. The 1930 Phillies also are second to the Giants on the league top 10 list (Table 2-22). The Phillies rank 4th in the league since 1973, but they ranked 10th in batting average in the 1993-97 period.

ERA--The Baker Bowl Phillies hold 5 of the top 8 spots on the top 10 list for peak ERA (Table 2-23), and the 1997 Phillies looked like they would make the list as well until their amazing turnaround. The 1930 Phillies set the all-time major league record for peak ERA, and not even the terrible Tigers of 1996 are close, even though the Tigers served them up to designated hitters. The Phillies were dead last in the league in ERA from 1903 through 1972, and they are next to last since 1973. They were 10th in ERA in the 1993-97 period.

Strikeouts--Even with their terrible ERAs, the Phillies usually ranked near the middle of the league in strikeouts. The 1997 Phillies set their peak behind the great performance of Curt Schilling. The 1997 Phillies make the top 10 list (Table 2-25), and the Phillies were 6th overall in the 1993-97 period.

Walks--The Phillies are last (highest) in the league in the 1903-45 period, first in the 1946-72 period, and last since 1973. Their peaks make the top 10 list (Table 2-27), and they were 3rd in issuing the most walks in the 1993-97 period.

Strikeout-to-Walk Ratio--With moderate strikeouts and high walks, the Phillies are 9th on the peak SO/W ratio list (Table 2-13), and far from the top 10 list. They also ranked 9th in the league in the 1993-97 period.

Table 3-25. Key Measures Summary for the Phillies

| | Per Game Peaks | | Total Year Peaks | | 1993-97 |
	Per Game	Year	Total	Year	Per Game
Runs	6.05	1930	944	1930	4.47
Home Runs	1.15	1977	186	1977	0.77
Doubles	2.21	1930	345	1930	1.76
Bat Avg.	.315	1930	.315	1930	.262
ERA	6.71	1930	6.71	1930	4.27
Strikeouts	7.46	**1997**	1209	**1997**	6.74
Walks	4.44	1928	682	1974	3.50
SO/W Ratio	2.40	1967	2.40	1967	1.93

Before WWII, the Phillies vied with the Braves and Browns for the title of the worst franchise in baseball. The Phillies won the 1915 pennant behind Grover Cleveland Alexander, and they also were second 3 times in the 1913-17 period. But after 1917 they had 30 losing seasons in 31 years, with only 1932 at .506 keeping them from having 31 straight losing seasons. They had the worst ERA in the league, and when they moved from Baker Bowl (which literally collapsed) to Shibe Park in 1938, they became last in runs also. In the 1938-42 period, they set the major league record for lowest winning percentage (.296) over 5 years.

New ownership rescued the franchise after WWII, and the Phillies won the 1950 pennant. They had many poor teams after that, but finally had great success between 1976 and 1983 with 5 division titles, 2 pennants, and their only World Series win in 1980. They declined again, but rose from last in 1992 to win the 1993 pennant. Then they fell to just over .400 in 1996 and 1997, and 1997 could have been much worse. Franchise stability is still a long way off.

Table 3-26 shows a summary of the key measures for the Pirates. Years from the 1990s are shown in boldface. Peak values and the years in which they occurred are shown on a per game and total year basis in the first two sets of columns in the table. The per game averages for each of the key measures from 1993 through 1997 are shown in the last column. The leaders for each measure from 1993 through 1997 are shown in Table 3-29.

Runs--The Pirates rank 3rd in the league in scoring runs both before and after 1973. They peaked in run scoring in the league's peak period of 1926 through 1930. Their per game peak (5.96) and total runs peak (912) both make the top 15 league list (Table 2-17). The 1929 and 1930 Pirates also make the list for both per game and total year runs, making the Pirates the only franchise in the league to have 3 teams on both lists. But the reputation of the Pirates for being a team that consistently scores runs at a high level suffered in the 1990s as the Pirates ranked 13th in scoring runs in the 1993-97 period.

Home Runs--The Pirates are only 6th in the league for the 1903-45 and 1946-72 periods, and although they left spacious Forbes Field for Three Rivers Stadium in 1970, they rank 8th since 1973. Their modest 1.00 per game peak came in 1947 when left field in Forbes Field was shortened by 30 feet for Hank Greenberg and Ralph Kiner. Greenberg hit 25 home runs in his last year, and Kiner hit 51 to tie for the league lead. The Pirates finished 2nd to the Giants (who set the then all-time league record in 1947), but the Pirates never did as well again. The 1966 Pirates set the total year peak with 2 more home runs in 6 more games. The 1947 per game peak is next to last on the league peak list (Table 2-4), and the Pirates were 13th in home runs in the 1993-97 period.

Doubles--The Pirates ranked 4th in the league in doubles in the 1903-72 period, and they set their per game doubles peak in 1925 when they set their runs peak. The Pirates rank 1st in the league since 1973, and the 1996 Pirates edged the 1925 Pirates for the total year peak. Both teams make the top 10 total year list (Table 2-21). The Pirates were 3rd in the league in the 1993-97 period.

Batting Average--In the 1903-72 period the Pirates led the majors in batting average, and the Pirates are tied for the lead in the league since 1973. Their 1928 peak is 4th on the top 10 list, but the 1922, 1925, and 1927 teams also make the list (Table 2-22). The Pirates are the only franchise in the majors to have 4 teams on the list. But they were 7th in batting average in the 1993-97 period.

ERA--The Pirates peaked in the league's peak year of 1930, and the 1930 (and 1953) Pirates make the top 10 list (Table 2-23). The Pirates are 4th in the 1903-72 period, and 6th since 1973. The large dimensions of Forbes Field helped, but the Pirates also had a lot of good teams before and after WWII. Their worst pitching on a sustained basis came in the early 1950s when left field was still shortened and the franchise had its worst teams. But they were nearly as bad in the 1993-97 period as they had the 2nd highest ERA in the league.

Strikeouts--The Pirates ranked relatively low in the league in strikeouts in all parts of the century. Their 1969 peak is 11th on the peak list (Table 2-10) and not near the top 10 list. The Pirates were 10th in the 1993-97 period.

Walks--The Pirates led the majors in fewest walks issued in the 1903-45 period, were 5th in the majors in the 1946-72 period, and are 4th in the league since 1973. Their peak years are low (good) on the league peak list (Table 2-12), and they were 6th in issuing the fewest walks in the 1993-97 period.

Strikeout-to-Walk Ratio--With low strikeouts and low walks, the Pirates stayed in the middle of the league over the century. Their 1991 peak is 11th on the league peak list (Table 2-13), and they were 10th in the 1993-97 period.

Table 3-26. Key Measures Summary for the Pirates

	Per Game Peaks		Total Year Peaks		1993-97
	Per Game	Year	Total	Year	Per Game
Runs	5.96	1925	912	1925	4.42
Home Runs	1.00	1947	158	1966	0.78
Doubles	2.07	1925	319	**1996**	1.77
Bat Avg.	.309	1928	.309	1928	.263
ERA	5.24	1930	5.24	1930	4.60
Strikeouts	6.94	1969	1124	1969	6.00
Walks	4.00	1950	625	1970	3.19
SO/W Ratio	2.29	**1991**	2.29	**1991**	1.88

The Pirates had 35 winning seasons in the 43 years from 1903 through 1945, the next best record in the majors behind the 36 posted by the Giants. But the Pirates are not thought of as the 2nd best franchise in baseball in that period because they won only 4 pennants and 2 World Series titles. The Pirates fell to the worst team in the league in the early 1950s, but they came back quickly to win the 1960 pennant. They had great teams in the 1970s with 6 division titles, and they won 3 straight division titles beginning in 1990. But of the 9 division titles they have won since 1970, they could convert only 2 into pennants. They have, however, won the Series 5 of the 7 times they advanced that far.

Unable to pay the salaries needed to keep the 1990-92 group together, the team became a candidate to move and by 1997 consisted of unknowns. Although the players consistently overachieved, especially in 1997, the Pirates did not have a winning season in the 1993-97 period and were last in winning percentage at .454. The franchise is clearly at a critical point in its long history.

Table 3-27 shows a summary of the key measures for the Reds. Years from the 1990s are shown in boldface. Peak values and the years in which they occurred are shown on a per game and total year basis in the first two sets of columns in the table. The per game averages for each of the key measures from 1993 through 1997 are shown in the last column. The leaders for each measure from 1993 through 1997 are shown in Table 3-29.

Runs--The Reds have the oldest runs peak in the majors. The 1903 Reds averaged 5.43 runs per game, and no franchise team has been able to top it since even though the Reds lead the league in scoring since 1973. This record is a little less astounding when it is realized that 1903 ranks 6th on the highest runs list for the National League (Table 1-4). Lots of runs were scored in 1903 even if it is in the "dead ball" period (the Reds actually finished 2nd to the Pirates in runs that year). The peak total runs record for the Reds came in the 1970s when the Big Red Machine was on the prowl. The 1976 Reds set the franchise high with 857 runs in the longer season. Both marks are 8th on the peak list (Table 2-2), but neither is near the top 15 list. The Reds had their lowest scoring year in the decade of the 1990s in 1997, but they still maintained their league lead since 1973 by ranking 3rd in runs in the 1993-97 period.

Home Runs--The Reds were last in the league in home runs in the 1903-45 period because what became Crosley Field was a pitcher's park and home runs were difficult for everyone. But dramatic changes in the park that favored hitters moved the Reds up to 3rd in the league in the 1946-72 period, and the Reds continued to feature big hitters after they became a top home run team in the 1950s. They are 2nd in the league in home runs since 1973 even after moving to Riverfront Stadium in 1970. The 1956 Reds tied the league record of the 1947 Giants both for most home runs per game and most total home runs. Those records stood until 1997 when the Rockies broke all prior league records. The Reds and Giants now remain tied behind the Rockies (Table 2-19). The Reds were 4th in home runs in the 1993-97 period.

Doubles--The Reds were next to last in doubles in the 1903-45 period, but 2nd in the 1946-72 and 1973-97 periods (they lead the league in doubles since 1946). But their per game peak is 8th on the peak list (Table 2-6) and their total peak is 12th. The Reds were 6th in doubles in the 1993-97 period.

Batting Average--The Reds have the oldest peak in batting average in the league, and are one of three original teams never to exceed .300 (Table 2-7). They rank 3rd in the league since 1973, and were 4th in the 1993-97 period.

ERA--The Reds are 5th in the league in ERA before 1973 and 8th after. Their peak came in the league's highest scoring year of 1930, and although it is 6th on the peak list (Table 2-8), it is not on the top 10 list. The strength of the Reds in the last 5 decades has been scoring runs rather than pitching, but their ERA was in the middle of the league in 7th place for the 1993-97 period.

Strikeouts--The Reds were next to last in the 1903-45 period but moved up to 4th since 1973. Their 1997 peaks are 9th on the league peak list (Table 2-10), but they are not on the top 10 list. The Reds were 7th in the 1993-97 period.

Walks--The Reds had the 3rd fewest walks in the 1903-45 period, but fell to 8th since 1973. They peaked during the same period the league peaked, and are 9th on the league peak list (Table 2-12). But they are far from the top 10. They were 7th in fewest walks in the 1993-97 period.

Strikeout-to-Walk Ratio--The Reds moved up to 5th since 1973 as strikeouts increased more rapidly than walks. Their 1964 peak is 7th on the league peak list (Table 2-13), and they were 5th in the 1993-97 period.

Table 3-27. Key Measures Summary for the Reds

	Per Game Peaks		Total Year Peaks		1993-97
	Per Game	Year	Total	Year	Per Game
Runs	5.43	1903	857	1976	4.75
Home Runs	1.43	1956	221	1956	1.02
Doubles	1.92	**1995**	284	**1990**	1.73
Bat Avg.	.296	1922	.296	1922	.266
ERA	5.08	1930	5.08	1930	4.21
Strikeouts	7.15	**1997**	1159	**1997**	6.65
Walks	4.10	1949	640	1949	3.22
SO/W Ratio	2.57	1964	2.57	1964	2.06

The Reds were a mediocre franchise before WWII. They did win 3 pennants and 2 World Series titles (including a 1919 win over the "Black Sox"), but their best teams did not come until 1939 and 1940 when they won back-to-back pennants. They became a big hitting team after WWII, and they also became a much more successful (and interesting) franchise. In the 1970s they won 6 division titles, 4 pennants, and 2 World Series titles as the Big Red Machine led the league in scoring runs. They also won isolated pennants in 1961 and 1990, winning their 5th World Series title in 1990.

The Reds are just behind the Dodgers in average winning percentage in the league since 1973, and in spite of the great success of the Braves in the 1990s, the Reds lead the league with 3 World Series wins over that period as well. They also have a big lead in the league in runs since 1973, although no one is near the Rockies since 1993. In spite of recent erratic management at the top, the last 3 decades have definitely been the best in the history of the franchise.

Table 3-28 shows a summary of the key measures for the Rockies. Years from the 1990s are shown in boldface. Peak values and the years in which they occurred are shown on a per game and total year basis in the first two sets of columns in the table. The per game averages for each of the key measures from 1993 through 1997 are shown in the last column. The leaders for each measure from 1993 through 1997 are shown in Table 3-29.

Runs--The Rockies were born in 1993 and their peak marks were set in the 1993-97 period by definition. The Rockies became the top offensive team in the league by 1995 and set their offensive peaks in 1996 and 1997. The 1996 Rockies are 8th on a per game basis on the top 15 league list and 4th on a total runs basis (Table 2-17). The 1996 Rockies scored more runs per game than anyone since the 1953 Dodgers, and they scored more total runs than any league team since 1930. It seems only a matter of time before they break the all-time league record of 1004. The 1997 Rockies just missed being the first National League team to lead the majors in scoring since the 1976 Reds. The Rockies easily led the league in scoring in the 1993-97 as their 5.33 per game rate was 16 percent above the league average.

Home Runs--The 1997 Rockies broke the league record both for home runs per game and total home runs (Table 2-19). The franchise became the only one in the National League to appear 3 times on the per game list as the 1997 Rockies pushed the 1966 Braves off the list. But in another decade the Rockies could well occupy all 10 places on the top ten list both for per game and total year home runs. The Rockies easily led the league in home runs in the 1993-97 period, and their rate of 1.23 per game was a huge 31 percent above the league average. This was in spite of an expected poor start in 1993 and 1994. The Rockies averaged 1.41 home runs per game between 1995 and 1997.

Doubles--As has been noted many times in this book, teams that hit a lot of home runs often hit relatively few doubles (they hit them over the wall rather than against the wall). The Rockies fit this pattern as well. Their 1996 peak is 9th on the league list (Table 2-6) and not near the top 10 list. But the Rockies were still 5th in the league in doubles in the 1993-97 period.

Batting Average--The peak for the Rockies leads all expansion teams, but it is only 9th on the league peak list because the batting averages of the 1920s are unlikely ever to be repeated (Table 2-7). In the 1993-97 period, the Rockies led the league in batting average by 17 percentage points, and in the majors only the Indians and Yankees had a higher average than the Rockies over that period.

ERA--As is often the case, the Rockies are as bad in pitching as they are good in hitting. The Rockies have 3 spots on the top 10 list and the Phillies have 5 (Table 2-23). It is probable that the Rockies will continue to add teams to the list, but they will probably not top the 1929 and 1930 Phillies. The Rockies easily had the highest ERA in the league in the 1993-97 period.

Strikeouts--Consistent with their poor pitching, the peak for the Rockies is last on the league peak list (Table 2-10) and last in the majors as well. The Rockies were also last in the league in the 1993-97 period.

Walks--The Rockies are low (favorable) on the league peak list (Table 2-12) because the other teams have had higher peak years in prior peak league periods. But the Rockies issued the 2nd highest number of walks in the 1993-97 period.

Strikeout-to-Walk Ratio--Low strikeouts and high walks produce low SO/W ratios. The Rockies are dead last in the majors on the peak list (Table 2-13) and also last in the league in the 1993-97 period. The Rockies are nearly as far below the league average in SO/W ratio as they are above it in home runs.

Table 3-28. Key Measures Summary for the Rockies

	Per Game Peaks		Total Year Peaks		1993-97
	Per Game	Year	Total	Year	Per Game
Runs	5.93	**1996**	961	**1996**	5.33
Home Runs	1.48	**1997**	239	**1997**	1.23
Doubles	1.83	**1996**	297	**1996**	1.75
Bat Avg.	.288	**1997**	.288	**1997**	.281
ERA	5.59	**1996**	5.59	**1996**	5.27
Strikeouts	6.19	**1995**	932	**1996**	5.79
Walks	3.85	**1996**	624	**1996**	3.70
SO/W Ratio	1.74	**1995**	1.74	**1995**	1.57

The Rockies have been an artistic and financial success since their birth in 1993. After 5 years the novelty of arcade baseball one mile up has worn off a little, but the Rockies continue to break offensive and attendance records. The 1995 Rockies set a record for winning percentage for an expansion team in only its 3rd year, and they made the playoffs. But although they had winning seasons, their 1996 and 1997 teams did not make the playoffs. As has been proven over and over again, one dimensional teams can win games but not titles.

Playing one mile up is not the only reason the Rockies are one dimensional. Focusing primarily on offense is also a problem. The Yankees were known as the "Bronx Bombers" when they dominated baseball for almost 4 decades, but the Yankees led the majors in pitching and defense more often than in offense. If the Rockies do not use as high a level of energy and resources in accumulating pitchers as they do in accumulating hitters, they will continue to be highly entertaining, but they will rarely, if ever, get to the World Series.

Table **3-29** shows the three top leaders from each league for the key measures in the 1993-97 period. All measures are shown on a per game basis.

Runs--The Indians, Yankees, and Mariners led the American League in runs while the Rockies, Astros, and Reds led the National League. The Rockies are close to the American League leaders, but the Astros and Reds are much farther behind the leader than is the case in the American League. This confirms the great difference between the Rockies and the rest of the National League. All the leaders in runs in the 1993-97 period except the Yankees ranked low in their league in runs between 1973 and 1992. The Mariners were last in this period and the Indians and Astros next to last (the Rockies did not exist).

Home Runs--The Mariners, Indians, and Orioles led the American League and the majors. The Rockies easily led the National League and were 19 percent above the 3rd place Giants while the Mariners in the American League were only 9 percent above the 3rd place Orioles. The Orioles are the only team among the leaders to also rank high in home runs between 1973 and 1992. The Indians were next to last before 1993 and the Mariners were 8th.

Doubles--The Red Sox led the majors in doubles in the 1993-97 period as they have done since 1946. The Yankees and Indians (one of the lowest teams in doubles since 1946) were not far behind the Red Sox. The Expos and Astros in the National League were also close to the Red Sox, but the 3rd place Pirates (and the rest of the National League) were far behind. The Expos were 3rd in the 1973-92 period, but the Astros were 8th before surging in the 1993-97 period.

Batting Average--The top 3 American League leaders have been in the top half of the league since 1973. The Rockies compare well to the American League leaders, but the Astros and Padres are far behind. It is notable that the Astros are among the league leaders in runs, doubles, and batting average in the 1993-97 period after being next to last in the league in runs in the 1973-92 period.

ERA--The 3 American League leaders are the only teams in the league to have ERAs above 5.00 in the 1993-97 period, and they also had the 3 lowest winning percentages in the league in the period (Table 4-2). In the National League, the Pirates had the league's lowest winning percentage to match their high ERA. The Cubs had a winning percentage of only .470, but the Rockies were a respectable .485. The Rockies can be expected to always lead the league in ERA whether they have a winning record or not. The unprecedented game of arcade baseball in Denver requires a new look at statistical relationships.

Strikeouts--The 3 leaders in the American League also are among the top 4 teams in the league in strikeouts since 1973, with the Mariners in first place since that time. In the National League the Dodgers and Astros lead the league and the majors in strikeouts since 1973. But the Braves were 10th in the league in strikeouts from 1973 through 1992 before becoming the strikeout leaders in the league and the majors in the 1993-97 period.

Walks--The A's issued a lot of walks because they had bad pitchers. But the Mariners and Blue Jays had power pitchers with lots of strikeouts who tend to issue a lot of walks. The Rockies had the league's worst pitchers and the Phillies had a mix of bad pitchers and strikeout pitchers. But the Marlins were below the league average in ERA and strikeouts. They just issued a lot of walks.

Strikeout-to-Walk Ratio--Of the 6 leaders in SO/W ratio, only the Braves and Astros were also among the strikeout leaders. The Braves had a ratio 9 percent higher than that of the Expos and 36 percent higher than that of the Indians. This was because the Braves matched the highest level of strikeouts with the 2nd lowest level of walks in the majors in the 1993-97 period.

Table 3-29. Key Measures Leaders for 1993-97 Period

	American League		National League	
	Team	Per Game	Team	Per Game
Runs	Indians	5.60	Rockies	5.33
	Yankees	5.41	Astros	4.86
	Mariners	5.40	Reds	4.75
Home Runs	Mariners	1.35	Rockies	1.23
	Indians	1.30	Braves	1.14
	Orioles	1.24	Giants	1.03
Doubles	Red Sox	2.02	Expos	1.92
	Yankees	1.93	Astros	1.91
	Indians	1.93	Pirates	1.77
Bat Avg.	Indians	.287	Rockies	.281
	Yankees	.284	Astros	.268
	White Sox	.277	Padres	.267
ERA	Tigers	5.29	Rockies	5.27
	Twins	5.29	Pirates	4.60
	A's	5.06	Cubs	4.32
Strikeouts	Mariners	6.90	Braves	7.32
	Blue Jays	6.65	Dodgers	7.06
	Red Sox	6.39	Astros	6.90
Walks	A's	4.09	Marlins	3.80
	Mariners	3.92	Rockies	3.70
	Blue Jays	3.88	Phillies	3.50
SO/W Ratio	Indians	1.81	Braves	2.46
	Yankees	1.80	Expos	2.25
	Orioles	1.80	Astros	2.18

Part IV
The Future

Key Measures Since the DH

Table 4-1 shows the key measures for the leagues before and after 1973, the year the designated hitter was born. The ratios of the higher league value to the lower league value for the 1973-97 period are shown in the last column. These data form the baseline for making projections about the future.

Runs--The AL scored 2.3 percent more runs per game than the NL in the 1903-72 period due to the edge the AL had in the 1930s (Figure 1-1). Since 1973 the AL has scored 7.8 percent (ratio of 1.078) more runs than the NL, and the AL increased its margin to 9.9 percent in the 1993-97 period (Figure 1-1). In spite of the 1993-97 outburst, the NL has scored fewer runs since 1973 than in the 1903-72 period even though the earlier period includes the "dead ball" era.

Home Runs--Contrary to most perceptions, the NL hit more home runs per game than the American League from 1903 through 1972. The NL edge over the AL was 4.1 percent. However, since 1973, the AL has hit 17.3 percent (ratio of 1.173) more home runs than the NL. Further, as shown in Figure 1-2 and Table 1-5, the AL continues to set new records while the NL has not been able to top its peaks of the 1950s. With the advent of the Rockies and arcade baseball in Denver, the NL may be able eventually to top its records of the 1950s, but they will stay well behind the AL as long as the DH exists only in the AL.

Doubles--Both leagues remained close in doubles and both increased their rate of doubles after 1973, but the AL increased its edge over the NL from 2.7 percent in the 1903-72 period to 3.9 percent (ratio of 1.039) after 1973. Both leagues also had some of their best years in doubles in the 1990s, but both were still well behind their all-time peaks of the 1930s (Table 1-6).

Batting Average--The NL just barely led the AL in batting average in the 1903-72 period, but the AL is well ahead since 1973. The AL also increased its average after 1973 even though the 1903-72 period includes the record peaks of the 1920s. The NL declined by a substantial 6 percentage points after 1973.

ERA--AL ERAs are higher in each period because AL runs are higher. But the AL ERA increase is greater than its runs increase, and the NL had an ERA increase with a decline in runs. This is because all runs after an error fails to end an inning are "unearned." Fewer errors mean a higher percentage of earned runs and a higher ERA. AL earned runs as a percentage of runs increased from 84.4 percent in the 1903-72 period to 90.6 percent since 1973. The NL went from 84.1 percent to 89.2 percent (the NL commits more errors than the AL).

Strikeouts--The NL leads by 6.9 percent since 1973 after the AL led by 1.8 percent in the 1903-72 period. The AL increased by 33 percent and the NL by 44 percent after 1973 as the style of play changed to the big swing at all times in the count. Both leagues set all-time records in the 1990s (Table 1-9).

Walks--The AL has led the NL in walks for nearly the full century. But although the AL is nearly constant before and after 1973, the NL has increased by 8 percent since 1973. However, the AL still issues 3.1 percent more walks.

Strikeout-to-Walk Ratio--The NL has been the consistent leader with lower walks and nearly the same or higher strikeouts. The AL hit its peaks before the DH, but the NL approached record highs in the 1990s (Table 1-11).

Table 4-1. Key Measures Comparison Since the DH

| | 1903-72 | | 1973-97 | | 1973-97 |
	AL	NL	AL	NL	Ratio
Runs	4.37	4.27	4.53	4.20	1.078
Home Runs	0.51	0.53	0.88	0.75	1.173
Doubles	1.44	1.41	1.57	1.51	1.039
Bat Avg.	.262	.263	.264	.257	1.027
ERA	3.69	3.59	4.10	3.75	1.095
Strikeouts	3.99	3.92	5.29	5.66	1.069
Walks	3.34	3.00	3.35	3.25	1.031
SO/W Ratio	1.23	1.32	1.58	1.74	1.105

The data in Table 4-1 show that the leagues were very similar in the 1903-72 period. The biggest difference was in walks. The AL issued 11.6 percent more walks than the NL and as a result the NL was higher in SO/W ratio by 7.3 percent. The DH was created in 1973 to stop the decline in runs that started in the late 1950s (Figure 1-1). As the AL learned to use the new tool, it produced an increase in runs and an even bigger increase in home runs. But the NL has had an overall decline in runs after 1973 in spite of the offensive surge of the 1990s. The NL also has had a decline in overall home runs since the 1950s.

With the DH, the AL scores more runs and hits more home runs than the NL. The offensive outburst of the 1993-97 period narrowed the home run gap a little, but the gap in runs grew in spite of the results of arcade baseball in Denver. The AL should continue its lead in the future, and trends for just the past 10 years indicate that the AL could increase the margins by which it leads the NL. Yearly trends for the key measures are shown in the following pages.

Figure 4-1 shows runs per game by year from 1987 through 1997 for the American and National leagues. The year 1987 was chosen as the starting point because it marked an offensive peak in both leagues. In the American League, runs per game in 1987 were the highest since 1950. In the National League, runs per game in 1987 tied with 1970 as the highest since 1961. The columns below the graph show the exact runs scored in each year and the ratios of American League runs to National League runs.

American League--Run scoring in the AL declined by 12 percent from 1987 to 1989, and 1989 scoring was the lowest in the AL since the strike season of 1981. But runs jumped with expansion in 1993, soared to their highest levels since 1937 in 1994, and then approached an all-time peak in 1996. Runs per game in 1996 were 10 percent above the 1987 spike, and 1996 was the highest scoring year in the AL (and the majors) since the league record of 5.67 in 1936 (Table 1-1). Runs declined in 1997 as AL teams played without the DH in games in NL parks in interleague play. The AL should remain at high levels, but more interleague play will increase the number of games played without the DH.

The AL was well ahead of the NL in scoring runs from 1987 through 1997. The closest approach came in 1990 when the AL led the NL by only 2.3 percent. But by 1996 the AL was ahead by 15.0 percent, the highest difference between the leagues since 1939. The margin declined to 7.1 percent in 1997 as NL teams got to use the DH in AL parks in interleague play. The margin should shrink more if NL teams play more games with the DH and the AL plays less.

National League--Following the 1987 spike, runs in the NL in 1988 fell to their lowest level since 1968. This is notable because 1968 was the "Year of the Pitcher" when offense fell to record lows due to the rule changes from 1963 through 1968 that favored pitchers. Offense was so poor in 1968 that the rules were changed in 1969 (when runs did not recover fully even after 1969, the AL went to the designated hitter in 1973). The NL recovered after 1988, but it hit a new low in 1992. Except for 3 years in the 1963-68 period, fewer runs were scored in the NL in 1992 than in any year since 1919, the end of the "dead ball" era. Thus, the highs and lows in the 10 year period of Figure 4-1 nearly encompass the highs and lows of the leagues during the century.

Expansion in 1993 pulled the NL out of its scoring dip, but from 1994 through 1996 runs increased only slightly each year before declining in 1997 in spite of the fact that NL teams got to use the DH in interleague play. The improvement in the 1994-96 period was due mainly to the Colorado Rockies. Except for the Rockies, the effect of expansion in the NL was spent by 1994 and the rest of the league was beginning a decline in scoring runs. If the Rockies fail to continue their high level of scoring, the NL may begin to decline on average in runs per game in the future unless expanded use of the DH in interleague play offsets it. A better solution would be the adoption of the DH in the NL.

Figure 4-1. AL/NL Runs Per Game by Year

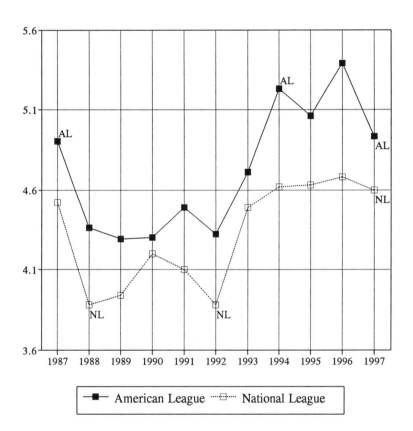

Year	AL Runs Per Game	NL Runs Per Game	AL/NL Ratios
1987	4.90	4.52	1.085
1988	4.36	3.88	1.123
1989	4.29	3.94	1.089
1990	4.30	4.20	1.023
1991	4.49	4.10	1.094
1992	4.32	3.88	1.114
1993	4.71	4.49	1.048
1994	5.23	4.62	1.131
1995	5.06	4.63	1.093
1996	5.39	4.68	1.150
1997	4.93	4.60	1.071

Figure 4-2 shows home runs per game by year from 1987 through 1997 for the American and National leagues. The year 1987 was chosen as the starting point because it marked an offensive peak in both leagues. In the American League, home runs per game in 1987 set an all-time record up to that time. In the National League, home runs per game in 1987 were the highest since 1961. The columns below the graph show the exact home runs hit in each year and the ratios of American League home runs to National League home runs.

American League--Home runs declined by nearly 28 percent in the AL between 1987 and 1988, a huge drop in one year. But 1987 represented a big increase from the early 1980s, and home runs remained at a relatively high level from 1988 through 1992. Thus, when home runs began to increase again with the expansion of 1993, they very quickly returned to record levels. The surge in 1994 marked the second best year ever in AL home runs per game at the time, and the league easily broke its 1987 record in 1996. Home runs in the 1993-97 period were far above any previous five year period (Table 1-1), and AL home runs should continue to be near record levels for some time to come.

The largest difference between the AL and the NL between 1987 and 1997 came in 1988 when the NL fell nearly 30 percent from its 1987 peak, an even bigger drop than that of the AL. It is notable that the leagues were nearly equal in 1990. The last time they were so close was in 1976, and the AL has never trailed the NL in home runs since the introduction of the designated hitter in 1973. The leagues were still close following expansion in 1993, but the AL surged ahead after 1993 as it set league and team home run records while the NL reached high but not record levels.

National League--The NL peak in 1987 was its 7th highest year ever at the time, but the 30 percent drop in 1988 quickly took the league out of record territory. Expansion pulled the National League back towards record levels, and each of the four years between 1994 and 1997 all made the league's top ten list, pushing 1987 off the list (Table 1-5). As is the case for runs, the Colorado Rockies are far ahead of the rest of the NL in hitting home runs. The Rockies just missed setting all-time records for team home runs in the NL in 1995 and 1996, and then they broke the league records in 1997 (Table 2-19). But no other NL teams from the 1990s could even make the team top ten list.

The NL set its all-time records for home runs in 1955 and 1956 (Table 1-5), and its five-year level from 1993-97 still trails its 1955-59 record for a five year period. The NL reversed a 40 year decline in home runs with its surge in the 1990s, but it has not yet matched its records set four decades ago, in spite of the outstanding efforts of the Colorado Rockies. Unless the rest of the league can get closer to the Rockies, the NL will continue to stay below its prior records. However, based on its present level of hitting home runs, adopting the use of the designated hitter would put both the league and the Rockies at record levels.

Figure 4-2. AL/NL Home Runs Per Game by Year

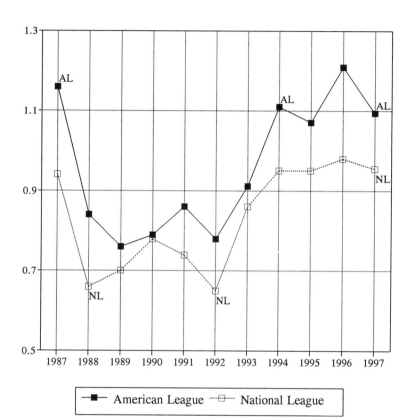

Year	AL HR Per Game	NL HR Per Game	AL/NL Ratios
1987	1.16	0.94	1.237
1988	0.84	0.66	1.273
1989	0.76	0.70	1.081
1990	0.79	0.78	1.013
1991	0.86	0.74	1.168
1992	0.78	0.65	1.206
1993	0.91	0.86	1.061
1994	1.11	0.95	1.167
1995	1.07	0.95	1.125
1996	1.21	0.98	1.236
1997	1.09	0.95	1.147

Figure 4-3 shows doubles per game by year from 1987 through 1997 for the American and National leagues. The year 1987 was chosen as the starting point because it marked an offensive peak in both leagues. In the American League, 1987 doubles per game were just below 1983, the highest year since 1941. In the National League, 1987 doubles per game were the highest since 1939. The columns below the graph show the exact doubles hit in each year and the ratios of American League doubles to National League doubles.

American League--Doubles declined after 1987, but they stayed relatively high and by 1991 they were back up to 1987 levels. With the offensive surge that started in 1993, doubles rose above the 1.80 level in 1993 for the first time since 1937. They peaked at 1.86 in 1986, the highest level since the record year of 1.94 in 1936. Both 1996 and 1994 moved onto the top 10 list in 5th and 7th place respectively (Table 1-6). Doubles in the five year period from 1993 through 1997 averaged 1.80 per game, just barely below the all-time record of 1.81 from 1935 through 1939. Faster runners on average and the use of the DH have put doubles in the AL at a record level, and they may have broken the all-time record over 5 years if not for the loss of the DH in interleague games in 1997. The future level of DH usage will determine if doubles set new records.

The largest difference between the AL and the NL between 1987 and 1997 came in 1991 when the AL returned to 1987 levels while the NL was reaching its low in the 10 year period. The ratio was nearly the same in 1996 when the AL surged and the NL remained flat, but in 1997 the leagues converged again. This reflects the loss of the DH to the AL and the gain of the DH to the NL in some of the interleague games. It also reflects the higher average level of speed in the NL because speed is more important in manufacturing runs in the NL.

National League--The NL fell from its 1987 peak to a low in the period in 1991, but it increased steadily from that point to a peak in 1994 that was its best mark for doubles since 1934. The Astros and Expos moved onto the top 10 list for per game doubles in 1994 (Table 2-21). After a brief decline, the NL climbed again in 1997. This was probably due to the use of the DH in interleague play. The higher rate permitted the Expos, Astros, and Marlins to set all-time franchise records for total doubles in 1997 (Table 2-6). Ironically, the Rockies, who were far ahead of the rest of the league in runs, home runs, and batting average, were well under the league average in doubles in 1997.

As noted above the NL was helped in 1997 by the use of the DH in interleague games. But the 1997 rebound also reflects the fact that the average speed in the league is higher than ever (as it is in all sports). Trying to take an extra base is more important in the NL than in the AL, because the average AL team hits more home runs than its NL counterparts. With increased interleague play offering more opportunities for the NL to use the DH, the NL should continue to hit doubles at a high level in the future.

Figure 4-3. AL/NL Doubles Per Game by Year

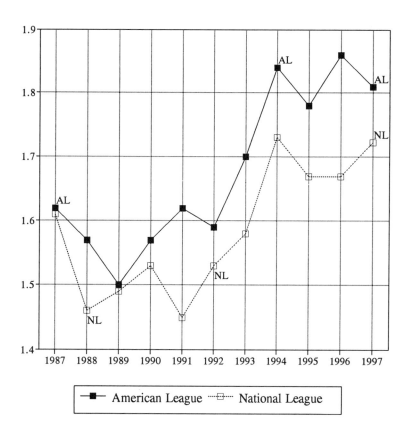

Year	AL 2B Per Game	NL 2B Per Game	AL/NL Ratios
1987	1.62	1.61	1.004
1988	1.57	1.46	1.078
1989	1.50	1.49	1.007
1990	1.57	1.53	1.029
1991	1.62	1.45	1.117
1992	1.59	1.53	1.039
1993	1.70	1.58	1.076
1994	1.84	1.73	1.064
1995	1.78	1.67	1.063
1996	1.86	1.67	1.113
1997	1.81	1.72	1.050

Figure 4-4 shows batting average by year from 1987 through 1997 for the American and National leagues. The year 1987 was chosen as the starting point because it marked an offensive peak in both leagues. In the American League, the league 1987 batting average was the 5th highest since 1950. In the National League, the league 1987 batting average was the 5th highest since 1961. The columns below the graph show the exact batting average for each year and the ratios of American League batting average to National League batting average.

American League--The league batting average dropped 6 percentage points between 1987 and 1988, and then remained essentially constant from 1988 through 1992. The league average rose together with the offensive upsurge that began with the expansion of 1993, and in 1994 it reached .273, the highest average in the league since .279 was recorded in 1939. The league average reached .277 in 1996, and then fell back to .271 in 1997. The five year average of .271 for the period from 1993 through 1997 was also the highest in the league since the period from 1935 through 1939.

The all-time highs for the AL were reached primarily in the 1920s, and the 10th ranked average is .282 in 1923 (Table 1-7). It is unlikely the AL will ever reach such levels again because it is unlikely pitchers will lose so many tools all at once as they did in the rule changes that took place in 1920. This is why both leagues set their batting average records in the 1920s.

The 15 points by which the AL led the NL in 1989 and 1996 tied the record set in 1930 when the NL was 15 points ahead of the AL. The NL hit .303 in 1930, the only time either league ever averaged over .300. Since the DH was born in 1973, the AL has never trailed the NL in batting average, and the gap has slowly increased with peaks being reached in 1989 and 1996. The AL should stay ahead of the NL unless the NL adopts the DH.

National League--The NL fell sharply from its 1987 spike, reaching .248 in 1988 and .246 in 1989. The 15 point drop between 1987 and 1989 put the NL at its lowest level since the "Year of the Pitcher" in 1968. Except for 1968 and 1963, the year the rules were changed to favor pitchers, the NL had not been so low since the league batting average reached .244 in 1909. The NL batting average was still at .252 in 1992 when the offensive outburst that began in 1993 took the league average to .264 in 1993 and .267 in 1994. This was the highest batting average in the NL since 1939. The league average declined in the next two years and then rose a little in 1997 as the NL got to use the DH in interleague play.

As in the AL, the NL will never again reach its peaks of the 1920s that culminated with the all-time record in 1930 (Table 1-7). But further usage of the DH in interleague play (or the adoption of the DH permanently) will help to reduce the gap between the leagues. Similarly, the quality of the big swing hitters coming up through the ranks should keep batting averages relatively high.

Figure 4-4. AL/NL Batting Average by Year

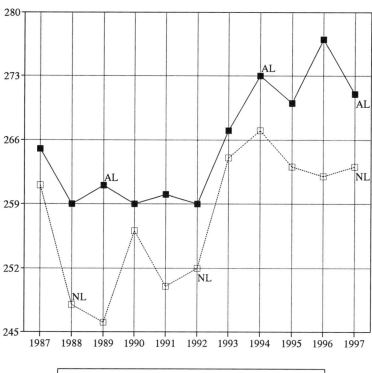

Year	AL Batting Avg.	NL Batting Avg.	AL/NL Ratios
1987	265	261	1.017
1988	259	248	1.044
1989	261	246	1.058
1990	259	256	1.010
1991	260	250	1.040
1992	259	252	1.031
1993	267	264	1.011
1994	273	267	1.021
1995	270	263	1.026
1996	277	262	1.056
1997	271	263	1.029

Figure 4-5 shows ERA by year from 1987 through 1997 for the American and National leagues. The year 1987 was chosen as the starting point because it marked an offensive peak in both leagues. In the American League, the 1987 ERA of 4.46 was the highest for the league since 1950. In the National League, the 1987 ERA of 4.08 was the highest for the league since 1953. The columns below the graph show the exact ERA for each year and the ratios of American League ERA to National League ERA.

American League--On a league basis, ERA would be expected to vary in the same way runs do. This is exactly the case for such a short period as 10 years, and thus the ERA variations in Figure 4-5 are quite similar to those shown in Figure 4-1 for runs. But the relationship between ERA and runs can vary widely over a long period of time because errors are constantly declining in both leagues. This reduces the percentage of total runs that are defined as "unearned," and thus the number of earned runs as a percentage of total runs constantly increases. As a result, when run scoring increased in the 1990s ERAs increased at a higher rate than would be expected based on the ratio of runs in the 1990s to runs in the prior high scoring periods of the 1920s and 1930s.

This is why 1994, 1995, and 1996 were 3 of the 5 highest ERA years in league history (Table 1-8) even though runs in these 3 years were only 3 of the top 14 years (Table 1-4). Errors are still declining in the AL (1995, 1996, and 1997 were the 3 lowest years for errors per game in league history), and thus ERAs will continue to increase even if run levels remain constant. The difference in ERA between the AL and NL will continue to track the difference in runs, but the difference in ERA will grow slightly more than the difference in runs because the AL constantly makes fewer errors than the NL.

National League--As in the AL, ERA values in the NL will continue to be higher than would be expected based on the comparison of runs in the 1990s to prior high runs periods in the 1920s. For example, 1996, 1994, 1997, and 1995 ranked 5th through 8th respectively in the top 10 highest ERA list for the NL (Table 1-8), while 1996, 1995, and 1994 only ranked 11th, 14th, and 15th respectively on the top 15 runs list (Table 1-4). 1997 did not make the top 15 runs list at all. 1997 ranks especially high on the ERA list compared to the other years in the 1993-97 period because 1997 errors in the NL were the lowest since the record low year of 1992. This puts 1997 ahead of 1995 for ERA even though runs in 1995 were well ahead of those for 1997 in the NL.

The NL will trail the AL in ERA as long as the NL does not adopt the DH permanently and continues to trail the AL in runs. Even if the NL adopts the DH and matches the AL in runs, the AL will still have a higher ERA because the AL commits less errors than the NL. It is tempting to say that the AL has fewer errors because the DH does not play in the field, but the AL has committed fewer errors per game than the NL in all but 3 years since 1959.

Figure 4-5. AL/NL ERA by Year

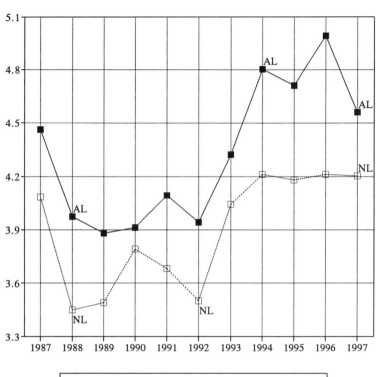

Year	AL ERA	NL ERA	AL/NL Ratios
1987	4.46	4.08	1.093
1988	3.97	3.45	1.151
1989	3.88	3.49	1.112
1990	3.91	3.79	1.032
1991	4.09	3.68	1.111
1992	3.94	3.50	1.126
1993	4.32	4.04	1.069
1994	4.80	4.21	1.140
1995	4.71	4.18	1.127
1996	4.99	4.21	1.185
1997	4.56	4.20	1.086

Figure 4-6 shows strikeouts per game by year from 1987 through 1997 for the American and National leagues. The year 1987 was chosen as the starting point because it marked an offensive peak in both leagues. In the American League, 1987 strikeouts per game were the highest since 1968. In the National League, the all-time record had been set in 1986 and 1987 was only 0.01 behind 1986. The columns below the graph show the exact strikeouts for each year and the ratios of National League strikeouts to American League strikeouts.

American League--At the time, 1987 strikeouts per game were higher than any other year in league history outside the 1963-68 period when the rules were changed to favor pitchers. Strikeouts fell as offense fell after 1987, but the AL was still near historic highs through 1992. Strikeouts rose sharply with the offensive outburst that began in 1993 as the big swing came to dominate the game. In 1996 the AL set its all-time high for strikeouts per game, topping the previous peak set in 1967 during the 1963-68 period. The AL then broke that record in 1997. It's inconsistent to blame pitchers for the big increase in offense in the 1993-97 period when pitchers were striking out batters at the highest rate in history. For a constant quality of pitching, the big swing trades more offense for more strikeouts.

In spite of the surge in strikeouts in the AL, the league was still well behind the NL in strikeouts per game. This is because of the lack of the DH in the NL. The AL and the NL were nearly identical in strikeouts during most of the century (Figure 1-6), and the AL led the NL in the high strikeout period of 1963 through 1968. But the AL has trailed the NL in strikeouts every year since the DH was born in 1973. This will continue to be the case as long as the NL lacks the DH. But the continuation of the big swing in the future means that strikeouts per game will remain at record highs in both leagues.

National League--The NL did not fall far from its record strikeout levels of 1986 and 1987 even though offense fell sharply after 1987 in the NL. In fact, the NL averaged more strikeouts per game from 1987 through 1992 than it did in the prior peak period of 1963 through 1968. This is why it appeared the NL was down for the count when it scored so few runs in 1992 (Figure 4-1). It is also another confirmation that the offensive outburst of the 1993-97 period was not due to poor pitching. NL pitchers did not suddenly lose their ability to pitch after dominating the league from 1988 through 1992. To the contrary they broke the 1986 strikeout record every year from 1994 through 1997, with each year being higher than the year before (Table 1-9).

The NL can be expected to continue to lead the AL in strikeouts as long the NL does not adopt the DH. Even interleague play which gave the NL the chance to use the DH did not keep the NL from setting a new strikeout record in 1997. This is the clearest signal possible that NL strikeouts will remain at very high if not record levels in future years.

Figure 4-6. AL/NL Strikeouts Per Game by Year

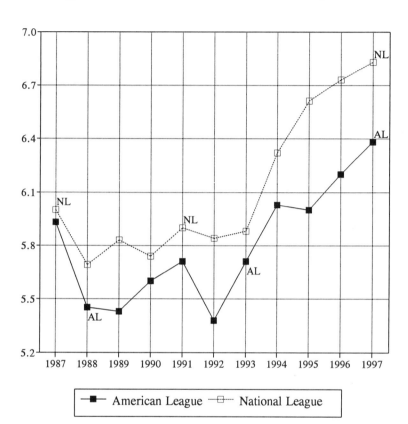

Year	AL SO Per Game	NL SO Per Game	NL/AL Ratios
1987	5.93	6.00	1.013
1988	5.45	5.69	1.045
1989	5.43	5.83	1.075
1990	5.60	5.74	1.026
1991	5.71	5.90	1.034
1992	5.38	5.84	1.086
1993	5.71	5.88	1.030
1994	6.03	6.32	1.047
1995	6.00	6.61	1.102
1996	6.20	6.73	1.084
1997	6.38	6.83	1.071

Figure 4-7 shows walks per game by year from 1987 through 1997 for the American and National leagues. The year 1987 was chosen as the starting point because it marked an offensive peak in both leagues. In the American League, 1987 walks per game were the highest since 1975 (the highest year since 1956). In the National League, walks per game were the highest since 1975 (the 3rd highest year since 1955). The columns below the graph show the exact walks for each year and the ratios of American League walks to National League walks.

American League--Walks per game fell in the AL as offense fell after 1987, but they were back up to relatively high levels by 1990. Then they increased sharply with the offensive outburst that began in 1993. At their peak in 1996, AL walks per game were the highest they had been since the 1947-56 decade when AL walks set all-time major league records. But walks per game in the 1990s in the AL are generally lower than in the 1930s, 1940s, and 1950s (Figure 1-7) in spite of the great increase in strikeouts and home runs and the return of run scoring to the levels of the 1930s. This is yet another indication that today's pitchers are better overall than their counterparts of the 1920s and 1930s.

Walks per game decreased in the AL in 1997, falling below the 1993 level even though 1997 strikeouts, home runs, and runs were well above 1993. This is partly due to the loss of the DH in interleague play, but it may also mark the beginning of the accommodation of AL pitchers to the era of the big swing. The AL led the NL in walks at nearly all points in the century, but walks were nearly equal in the 1970s and 1980s in spite of the DH. The leagues were equal in 1989 (the NL actually led if you go out to enough decimal places), but the AL surged to a big lead when the offensive outburst started in 1993. The AL decline in walks in 1997 moved the AL close to the NL, and the AL is likely to stay closer in the future as the use of the DH varies in interleague play and AL pitchers accommodate to the big swing era.

National League--Walks per game in the NL fell sharply after 1998 as offense declined, and they did not get back above the 1987 level until 1997 in spite of the 1993-97 offensive outburst. In the 10 years from 1987 through 1996 NL walks declined on average while offense and strikeouts increased dramatically. Walks per game in the NL in the 1990s are still near historically high levels for the century (Figure 1-7), but walks per game in the NL have essentially remained constant for the last 3 decades after falling and rising in the 1960s in response to the rule changes in the 1963-68 period that favored pitchers.

It's not clear why the NL remains relatively constant in walks over long periods of time in spite of huge variations in offense and strikeouts. But as noted many times in my previous books, walks have varied in strange ways in both leagues over the century. The most reasonable prediction for the future is that the prior variations will continue. Walks in both leagues will probably continue to be consistently inconsistent.

Figure 4-7. AL/NL Walks Per Game by Year

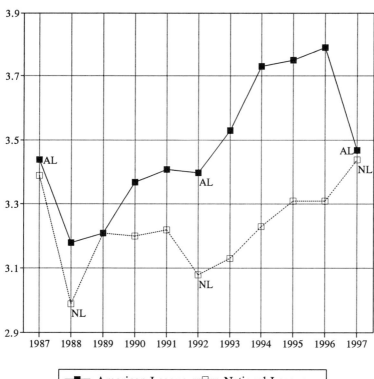

Year	AL Walks Per Game	NL Walks Per Game	AL/NL Ratios
1987	3.44	3.39	1.017
1988	3.18	2.99	1.064
1989	3.21	3.21	1.000
1990	3.37	3.20	1.052
1991	3.41	3.22	1.057
1992	3.40	3.08	1.105
1993	3.53	3.13	1.128
1994	3.73	3.23	1.152
1995	3.75	3.31	1.132
1996	3.79	3.31	1.146
1997	3.47	3.44	1.008

Figure 4-8 shows SO/W ratios by year from 1987 through 1997 for the American and National leagues. The year 1987 was chosen as the starting point because it marked an offensive peak in both leagues. In the American League, 1987 SO/W ratios were the 10th highest ever at the time. In the National League, SO/W ratios in 1987 were continuing an upsurge that started in 1984. The columns below the graph show the exact SO/W ratios for each year and the ratios of National League SO/W ratios to American League SO/W ratios.

American League--SO/W ratios in the AL fell steadily after 1987 as strikeouts declined (Figure 4-6) and walks increased (Figure 4-7). Ratios stayed low compared to 1987 even after the beginning of the offensive outburst in 1993 because a sharp increase in strikeouts in 1993 was matched by a sharp increase in walks. The all-time league record of strikeouts in 1996 finally started the SO/W ratio curve moving upwards again, and the sharp decline in walks in 1997 combined with another all-time league record for strikeouts put 1997 SO/W ratios in the AL far above 1987 levels.

The AL set its all-time highs in SO/W ratio in the 1963-68 period when strikeouts soared due to the 1963 rule changes favoring pitchers. The birth of the DH in 1973 cut AL strikeout levels, and SO/W ratios have stayed well below their highs of the 1963-68 period ever since. The strikeout peaks in the 1993-97 period were associated with an increased level of walks, and thus even these years could not match the SO/W ratios of the 1963-68 period until the 1997 spike in SO/W ratio knocked 1987 off the top 10 list and put 1997 ahead of 1965.

Primarily due to higher walks the AL has trailed the NL in SO/W ratios for most of the century. The difference between the leagues increased when the DH was born, and the AL will remain well behind the NL in the future as long as the NL does not adopt the DH.

National League--SO/W ratios were increasing in the NL in 1987 and they stayed above the 1987 level in the 1990s as the rate of change in strikeouts was usually more favorable to increasing SO/W ratios than the rate of change in walks. The surge in strikeouts in the NL in the 1993-97 period was not accompanied by a surge in walks, and the NL exceeded 2.0 in SO/W ratio in 1995 and 1996 for the first time since the all-time record year of 2.22 in 1968 (Table 1-11). The AL has never exceeded 2.0 in SO/W ratio, and until 1995 and 1996 the NL had done so only in the 1963-68 period. The NL fell just below 2.0 in 1997 partly due to the use of the DH in interleague play, and with the planned expansion of interleague play in the future, the NL may not exceed 2.0 again.

SO/W ratio has long been a measure of the effectiveness of a pitcher, and the fact that both leagues have historically high SO/W ratios in the 1990s in spite of the high offense level and the lack of the favorable rules of the 1963-68 period confirms again that today's pitchers are better overall than their predecessors. The big swing is the key to the offensive outburst of the 1993-97 period.

Figure 4-8. AL/NL SO/W Ratio by Year

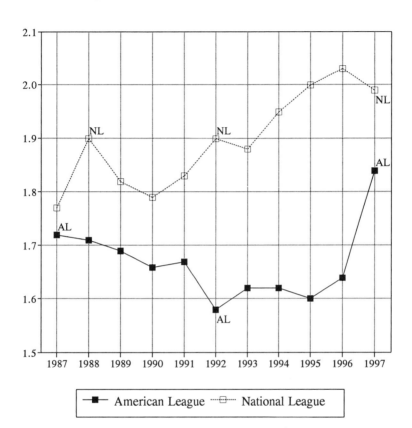

Year	AL SO/W Ratio	NL SO/W Ratio	NL/AL Ratios
1987	1.72	1.77	1.030
1988	1.71	1.90	1.111
1989	1.69	1.82	1.075
1990	1.66	1.79	1.079
1991	1.67	1.83	1.093
1992	1.58	1.90	1.200
1993	1.62	1.88	1.162
1994	1.62	1.95	1.206
1995	1.60	2.00	1.247
1996	1.64	2.03	1.243
1997	1.84	1.99	1.081

Table **4-2** shows the average winning percentage for American and National League teams for the 1993-97 period. The peak percentage for each team during the period and the year the peak was reached is also shown. Because all peaks are in the 1990s, the peak year is not shown in boldface. Further, the National League is discussed first because the Braves were the top team in the period.

National League--The Braves led the majors in winning percentage in the 1993-97 period with an average of .616, the best average over 5 years in franchise history. Their peak was .642 in 1993, the highest winning percentage in franchise history for one year. Their lowest percentage in the period was .593 in 1996. The fact that their low was close to their average demonstrates the consistency of the Braves in the 1993-97 period. They were clearly the best team in baseball, and they won a record sixth straight division title in 1997.

The Expos were in second place, and they also set franchise records for highest average over 5 years and highest percentage for one year (1994). But the Expos were 74 percentage points behind the Braves, and the Expos did not make the playoffs even once in the 1993-97 period (the playoffs were canceled by the strike in 1994 when the Expos led the majors in winning percentage). The Astros and Dodgers were next, and they were the only teams other than the Braves (and Yankees) to finish at .500 or better every year in the 1993-97 period.

The expansion Rockies finished ahead of 6 other teams and the expansion Marlins led 4 teams. Both the Rockies and Marlins also made the playoffs once. If not for their great comeback in the second half of 1997, the Phillies would have finished last overall in spite of winning the pennant in 1993 with the 4th highest peak in the period. As it was, the Phillies were above .500 only in the year they won the pennant. The Pirates finished last and were the only NL team to fail to get above .500 for any year in the 1993-97 period.

The Braves of the 1990s made a complete turnaround from the 1973-90 period when they had the worst record in the league. At the other end of the scale, the percentage of .530 for the Dodgers in the 1993-97 period is near their league leading percentage of .538 for the full 1973-97 period. The Dodgers have continued to lead the league over various sustained periods of time since 1940.

American League--The Indians had the highest average in the AL in the 1993-97 period (.579) as well as the highest peak in the majors (.694) when the won the 1995 pennant. The Indians (twice) and the Braves (three times) were the only teams in the majors to be above .600 more than once in the 1993-97 period. But the Yankees were not far behind the Indians in overall average, and the Yankees were the only team in the AL to have a winning record every year in the period. The lowest year for the Yankees in the period was .543 in 1993, a minimum that was topped only by the Braves. The Blue Jays were as inconsistent as the Phillies, peaking at .586 when they won the 1993 pennant, but then falling to .389 in 1995. The Blue Jays were above .500 only in 1993.

The Indians, like the Braves, rose dramatically to the top in the 1993-97 period. The Indians were 13th in the league in winning percentage from 1973 through 1992, leading only the Mariners who were last in the majors in that period. The Mariners similarly improved greatly in the 1993-97 period and had by far their best teams in franchise history. The Indians, however, did not quite match the success they had in the 1948-54 period. The Yankees had a lifetime winning percentage of .569 from 1903 through 1989, a near match for their .574 from 1993 through 1997. The Yankees lead the majors in winning percentage both before and after WWII, and they remain consistent winners decade after decade in spite of the poor years they had at the beginning of the 1990s.

Table 4-2. AL/NL Teams Winning Percentage 1993-97

American League				National League			
Team	Avg.	Peak	Year	Team	Avg.	Peak	Year
Indians	.579	.694	1995	Braves	.616	.642	1993
Yankees	.574	.619	1994	Expos	.542	.649	1994
Orioles	.546	.605	1997	Astros	.530	.574	1994
White Sox	.533	.593	1994	Dodgers	.530	.556	1996
Mariners	.514	.556	1997	Reds	.518	.590	1995
Red Sox	.513	.597	1995	Giants	.511	.636	1993
Rangers	.506	.556	1996	Cards	.486	.543	1996
Royals	.489	.557	1994	Rockies	.485	.535	1995
Blue Jays	.476	.586	1993	Phillies	.476	.599	1993
Angels	.468	.538	1995	Marlins	.474	.568	1997
Brewers	.463	.494	1996	Cubs	.470	.519	1993
Tigers	.443	.525	1993	Mets	.462	.543	1997
A's	.443	.481	1996	Padres	.459	.562	1996
Twins	.439	.481	1996	Pirates	.454	.488	1997

In spite of the offensive surge in the 1993-97 period, the common theme for the Braves, the top team, and the Yankees and Dodgers, who won every year in the period and who lead their leagues in wins since 1920 and 1940 respectively, is pitching. The Braves and Dodgers had the lowest ERAs in the NL and the Yankees had the lowest ERA in the AL in the 1993-97 period. This is new for the Braves, who were next to last in ERA in the NL for the 1973-90 period. But it is normal for the Yankees and Dodgers, who lead their leagues in ERA over the same long periods they lead in wins. You can't have too much pitching.

As noted, the Yankees and Dodgers continued to win in the 1993-97 period just as they had for the last 75 and 55 years respectively, while the Braves, Indians, and Mariners made complete reversals of form in the 1993-97 period. The Braves gained 154 percentage points, the Indians 121, and the Mariners 87 compared to the 20 years just before the 1993-97 period. Most other teams stayed within 30 percentage points of their prior performance, but the White Sox gained 43 points and the Expos 42. The Pirates led the National League with a drop of 66 points, while in the American League the Royals and Brewers were down by nearly 40 points, the Twins by 48, the Tigers by 64, and the A's by 73.

In the era of free agency, teams can improve their performance dramatically in a short time by aggressive and intelligent spending in the free agent market. The Yankees and Dodgers show a franchise can win for long periods in spite of changes in the game if top management is competent and remains committed to winning. It is the same in baseball as in any sport or business. Prior losers can become big winners with capable new management, but prior winners can turn into big losers with new but incompetent management. There is no way to forecast how a franchise will survive in terms of management changes.

But it is possible to forecast what is required for winning. Connie Mack was right when he said pitching was 75 percent of the game. The percentage may even be higher in the era of big swings and the DH (both of which will remain in the future). Pitching especially separates losers from winners when big hitters make it possible for nearly all teams to score runs. The Braves proved the importance of pitching in the 1990s, just as the Yankees and Dodgers proved it over prior decades. The Yankees and Dodgers have had many great hitters, but when they were winning it all they also were among the leaders in pitching. The Dodgers have led the majors in pitching since they moved to Los Angeles, but they also have stayed near the top of the league in home runs. The Yankees were legendary for power in the 1920s and 1930s, but they were also among the leaders in pitching and defense. Their key in their most successful times in the late 1940s and the 1950s was pitching and defense even thought they still led (by smaller margins) in runs. The Yankees are still second in the league in runs since 1973, even though other teams have surpassed them in hitting home runs. The key to their success in the 1993-97 period was once again pitching and defense.

Balance is the key, but balance should start with pitching. Since 1940 the Red Sox have led the majors in runs, but they have won only 4 pennants and no Series titles since then because of poor pitching. In the 1993-97 period the Mariners and Rockies proved again that even great power is not enough. The Braves, who lead the NL in home runs since 1946, had the league's worst record since 1973 until they developed great pitching. If you focus on pitching first, and then consistently add just enough hitting, you can win for decades. It has always been this way in baseball, and this is the way it will be in the future.

Index